Marketing Your Financial Planning Services

Marketing Your Financial Planning Services

A Guide for Professionals

H. STANLEY JONES *CPA*

Jones & Associates
Inglewood, California

John Wiley & Sons
New York • Chichester • Brisbane • Toronto • Singapore

Library of Congress Cataloging in Publication Data:
Jones, H. Stanley.

   Marketing your financial planning services: a guide for
professionals / H. Stanley Jones.

       p.   cm.
   Bibliography: p.
   Includes index.
   ISBN 0-471-85649-5
   1. Financial planners—United States—Marketing.   I. Title.
HG179.5.J66   1988
332.6′2—dc19   87-26373
                                                                          CIP

0-471-85649-5

Dedicated

To the three most important women in my life . . .

My mother, Doris
My wife, Roberta
My daughter, Debby

Preface

ABOUT THIS BOOK

This is a guide for Financial Professionals who want to develop and market a Personal Financial Planning Service. By the term Financial Professional, I mean the broker, CPA, insurance agent, lawyer, trust officer, or real estate agent.

As a Financial Professional, you are already expert in one or more phases of the Personal Financial Planning process. You are also well informed about those phases that lie beyond your current area of expertise. This book will help you organize your resources and skills to develop a complete and consistent Personal Financial Planning Service.

This is not a detailed textbook that will transform you into a competent Financial Planner. There are ample courses, books, and training agencies to help you with that job. In this book, I want to give you the underlying ideas, ideals, strategies, and techniques that will guide you in the development of your target service.

After you have defined, developed, or refined your service, you will need to market it. Financial Professionals can be surprisingly deficient in marketing skills and techniques. However, in an increasingly competitive marketplace you need to acquire and sharpen these skills to survive. For this reason the book discusses strategic marketing in general, with specific applications to a Personal Financial Planning practice.

I want the independent Financial Professional and the small practice to benefit from this book's "do-it-yourself" approach.

THE PROBLEM THAT ETHICS BUILT

I have been planning and collecting material for this book for several years. I started at a leisurely pace that could have extended the work into a retirement hobby, but a growing sense of urgency diverted more and more of my energy toward getting this material into your hands. As I continued my Personal Financial Planning practice and monitored the related services and market, I saw a problem emerge that needs correction.

The Financial Professional has hesitated to enter the client solicitation arena with an aggressive, highly visible stance because of notions of professional deportment. These notions were reflected in and reinforced by various governing and regulatory bodies through codes, laws, and rules about advertising and solicitation.

The informal or codified ethical rules we created no longer serve us or our clients well. There is a need and desire for quality Personal Financial Planning Services. Our existing clients and potential clients want this service, but we have kept ourselves from telling them that we could provide such services. That left a gap.

Both nature and business abhor a vacuum, and into this gap has poured a stream of unqualified, self-proclaimed Financial Planners. These opportunists offer products that ultimately cannot satisfy the consumer's need. However, without regulatory constraints, they are free to continue trying.

Our professional position is an awkward one. Our code of ethics, originally designed to protect consumers, is now in fact putting them in jeopardy. Consumers are being drawn to single-product vendors, lulled into a false sense of security by prestigious but unfounded titles, and are entrusting their entire financial futures to inept or tunnel-visioned amateurs.

Until our regulating bodies catch up (and they will), we must strive to fill the gap in a professional and ethical manner. I hope this book will encourage you to develop and make available the kind of Personal Financial Planning Service needed by your clients.

No matter what the codes and rules say, in today's environment it is unethical for the Financial Professional to avoid offering quality Personal Financial Planning Services in an aggressive fashion.

THE DOUBLE-EDGED SWORD

I want this book to be a double-edged sword, able to cut both in and out. One edge should cut into our practice, defining an ideal Personal Financial Planning Service. Such an ideal acknowledges the Financial Planner as a dream mechanic. His primary function is to learn what is truly in the heart of the client, and to develop a plan that can make those dreams into reality. The ideal Personal Financial Planning Service integrates the broad aspects of the client's financial life into a harmonious whole. Finally, a good financial plan is a living entity that evolves in response to time and change.

The other edge of the sword should cut out from the practice and into the market. I want to show you how to develop and implement an optimal marketing strategy. The marketing plan must be created and executed from a clearly defined ethical stance.

I hope you will come to feel my sense of urgency about correcting the problem that we have all helped to create. Motivate yourself with the potential profit, the fun of developing new skills, the rewards of human interaction. Or motivate yourself as I have, with the moral imperative to offer a needed service, of high professional quality, delivered with the knowledge that you have fully satisfied the needs of your client.

A FINAL WORD

The use of the male personal pronoun in this book should not be construed to mean that all Financial Planners are men. Such is far from the truth. Although *he* and *him* are used to avoid awkwardness and conform with standard usage, they apply to both men and women.

Acknowledgments

Over the years many people have contributed in various ways to the production of this book. My deepest thanks and appreciation for all their dedicated assistance and help to those most closely involved in the final stages. They include Kathy R., David C., Steven K., and John H.

Contents

1

Fad or Future?

THE GROWING NEED, THE SPRAWLING SERVICE

What do personal computers, satellite dishes, and personal financial plans have in common? First, they are all products of the 1980s. Second, they are items with high consumer appeal. And third, depending on how they are built, packaged, purchased, and put to use, they can be either a major asset or an expensive liability.

Why has the subject of Personal Financial Planning captured the interest of the U.S. consumer? Is the fascination associated with this new status symbol a passing trend, or is it based on a new but enduring need? To get a clear answer to these questions, we'll need to find out where we have come from, and where we are now.

From the 1950s until the late 1960s, real productivity and discretionary income were growing at a modest but perceptible rate. From then through 1980 they were flat. With inflation and taxes, we found ourselves in the puzzling situation of earning more money, yet having fewer dollars to spend, with a dwindling return of value. It felt as though we switched from a candle to a wide-beam flashlight, only to discover that our batteries were running down.

As we experienced increases in income with decreases in available cash, smarter use of our resources became highly desirable, or even necessary. Alas, it has also become harder to be smart about finances. Personal monetary situations have gotten more complex over the years,

1

particularly concerning income tax issues. When your accountant no longer prepares his own return . . . .

Not only taxation, but the entire economic environment is complex and rapidly changing. More and more we have come to rely on the advice of specialists and experts. Complexity is here to stay, and so is the need for Personal Financial Planning.

The concepts behind Personal Financial Planning are not new. Various fragments of the service have been provided for years by estate planners, insurance agents, accountants, and so forth. What is new is the packaging of this product.

Today's Personal Financial Plan merges various wedges of service into a highly consumable pie. Instead of employing the services of five or six separate financial professionals, consumers can avail themselves of all services under one roof. The image of the complete pie is particularly accurate, as the circle emphasizes the completeness and integration inherent in a good plan. And who is the master chef? Enter the Financial Planner.

Financial Planning is a new profession that reflects the highly diverse and demanding environment that spawned it. To stretch the pie analogy a bit further, imagine that the pie is made of wedges with different fillings, different crusts, yet baked all as one. And all pieces of the finished pie must complement each other! Let us try for a recipe.

Financial planning is the process of coordinating a broad range of financial services, products, and strategies. These must be consistent with the client's goals and values. The process must develop and maintain a plan of action to reach the client's personal objectives. The plan must respond to changes in goals and environment, and reflect the client's stage of life; it must also include transfer of wealth at death.

Personal Financial Planning emerged almost naturally out of the mutual fund era of the 1960s, with the cross selling of insurance and mutual fund investments by vendors on both sides. Astute financial professionals and consumers began to wonder why consumers wanting diverse finanial services had to shop at a multitude of "stores." However, it was not until the early 1980s that the consumer at large became aware of the new services and the benefits available from them.

In 1981 Sears Roebuck & Co. (Sears) purchased the brokerage of Dean Witter Reynolds, Inc. (Dean Witter) and the Coldwell Banker real estate organization. Combined with its already successful Allstate Insurance company and Allstate Savings and Loan, the Sears Financial Network became an overnight leader in the financial services industry.

Sears' 1982 announcement of its Financial Network sent a clear signal to traditional financial institutions that the "department store of financial services" was a reality. More importantly, the same message reached the considerable Sears' customer base. The department store shopper was soon exposed to similar services offered by J.C. Penney Co., Inc. (Penney), K-Mart Corporation (K-Mart), and Kroger Co.

The proclaimed purpose of these programs is to help the consumer save as well as spend and invest. This is not so much a humanitarian gesture as a sophisticated grooming and maintenance of the Great American Consumer.

Other exposures of Personal Financial Planning Services to the general public occurred through the media, notably through the Public Broadcasting Service (PBS) television series, *Profiles of Success*. The emergence of the Personal Financial Planning Service of the 1960s further stimulated the evolution of the financial services industry as it is known today.

Large traditional financial institutions responded by the early 1980s. Merrill Lynch, E.F. Hutton, Cigna, and Anchor National Life are but a few who joined the new trend. Merrill Lynch converted the broker into a financial adviser, who was to be the hub of a network of salaried sales assistants and professionals specializing in insurance, lending, and tax matters. Prudential-Bache began marketing "total financial planning" in early 1983.

Deregulation in the 1970s and 1980s has also had an effect on traditional institutions, unleashing their capabilities as multiple product and service vendors. Many banks, Savings and Loan institutions (S&Ls), credit unions, finance companies, and real estate companies now see themselves as "financial services" institutions.

Further, the new environment has encouraged the development of operating networks of related services. For example, in 1983 Southmark Corporation, a Dallas-based real estate firm, purchased University Group and reorganized it into Southmark Financial, which provides broker-dealer services to a nationwide network of independent Financial Planners.

As the established institutions evolved, brand-new corporations crystallized that were specifically dedicated to comprehensive Personal Financial Planning Services. Companies like Equitec Financial Group, Consolidated Capital, and Integrated Resources, Inc., materialized in response to growing consumer needs.

By the mid-1980s, the diversification and integration brought about by the new financial services had become acceptable to the Wall Street establishment. Following the traditional financial service firms, came the entry of the sleeping giants of the industry, the Certified Public Accountant (CPA) firms. CPAs had already been doing income taxes, estate taxes, pension plans, and financial statements. The obvious next step was comprehensive Personal Financial Planning.

One group study course offered by the American Institute of Certified Public Accountants (AICPA), "The CPA as a Personal Financial Planner," was offered almost 80 times in 1984. The California CPA Foundation for Education and Research has even developed its own curriculum to educate CPAs in Personal Financial Planning. In June 1985 it introduced a new "Advanced Personal Financial Planning" Certificate Program with 7 modules that requires a total of 88 class hours. Response was unprecedented: 1129 CPAs signed up for the first module at 18 California sites!

A significant indicator of the growth of an industry is the growth of its related professional associations. The International Association for Financial Planning (IAFP) is the largest organization representing the Personal Financial Planning Service industry.

There is a desire to formalize the concept of the professional Financial Planner, but the field is still too young for this. Thus, the membership of IAFP is not homogeneous in composition. It views itself as a professional organization acting as a forum for financial professionals participating in the financial planning process, including:

- Financial planners
- Stock brokers
- Bankers
- Trust officers
- S & L officers
- Credit union managers
- Mutual fund salespersons
- Insurance agents
- Pension specialists
- Real estate professionals
- Bankers
- Tax shelter representatives
- CPAs
- Estate tax planning attorneys

As might be expected, the organization has experienced tremendous growth in the 1980s. From 1980 to 1985, the IAFP grew from 6150 to 22,176 members. But frantic growth in response to consumer need is not without its problems. One of the twenty thousand members of the IAFP is Boris "Bo" Regaard of Tampa, Florida. Boris is a dog. Literally. His owner, also a Financial Planner, registered his dog with the IAFP to make a point: Just because a person calls himself a Financial Planner doesn't mean that he is one.

Our response to client needs has been a haphazard, rather than an organized and harmonious, growth. As a result, consumers are often confused when trying to select a Financial Planner. If selecting a Financial Planner becomes more confusing than doing their own plan, we are failing in our responsibility as professionals.

Part of the confusion seems unavoidably bound up in the newness of the field. There has scarcely been time to define Personal Financial Planning or the Financial Planner. Accordingly, there are various and diverse notions of what a Financial Planner is supposed to do.

The scramble to serve clients poses difficult problems not only for the consumer, but often for the entrant supplier. Many firms have been wrestling with the following difficult issue: To what extent do we want to be involved with financial services product implementation, which may involve commissions and licensing, and may deteriorate our position of impartial objectivity? Licensing and financial planning regulation is another issue. If the practitioner does not rush to regulate himself, government will do so, with the associated complications and inefficiencies. California's legislature is pioneering research to develop possible model legislation that could regulate California Financial Planners as professionals.

Financial Planners cross many traditional professional lines. They must be licensed in each of the areas from which they receive commissions. This is not always an easy matter for the busy professional. Licenses, governed by each state, typically require passing examinations and sometimes completing course work. Those who charge a fee for investment advice must generally register as an investment adviser with the federal Securities and Exchange Commission (SEC) though no examination is required.

Now you have an idea of where we have come from, where we are now, and some of the problems we face. Let's take a closer look at the factors that generate the need for Personal Financial Planning.

FINANCIAL FACTORS

Though few people realize it, Personal Financial Planning has become essential for financial survival. Consider, for example, an average group of 100 people who have survived to age 65. Of this group, only one person is wealthy, and only four people are financially independent. Of the remaining 95 people, 51 are totally dependent on either government or private subsidy. Saddest of all, 44 members of this group must continue to work in order to survive. This is a dismal deviation from the American Dream.

What goes wrong? Thousands of dollars have passed through the hands of everyone reaching age 65. What makes the difference between independence and dependence, wealth and poverty? We fail to establish goals, fail to plan for them, and fail to follow the plan.

A hoard of economic goblins threatens our economic standard of living in the 1980s:

- Price inflation
- Progressive federal and state income taxes
- The high cost of borrowed money
- Excessive use of consumer installment credit
- Periodic downturns in the economic system
- Failures in important saving and investing areas
- Decline in liquidity and savings positions

Personal Financial Planning must defend us against each of these threats. Of all factors, inflation and taxation are the most significant since they are clearly experienced and readily understood by the general public. They can be the keys to understanding your potential client.

Inflation, formerly an obscure economic concept, is now very prominent in the public consciousness. It is often directly related to the employee's wages through cost-of-living factors. Inflation, a hot topic, has received abundant media coverage and has become one of the key political issues.

Everyone is aware of inflation's current impact and is concerned about being able to ride the crest of this wave in the future instead of being drowned by it. Yet few have the tools and know-how to act effectively. For example, the Individual Retirement Account (IRA) presented a perfect tax shelter and retirement savings combination. Yet according to a 1982 report released by the Employee Benefit Research Institute, only 57.6 percent of employees earning in excess of $50,000 established an IRA in 1982.

Inflation has increased the value of our previously acquired assets, but dramatically decreased the purchasing power of our current dollars. We can expect consumer prices to increase at least 8 percent each year in the next decade. This means that in 1985 our 1980 dollar bought only 71 cents of goods or services. By 1990 that same 1980 dollar will amount to only 56 cents of purchasing value.

Inflation has reduced the real purchasing power of our income and savings. Our saved dollars have deteriorated in value, much like a set of sterling silver dishes that cannot be protected from corrosion.

From 1970 to 1980 the average income rose from about $6000 to $11,000 per annum, in current dollars. But in the same period, the average income rose from about $6000 to $6000 per annum, in 1970 dollars. That's not a misprint. It's a forceful way of saying "no improvement." While our ability to purchase value has *not* changed, our ability to be taxed at higher brackets *has*.

Tax laws are constantly changing and are hopelessly confusing. Proposed changes in the current administration will see middle and high-middle income families hardest hit. These are the people with the ability, (i.e., the discretionary income) to use a Personal Financial Plan. How hard and how long this sector of the population will be taxed is uncertain. It is hard to imagine moving from our present position to a worse one.

At the federal level of government, U.S. income tax-payers have been subject to rates ranging from 14 percent to 70 percent. Added to these incredible tax burdens are the income tax provisions of many states. In California, for example, the taxpayer is subject to additional income tax rates of from 1 percent to 11 percent.

These tax burdens are staggering, but even worse is the simultaneous impact of inflation and progressive income tax rates on take-home pay. As inflated dollar incomes increase, so does the level of taxation. This turns the American Dream into a nightmare.

Typical personal or family dreams include: owning your own home, being a two-car family, taking an annual family vacation, sending the kids to college, and having a comfortable retirement. These are the goals we vaguely expected to be reasonable accomplishments. Notice that typical goals are centered around those things that require money. With inflation and taxation, how many Americans can expect to achieve this dream? Personal Financial Planning is the tool that can repair our broken dreams, but we must have the tool in our hands to begin the work.

These are common economic experiences we have all had in the last decades. What psychological impact have these had?

PSYCHOLOGICAL FACTORS

Marketing is far from a pure science. To reach consumers we have to understand their experiences. We have to look at the emotional factors behind the need for Personal Financial Planning. Remember that a good Personal Financial Planning Service hinges on satisfying the dreams, the emotional needs of the client. What are the emotional factors? There are both threats and incentives to plan financially.

In the consumer's mind financial security is closely related to employment. Formerly, employers provided a major portion of security, from the start of our productive years to our retirement. However, in harder times companies have become less humanitarian. If a corporation has any social responsibility, providing a job at all comes before providing a lush benefit package and retirement plan.

It is regrettable, but a more ruthless kind of corporate personnel policy is developing. Phenomena such as dismissals before vesting and curtailment of traditional retirement benefits are indicators of the emerging stance of letting employees fend for themselves. The emotional impact of such changes ripples out to work peers, family, and friends, and spreads a general feeling of insecurity. Financial planning is gaining popularity with companies as an executive perquisite, according to the Hay Group, a benefits specialist. From 1979 to 1985, the portion of companies offering Personal Financial Planning as a benefit rose from 22 percent to 31 percent (see Bohn in Bibliography). But is this move intended to augment benefits, or to eventually replace them?

Recall the tax situation. The success of tax preparation specialists shows that people feel unable to complete more complicated returns. This inability to deal with complexity is not felt only by the humble wage earner, nor is it confined to tax issues. Even the top managers who handle corporate finances cannot do their own Personal Financial Planning. A recent study (1985) shows that 83 percent of executives earning over $50,000 per annum feel insecure about their ability to make personal financial decisions (see Mattauch in Bibliography). We are overwhelmed by this complication, and perhaps resent it, but we also have a certainty that complexity is now a permanent feature of our financial lives. Further, as a society we have experienced an increase in the fluidity—the speed and number—of changing tax issues. The general public has a frightening prospect for the future. Finances have become so complicated, always changing, that it's difficult to plan sensibly. Remember how you felt when you realized that the IRA was mortal?

Coupled with the new hard-line business attitude toward retirement benefits is another ominous prospect. That is the statistical certainty that the social security plan will not meet the needs of the postwar baby boom.

All these experiences combine to create a continual sense of being only one step ahead of financial disaster. Consumer debt has risen dramatically in the last five years, but is not the answer. It is just one more gnawing worry to cause a sleepless night. We borrow to keep pace with our dreams, hoping somehow that things will improve, but deeply certain that they will not. We want to react sanely to these threats, but it seems impossible to keep pace with all the information currently available to us in the decision-making process. All this paints a dark and negative picture.

There are positive psychological forces working here—positive in the sense of encouraging rather than forcing a smarter use of financial resources. What used to be a matter of keeping up with the Joneses is today more a question of outdoing the Joneses. Whether or not this is sane or right, it is a force operating in the hearts of the public. Even though we are encouraged to want more, few people have the expertise to get more. This leads to another emotional experience: the frustration of never seeming to get closer to achieving our dreams and goals.

The American Dream really is our dream. We have created it, and we maintain it. It is our society, selling itself in a ghostly fashion. It is circular, but we are the ones going around and around.

The influence of the media to propagate and strengthen our dream has been felt, but poorly understood. Our profit-motivated society has a powerful tool in the media. However, the media are being used with little regard to ultimate effect. The more we see, the more we want. The media sell us on a certain life-style through emotionally charged messages. We want more, and we want the tools that will help us get more. Again, the issue is not one of right or wrong. As professionals, we must simply and realistically see the effect on our client.

We also want to do a good job of providing and caring for those in our charge: spouse, children, parents, even friends. We would like to ensure that our families, whether traditional nuclear or newer arrangements, are financially healthy.

Like life insurance, a financial plan is often bought and sold as something we do for those we love. It provides a financial future for all members of the family throughout every stage of their lives, and is a gift we want to be able to give.

The tools needed to make optimal financial decisions are no longer obscure. The marketing of Personal Financial Planning by traditional financial institutions, by department stores, and by single-product vendors is pushing the service to the fore of public awareness. It's out there, and the public knows that tools are available. But what have they got, what do they want, and what can they get?

Several themes emerge. Because of heartless companies and the failing social security scheme, we hear: "Who is going to take care of you if not you? Nobody; not government, not your employer." So we begin to realize that if security is important to us, we must secure it for ourselves. There is a general feeling of fear and distrust throughout the world caused by terrorist attacks, loss of faith in our government, failure of certified safe products. The world—even the United States—is no longer a safe place.

Yes, we want to do something, but how? The problems we face are emotionally charged, complex, and intimidating. Unfortunately, so is the solution. We are overwhelmed by the availability of financial products and services.

Personal Financial Planning should provide a sense of comfort, a sense of "being taken care of" rather than "being taken for a ride." Beyond easing our fears about security, Personal Financial Planning should enable us to move forward in pursuit of our dreams. Any service designed to fill such needs must provide proof that these dreams can become realities.

THE CONSUMERS

Now it's time to meet the people we've been discussing. Successful marketing of Personal Financial Planning Services, like any other intangible service, is a meshing of service with need. Need is a human experience, that is unique to each person. Who is the buyer of Personal Financial Plans? To make sense of large statistical arrays, we need to classify the information presented.

There are several ways to classify consumers for analysis. But remember, this process is only for analysis. Statistics are not people. Regardless of means and norms, almost in defiance of standardized profiles, your clients will emerge as unique individuals. You will need generalized evaluations to develop a marketing strategy, but you must use them to develop empathy, rapport, understanding, and compassion for the people with whom you want to work.

Consumers may be classified by age, education, income, geographic location, cultural background, philosophy, religion, occupation, and family situation. The ways of classification are endless, and must be chosen according to purpose. Our purpose here is to gain a sense of the market for Personal Financial Planning Services and of the type of consumer who comprises the market. With this purpose in mind, we will use the following criteria: age, education, income, and occupation.

The measure of chronological age is helpful, but if we combine this with the family situation, we get a more germane means of classification that we might call the *stage of life*. Here are the stages of life. As you read each description try to associate the generalization with someone you know.

1. Employed Before Marriage.   The consumer has completed his formal education and entered the work force. He is basically concerned with himself, with securing his living situation and rapidly developing his career. He has few concerns and responsibilities.

2. Married Without Children.   The next step in the American Dream is accomplished by finding a mate. Now the consumer begins to deal with a household and develops dreams of the future. Responsibility increases, whether the couple has a single or double income. A rush of new capital must be deployed sensibly in establishing the household.

3. Married With Children.   With the advent of children comes a dramatic increase in expenditure. There may also be a significant rise of income during this stage as the consumer's career develops. The addition of a child to the family presents the most acute and penetrating sense of responsibility to the parents, and protection becomes important. This will force new and more detailed planning and dreaming for the children's future education and benefits.

4. Children Have Left the Nest.   The consumer's earning power is likely to be at its peak. The first pass of the American Dream has been completed, and second careers are often considered. It is important to the consumer that things remain secure and stable as attention returns to the couple and thoughts of their future lives.

5. Retirement.   The consumer has left the work force, with the major task of his working life completed, and now he wants to know what is left for him. He may have embarked on a second career for growth or financial reasons. Maintaining a comfortable income is a concern. There is now greater freedom and independence, reminiscent of the early stages of his life, and an associated desire to take chances. The benefit of maturity and experience will help him avoid extremes.

Education is an important factor in the consumer's makeup. With higher education comes the ability to handle complexity and abstraction. The simple classes of formal education will serve here: none, high school, college, or postgraduate.

It is deceptively simple to categorize by annual income. We must note that gross annual income is an indicator but not the key element in being a consumer of Personal Financial Planning Services. The real key is discretionary income. If we add a measure of minimum net worth, we add the dimension of measuring the consumer's immediate need for Personal Financial Planning with his capability to exercise a plan.

Occupations are the least difficult means of classification. Rather than listing various professions, we can simplify this classification to the following divisions: labor, trades, technical, and executive.

With these classifications established, we can profile those who have been buying Personal Financial Planning Services. Purchasers of the original forms of fragmented planning services were typically age 50 and over. These were people in the latter stages of child raising, empty-nesters, and retirees. More recently, the consumer is in earlier stages of life, either married with children, or even newly married, ranging in age from the mid-thirties and up. The typical consumer has one or more children.

There is still little marketing of Personal Financial Planning Services to people under age 30. The single wage earner has too much of a sense of the present to be genuinely concerned with financial planning for the future. For these people, primary goals are to find an apartment, buy a car, and enjoy life.

Most people aren't ready to start thinking seriously about the future until their early thirties. The newly married and new parents are faced with real and immediate expenses. Their goals become a permanent home or an education for the child.

It is harder to typify the education of our typical consumer. Consumers are inclined to have post high school educations, though not necessarily degrees. The exposure to business and finance seems as significant as college education in influencing people to seek and buy financial expertise.

According to a survey done by Money magazine, 93 percent of those individuals who earned in excess of $50,000 in 1985 bought outside financial advice (see Beasley in Bibliography). Annual income of the buyers of Personal Financial Planning Services is above average, in the $30,000 to $40,000 range for single-income families. However, this category must be tempered by consideration of regional norms. Combined annual income for double-income families is typically in excess of $50,000. Remember that annual income is useful only as an indicator of discretionary income.

As you might expect, entrepreneurs and executives are the largest occupational category of Personal Financial Planning Service consumers. These are people who understand the value of financial services due to their own business experience. They also understand that in order to make money you have to spend money.

This is the nature of the consumer, the person who has bought the service we can provide. But let's do more than look at the past. We can try to get a feeling for what will happen in the future, or at what we could cause to happen. Rather than confining our efforts to an existing market, let's prepare ourselves to extend the market.

Understanding the power of time and compounding, we know that the earlier we start a savings-and-investment program, the greater chance we have for independence or wealth in our lives. Graduates of dental, legal, medical or other professional schools are typically in debt, but they generally aren't for long. Such people are ideal clients, the kind we would groom for discretionary income. This is the youngest stage of life, the "employed before marriage" group. Why not offer them the rudiments of a plan that can grow in scope and power as they grow? As the inexorable economic forces of the 1980s continue to assail their parents, the importance of Personal Financial Planning will become obvious to the new graduates.

Have the uneducated excluded themselves from the market by their fear of the unknown? Basic introductory and education programs offered as part of a Personal Financial Planning Service could make effective inroads to people who could benefit from the service.

Discretionary income is the main ingredient in operating any financial strategy. However, people who currently have no operating leeway can be groomed for success. A preplanning service to develop discretionary income capabilities will also develop the market.

Overcome your notion that professional occupations have the greatest financial rewards. Think back to the last plumbing or carpentry bill you paid. A marketing strategy that acknowledges the financial power and growing acumen of the nonprofessional is essential.

THE MARKET FOR PERSONAL FINANCIAL PLANNING SERVICES

The growth of Personal Financial Planning Services since the early 1980s has been phenomenal. In 1983 alone, there was a 43.5 percent increase in the number of individuals and companies that registered their investment advisory services with the SEC. It is estimated that there are more than 200,000 Financial Planners today, not including those who provide Personal Financial Planning related services (bankers, estate attorneys, insurance agents, investment brokers, accountants, etc.). However, Personal Financial Planning is as yet a fairly untapped market!

Less than 25 percent of the nearly 10 million U.S. households where annual incomes are in excess of $50,000 take advantage of any form of financial consulting or planning services. For financial professionals there is still a substantial market to be reached, merely by expanding existing services.

The reasons for growth in popularity of Personal Financial Planning are partially fad. A gush of media publicity has made the area a new status symbol. But as we have seen, Personal Financial Planning is primarily a necessity. Inflation, changeable tax laws, a volatile economy, and the constant influx of new economic and financial information are the financial and psychological factors that drive the need.

The percentage of the market you will be able to tap will be entirely dependent on two things: potential market and market share. Your potential market is the number of households or earning units within your service area who are earning sufficient incomes to afford and warrant the use of your services. We can express the basic factors in a simple equation.

$$C + P = F \rightarrow PM$$

C = cost of developing a Personal Financial Plan
P = profit you need to make
F = fee you must charge or commission you must earn
PM = those consumers who can afford, or are willing, to purchase your services at that price

Obviously, the higher your fees, the more you limit your potential market.

Market share is the percentage of the potential market you are able to capture through various public relations and marketing approaches. A more detailed formula follows:

$$C + P = F \rightarrow PM * MS = CB$$

MS = market share (a percentage)
CB = client base

It is the actual client base, that is, those clients you will provide service to, that will determine your success. For example:

$$\$500 + \$1000 = \$1500 \rightarrow 100,000 * 1\% = 1000$$

Your strategic marketing plan will be determined in part by the market share you are trying to capture, in order to establish your client base.

CAPTURING YOUR MARKET SHARE

Currently, Personal Financial Planning is a highly unregulated field, and literally anyone can call himself a Financial Planner. Since the title Financial Planner tends to open doors with its air of sophistication and professionalism, the consumer becomes vulnerable to the sale of shoddy services and products. The Better Business Bureau and North American Securities Administrators Association issued a joint alert in August, 1985, warning the public about the fraudulent abuse/misuse of the title Financial Planner. However, the unethical single-product vendor is not your only competitor. The phenomenal growth of the IAFP and registration with the SEC are indicators of those individuals who are trying to provide an ethical, professional service. These figures do not include the traditional and nontraditional institutions who are also vendors of Personal Financial Planning Services.

Even among the bona fide financial service institutions, there is often a tendency to view Personal Financial Planning as just another marketing tool for fragmented financial products such as insurance, tax services, stocks, mutual funds, wills, real estate investments, or retirement plans. True, these are all valid slices of Personal Financial Planning, but they are not the whole pie.

Why are banks now hiring retailing consultants? Imagine walking into your bank's local branch office and seeing a collection of boutiques offering departmentalized services such as insurance, real estate, travel, discount stock brokerage, tax preparation, legal, and financial consulting. This is not a fantastic dream, but an already emerging reality.

Huntington National Bank of Columbus is developing a life-style marketing plan similar to strategies used by Sears. First Union National Bank in Charlotte, North Carolina, now shows videotapes of its financial products. Valley Bank of Nevada has hired a large sales force with no banking background to scout out wealthy and small business customers.

Next to CPAs, bankers have the highest public confidence ratings. This, coupled with their already large client bases, makes them formidable competitors. Banks have large resources with which to start Personal Financial Planning departments and to fund marketing campaigns. Their greatest weakness is the lack of personnel qualified to offer comprehensive services.

Insurance companies now admit that they did not invent Personal Financial Planning, but they are making up for the boast. They have a committed agent force, and are converting these agents to Financial Planners. The training takes time, but these competitors have extensive resources and draw from a diverse product base. Fighting an uphill battle against the common perception that they will do almost anything to sell more insurance, insurance companies are now doing almost anything to sell Personal Financial Planning Services.

Brokerage firms effectively manufacture many of the products used in the implementation of a Personal Financial Plan. This is both a strength and a weakness since their capacity to provide products is marred by potential conflicts of interest over their products.

CPA firms have been slow to enter the Personal Financial Planning Service market because of their rigid ethical strictures. Their advantages are obvious: established relationships with existing clients, expertise in many areas of the Personal Financial Planning process, ability to attract qualified personnel. Despite these advantages, there is hesitation to give specific advice that would require licensing and registration.

There is also competition from department stores. Because of their ability to access the consumer, department stores are able to secure deposits by the billions through aggressive selling.

In the flurry to offer new services, the financial professional has failed to capture a fair market share. There are great risks to our clients and our livelihood in taking a noncompetitive or passive stance. There is a real need for our services, and if our clients cannot obtain them from us, they will go elsewhere.

Why is the independent financial professional absent from the market place? One reason is the consumer's attitude about our ability to provide the service. Studies point out the negative public perception of various financial professionals as Financial Planners.

Lawyers are considered too specialized. Stockbrokers have a conflict of interest with commissions. Bankers have narrow capabilities and are too conservative to provide effective, dynamic plans. Insurance agents are self-serving, rather limited in education to do financial planning. Certified Financial Planners have questionable certification and lack objectivity. Certified Public Accountants (CPAs) are viewed as too narrowly trained for broad financial or business advice.

Please note that public perception, a result of information available, is not fact. The financial professional is failing to provide enough information about his capabilities.

Why are we hesitant to embark? The factors most often quoted in surveys are: failure to recognize opportunity, fear of the unknown, lack of time, poor public relations or marketing efforts, and limited resources. Yet the majority of innovative Personal Financial Planning organizations have three or fewer partners and use independent broker-dealers for implementation. There are emerging support networks for the independent Financial Planner, including: Financial Service Corporation International (Atlanta, Georgia), Private Ledger (San Diego, California), Integrated Resources, Inc. (New York, New York), Anchor Financial Services (Phoenix, Arizona), and Southmark Financial (Dallas, Texas).

Opportunity is knocking, but someone else is answering the door. That is what this book is about. There are hard questions for the financial professional to consider. Are you willing to learn a new profession? How can you use your existing expertise to participate in the fastest growing sector of financial services?

If you are ready to enter the market, you must overcome your historical low visibility. You must learn to use public relations and marketing techniques to sustain public trust in your accuracy, effectiveness, and confidentiality. You must outgrow any shyness of the limelight.

Marketing and public relations are both soft skills, relying on qualitative rather than quantitative methods. This may require a drastic change in your thinking, a drift from figures to features, from the abstract to the unique and human. The central issue will be how to develop the service and market it.

The ideal role for a Financial Planner is to be the financial coordinator of a client's many financial and tax needs, calling on specialists when appropriate. During the development and marketing processes, we must keep in sight two primary goals:

1. *Ethics.* Maintain the highest possible ethics, codes of conduct, integrity, sincerity, and professionalism.

2. *Aggression.* Capture your fair share of the Personal Financial Planning market without apology or hesitation.

In balance, these ideas will enable you to conduct a campaign which is in keeping with your professional sense of ethics but aggressive enough for you to succeed.

2

What Is and What Should Be

INTRODUCTION

If you plan to provide a Personal Financial Planning Service, you will be competing for business. Your competitors will be highly reputable firms, individual practitioners, even your own clients. The advent of personal computers has brought with it a variety of low-cost software packages that are intended to let the layman perform complicated planning functions in the privacy of his own home.

To market your service successfully, you must distinguish yourself from the rest. The distinction must be apparent in your service, your methods, your person. Study the competition to find out what works so that you can do it better and to find out what does not work so that you can avoid doing it at all cost.

Further, you must understand the public perceptions of Personal Financial Planning, Financial Planners, and of your own profession. What are the strengths and weaknesses of the competition, of your profession? What can you do to eliminate real or perceived shortcomings?

To get a feeling for all this, let's outline the ideal Personal Financial Planning Service in terms of what clients want and expect. With the ideal in mind, we can survey what is currently available to the consumer, noting areas where you can differentiate your service by improving toward the ideal. Before we can define the ideal Personal Financial Planning Service, we need to understand what planning is in general and to sharpen some terms that can aid our understanding of the client's experience.

FANTASY, DREAM, GOAL, AND PLAN

The most exciting image of the Financial Planner is that of dream mechanic. His work can make dreams come true. But how? What are the tools of this trade? Here are some conceptual tools that have served me well over the years. These are special definitions of the words fantasy, dream, goal, and plan.

A fantasy is a possibility that goes through your mind. You may decide to associate yourself with a fantasy, or you may not. It is simply one of the endless number of possibilities for your life. Since we have no fixed association with our fantasies, they come and go freely, and remain light and flexible.

A dream is a fantasy to which you have attached yourself. Your mind returns to a dream often, and elaborates on the details. Dreams are closer to your heart than fantasies; they carry your emotions. This makes them heavier than fantasies, slower to change, and less flexible. A dream is something that you seriously wish would happen in your life. You may even take steps to bring a dream into reality.

Steps or actions taken in your life can turn dreams into goals. Goals are fully realized dreams, with all the wealth of detail and solidity of this world. However, goals are set in the future. They are realistic images of dreams that will come to pass if you take appropriate steps and actions. A goal is a dream that you intend to realize, and the steps you must take to do this are called a plan.

A plan is a model of reality that you must build to help you reach your goals. It is a list of steps, a chart of action, a road map that leads the way to each goal.

Here's an example that shows how these ideas work together. Like all young boys, I wondered what I would be when I grew up. No, I never expected to be a Financial Planner, but I fantasized about being a detective, a railway engineer, and a famous author. These were my career fantasies. Few of them stayed with me as I grew. Only one of them held much emotional appeal over the years.

I continued to fantasize about the life of an author. The fantasy became a dream as I imagined in more detail the life of quiet introspection, the freedom of working at home, and the gratification of having others read my thoughts. As I continued my professional career, the desire to share my ideas with others and to become a respected authority shaped and nourished the dream.

Finally, I decided to write this book. In order to do this, I would have to set aside the time, do the research, and create the manuscript. When I took these necessary steps, my dream of writing as a career became a goal. When I realistically planned my life to accommodate this goal, it happened.

Fantasy, dream, and goal are not elements in a hierarchy of desirability. Dreams are not more valuable than fantasies; goals are not better than dreams. All three play an important role in Personal Financial Planning. As a Financial Planner, you must recognize the differences among the three, and be prepared to work with each.

You should present fantasies to clients whose dreams are needlessly restricted. Offer alternates and encourage clients to reach out to the full scope of possibilities. Help clients sort out their dreams from their fantasies.

The mechanical part of Personal Financial Planning is to convert dreams to goals. Once you have identified the goals, help clients build the model of reality that includes each goal. This is the Personal Financial Plan.

Converting a dream to a goal requires a plan of action, but it must be appropriate action. To this day, I can still hear my father swear that he would give his right arm to be able to play the piano. Playing the piano may have been a good dream, but according to his plan, the goal reached would have been unworkable. Sometimes you will have to show clients that their fantasies cannot become realistic dreams, or that their dreams must change shape to become goals. But some fantasies are worthwhile dreams, and Personal Financial Planning can make dreams into goals that come true.

A plan is a model of reality. Models can involve time, and can be open to, or sealed against, the effects of change. Consider a photograph. It is a static, two-dimensional representation of reality. Over a period of time, a photograph gives a poorer and poorer representation of a person because the person changes but the photograph does not. Any plan that involves the life span of clients, not just their current position, will involve time and must be open to change. If you doubt the need for changing a plan in response to a changing environment, consider using a 20-year-old road map on your next vacation drive.

For these reasons, a good Personal Financial Plan is not a static product, but part of an ongoing process of modeling, action, feedback, and modification. The planning you do as a Financial Planner has to be temporal and open. The plan document you produce as a product must always be one of a series of revised and improved documents.

The image of the Financial Planner as a dream mechanic haunts me. The Financial Planner must envision, or even help create, the clients' dreams. He must then have the know-how to help clients turn dreams into goals and set goals into a plan that will ultimately achieve the dreams.

Please note that we are discussing the clients' goals and dreams, not yours. The job of dream mechanic requires you to free your mind from your own value systems and give full credit to the individual, unique, and even idiosyncratic dreams of your clients. You can show them how to dream, but the dreaming must be theirs. Could you help a client whose dream is to work nine months of each year and to travel for three? Think about it.

You may be wondering what fantasies and dreams and temporal modeling have to do with marketing a Personal Financial Planning Service. The connection really is simple. The service you intend to sell must meet the emotional needs of your clients. The emotional needs of your clients are filled when their dreams become goals. If you can grasp this, you understand the living heart of the matter; and you will succeed.

Now we can sketch out the ideal Personal Financial Planning Service, from four perspectives:

- The service
- The planner
- The process
- The product

We are working at the fantasy or dream stages of your Personal Financial Planning Service. To make these fantasies more real, let's talk about the ideal service as if it were already a fact. This will help you convert parts of the fantasy into your own dreams.

THE IDEAL—WHAT SHOULD BE

The Ideal Service

Personal Financial Planning treats our financial health as holistic medicine treats our physical health. When clients go to their Financial Planners, they seek services similar to those provided by their physicians. They are buying experiences more than things. Because of the holistic nature of Personal Financial Planning, the Financial Planner is responsible for delivering everything that goes with the plan—the full service.

The successful sale of any service depends on the benefit gained, or the loss avoided, by the client. We can define our ideal Personal Financial

Planning Service by describing the benefits the client wants to gain. These fall into eight categories:

- Security
- Direction
- Advice
- Expertise
- Objectivity
- Coordination
- Time
- Value

Security. This is the most important gain that clients can obtain from our service. Security may not be foremost in their minds, but it will ultimately satisfy their real needs for happiness. Security comes when clients see their dreams converted to goals—goals that can and will be reached by the plan. Security itself is not a goal, but a state of being; it requires constant maintenance. Clients don't want to be secure for only a year; they want to be secure for a lifetime.

That's why the ideal is a service, not a product. Our services must be living entities and include periodic reviews, a constant watch on investments, a monitoring of tax problems, and the like. Our service provides whatever it takes to let clients know that they are "covered."

This relieves clients from the pressures of constant decision-making. For example, Personal Financial Planning includes tax planning, and tax laws are fluid. Since our service produces a dynamic plan, which is reviewed and revised as required, it prevents yesterday's spacious tax shelter from becoming today's cluttered shack.

Direction. Consumers want to know what to do. This seems simple, but we must never overlook this essential part of our service. We must give clients direction. The ideal service provides them with direction at whatever level of detail they need in order to act on the plan.

Direction involves more than plan implementation, however. We must tell the client when periodic reviews are needed; how to report changes in their lives, goals, or dreams; and how to react to changes in the economic environment. Beyond this, our service must be a catalyst, motivating the client to act through the plan.

Advice. Our service offers clients a trusted financial adviser and friend. People can interact with people within our "high touch" rather than "high tech" framework. True, consumers want to buy the work of an expert and objective professional. But more, they want to talk to a person who has a sincere concern for their financial well-being.

Expertise. Consumers of our service expect to gain the expertise of professionals. To deliver this level of expertise, we gather and analyze information, producing plans that enable clients to reach their goals.

In an area as complex and diverse as Personal Financial Planning, the expertise needed will often be specialized and varied. This expertise is not crammed into any individual Financial Planner. Rather, our ideal service connects clients with a network of expertise that is coordinated by the Financial Planner.

This network, which assures clients of the level of expertise with which they are connected, is both visible and flexible. When we work with clients' own bankers, insurance agents, or tax preparers, we gain their valuable trust and familiarity.

Objectivity. A defining feature of professional service is its high level of objectivity. Our service will shape, adjust, and regulate itself by working to create client trust in its objectivity.

Our objectivity shows in our willingness to provide an overview and to clarify or refine goals, without imposing our personal standards or risk tolerance levels on clients. Plan options are offered in a clearly unbiased fashion, with a disclosure of how these might affect commissions or fees. Clients are not obligated to purchase only those products available from our service, but may go to their preferred vendor.

Clients experience the objectivity of our service when we recommend the services of another financial professional, or when they are free to choose their own specialist experts.

Coordination. Expertise is required in many areas, of which estate planning, accounting, insurance, and law are but a few. Since it is difficult for one individual to master all these areas, the client must be aware of our service as a coordinating center. We can offer the client our own coordinated range of expertise, or we can offer to coordinate with the client's preferred financial professionals.

Along with a coordination of expertise, our service reflects an awareness of the interaction of all components of the plan. The service embraces and coordinates such diverse factors as salary and benefits, savings, debts, stocks, mutual funds, home equity, life insurance, disability insurance, home and car insurance, income taxes, social security taxes, estate and gift taxes, trusts, real estate investments, tax-sheltered investments, and retirement plans.

When these factors are coordinated by our ideal service, they become the financial nuts and bolts of the machinery that will manifest the client's goals. Our service coordinates all levels of planning, implementation, and maintenance.

Time. Clients may or may not have the expertise to do their own plans, but if they are interested in buying our services, they most certainly want to gain time. So we make sure that our ideal service gives clients the information they need, with a minimal investment of their own time.

This applies to our help with the data-gathering and goal-setting steps of the process. It also applies to the final report itself, where the volume of material is not of value, but rather the analyzed and condensed information. The information we present to clients is tailored to match their preferred mode of comprehension. How is it be easiest for them to consider alternatives? Our service lets them play *what if* in an easy but meaningful way.

Value. Of course, clients want value. Value is related to service and cost in this way:

$$V = S/C$$

Value (V) is the level of service (S) divided by the cost (C) of the service. The higher the level of service, the more the perceived value; the lower the cost, the more the perceived value. And vice versa.

Our ideal Personal Financial Planning Service lets clients know what levels of service are available and at what cost. This might take the form of a written fee policy or a schedule of service levels that we discuss with clients. When clients buy the service, they have a clear idea of exactly what will be charged and on what basis.

This brings us to a consideration of the methods of compensation for our ideal service. There are three principal methods in use today: fee only, commission only, and a combination of fee and commission.

The fee-only service gathers information, analyzes it, and produces a plan that enables each client to reach his goals. The client pays the service fee whether or not he implements the plan or any portion of it. Usually, the fee charged is based on the complexity and depth of the plan created, as well as the time needed to collect and analyze the information.

A commission-only service performs the same gathering, analysis, and planning functions, but depends on commissions from product sales for compensation. Financial professionals who offer this service must be licensed for the products they sell. Rather than direct the client to others for specific products, they sell the instruments for which they are licensed.

Fee-and-commission services do the work that leads up to and includes the plan for a fixed fee. They also earn commissions on the sale of products required for plan implementation. Since this kind of service has the potential to earn commissions with each client, the set fees are usually lower than those charged by a fee-only service.

At this point, you have probably surmised that our ideal service works with all these modes of compensation. Our service uses the method that maximizes the value received by the client.

To define an ideal Personal Financial Planning Service, we have looked at the benefits that the client can gain. If this glimpse at an ideal service has given you a few moments of doubt, please consider them as a warm-up. Now we're going to turn to a mirror to see if we can find the ideal Financial Planner.

The Ideal Planner

Being a Financial Planner is not purely philanthropic. Since you are thinking of becoming one, you obviously feel that it can be profitable. However, if you are motivated purely by profit, you will not be a good Financial Planner. Yes, there is ample financial reward in this profession, but if this is your prime motivation, you will fail.

The greatest opportunity offered to the Financial Planner is not financial gain, but the opportunity for learning, growth, and human satisfaction. The job can be a platform for you to develop professionally and personally. If you motivate yourself with the excitement of helping people reach their goals and of providing them with security in uncertain times, then you will differentiate yourself from your competitors and you will succeed.

Personal Financial Planning can be your introduction to the softer, more human side of the financial industry. The challenge that a Financial Planner faces is to match the plan to the heart of the client. To meet this challenge, you must acquire "people" skills, in addition to marketing and technical expertise. As we define the ideal Financial Planner, we'll be focusing on personal attributes and roles played, as well as professional and technical requirements.

In order to run the ideal Personal Financial Planning Service and to deliver a good Personal Financial Plan, the Financial Planner must be more a capable psychologist than a button-pushing technician. Earlier we used the image of a dream mechanic to visualize the Financial Planner. Here's a more concrete image that will help us focus on the ideal.

The ideal Financial Planner is the quarterback of a team of financial experts. He is responsible for developing and coordinating his team. He is also the single point of human contact between the client and the expert team. While the ideal planner may have his own areas of financial expertise, his main skill is in coordinating the people who play and the client for whom they play.

What does the consumer of Personal Financial Planning Services look for in his Financial Planner, his quarterback? He wants a trusted, objective, and expert professional. This professional must serve as:

- Coordinator
- Counselor
- Educator
- Motivator
- Watchdog

Let's look at these things one at a time.

Trusted, Objective, Expert Professional. The client wants the services of a professional. As the ideal Financial Planner, you have the special training, education, knowledge, and skills to do your job with a degree of perfection. You are expert enough as a financial professional to coordinate the diverse specialists on your team. You are expert enough in human skills to advise, educate, and plan with your client from a shared perspective.

More importantly, as the ideal planner you can actually help clients experience your professionalism. By understanding your clients and how their minds work, you can provide an experience of professionalism tailored to their individual needs. For example, your level of technical education and ability is evident from your certification and credentials. However, your skills as a coordinator are demonstrated to the client during the actual process of creating and implementing the plan.

As the ideal Financial Planner, you are affiliated or registered with a reputable agency, such as these:

Institute of Certified Financial Planners (ICFP)

Institute of Chartered Financial Analysts (ICFA)

International Association for Financial Planning (IAFP)

National Association of Personal Financial Advisors (NAPFA)

National Association of Securities Dealers (NASD)

Securities and Exchange Commission (SEC)

You may hold one or more of these designations:

Certified Employee Benefits Specialist (CEBS)

Certified Financial Planner (CFP)

Chartered Financial Analyst (CFA)

Chartered Financial Consultant (ChFC)

Chartered Life Underwriter (CLU)

Chartered Property and Casualty Underwriter (CPCU)

Enrolled Agent (EA)

Registered Health Underwriter (RHU)

Registered Investment Adviser (RIA)

Registered Representative (RR)

Residential Manager (RM)

As we saw in defining the ideal service, a professional spends a majority of time in Personal Financial Planning activities. Therefore, as the ideal Financial Planner, you will make your living by doing financial planning. The groups you will be affiliated with will provide additional evidence of your commitment to professionalism and your specialized education.

Some clients place little value in diplomas and certificates. To them the real measure of ability is results. You can demonstrate your experience and success via personal and professional referrals. As the ideal Financial Planner, you should offer these to the client who values them.

For clients who place their own evaluations above credentials and references, you can demonstrate your professionalism in a sincere interest for their financial well-being. A true professional has the interests of his clients at heart, and will give the best advice possible even if it means losing a commission or an additional fee.

Clients can experience the professionalism they seek through any or all of these vehicles. As the ideal planner, you are a generalist, not a specialist in the technical aspects of finances. You have a broad exposure to business and finance. You may be very knowledgeable in one or more areas, but your strength lies in comprehending and organizing the areas of special expertise into a coherent whole.

This is the image of the quarterback. The planner is a generalist, with access to a team of specialists in diverse areas such as law, tax consulting, estate planning, risk management, pensions, and profit sharing. It is this position that lets the planner offer objectivity.

Objectivity shows in your ability to synchronize perspectives, values, and dreams with the client. Picture the quarterback in his stance behind the center. Before the play begins, he glances up and down the lines, swiveling his head to ensure that all is ready. The ideal planner also swivels his head, but in a multiplicity of directions and dimensions. You can shift your focus from technical details to the overview, from generally accepted value systems to the unique values of your client.

The "swivel head" of the ideal Financial Planner is what generates the experience of objectivity for the client. You can adopt any level of detail and support any dream of the client. Without expressing personal preferences or standards, you can offer the overview, and clarify or refine goals. You can do all this while keeping within the values and risk tolerance of the client. The client sees you as unattached to any one product or strategy, free of bias, but not without purpose. As ideal Financial Planner, your objectivity operates under the ultimate purpose of maximizing client happiness. From such a position, you act as a buyer on behalf of your client—instead of a seller of financial products or services.

The final attribute needed in the Financial Planner is trust. The consumer of a Personal Financial Planning Service wants to find a trusted adviser. The factors that build an experience of objective, expert professionalism also build trust, but this happens over time. There are additional factors that build trust quickly.

The ideal Financial Planner is dedicated to serving local clients. You enjoy a solid reputation in the community, and are already a familiar name to the client. You have a reputation for being committed to the confidentiality of your client's affairs.

This exhausts the key attributes of the ideal Financial Planner as a professional. Now we turn to the roles he must play for his client.

Coordinator.　　You must coordinate on many levels. You help assemble data, make analyses, and produce a well-written, concise report that coordinates all information. As quarterback of the expert team, you coordinate the work of the professionals needed to build and implement the plan.

This means that you have enough familiarity with the technical areas to be able to understand and properly coordinate the players, the products, and the results via the medium of the plan. When you hit an area in which your expertise is shallow, you work with as many other professionals as are needed in order to develop a good plan.

Human Counselor. Clients are worried about their financial futures. They want to trust someone, not only on the basis of accredited or demonstrable skill, but on the basis of whom they are as a person. The most important aspects of trust are built by your interaction with clients. You must be counselor and friend. This stance allows you to bring objectivity and independence to the planning and implementation process.

Your presence as friend and trusted counselor means that you must swivel your head to get a clear picture of what clients want. Don't let your technical ego overwhelm your objective. Don't be so busy posing as a source of knowledge that you lose your clients' rapport. Don't boost your ego at your clients' expense, unless your interest in Personal Financial Planning is academic and not as a profession.

This means that you should be humanly accessible, both in the office and outside of it—not brusque or hard to reach. Your sincere concern should show in each interaction with a client, and you should always have time (or should set aside future time) to talk.

You also serve the whole client. Though each client may be embodied in a single person, he or she is often connected to a family unit. You should know the family, and how it meshes its dreams together. You should involve both spouses or all key family members in the planning process.

Your philosophy can coincide with that of the client, whether conservative or liberal. You can focus on preservation of wealth or accumulation of wealth, depending on the client's needs.

To become a trusted financial adviser, you should do several things. Be a sounding board. Listen and advise the client about the choices to be made. There is a fine line between recommending a course of action and making a decision. Clients must always make the decisions, but you must help them feel out the results of each decision to the level of detail with which they feel confident.

The sounding board idea is important so that your clients can develop their ideas and test alternatives and so that you can understand your clients' real dreams and needed goals. This means that you must be an active listener. Beyond the proper credentials and training, the most important quality you can develop as the ideal Financial Planner is the ability to really hear what your clients have to say. A good Financial Planner is a good listener.

Educator.   Often you must expose clients to new ideas and concepts. It is not enough that you have an understanding of the situations and strategies involved. You must be able to convey this understanding to clients at levels that enable them to make their own decisions. This touches on your skills as a head swiveler again. You must tailor and format information to match the comprehension needs of clients.

Personal Financial Planning is often shown as a pyramid. Building blocks such as risk management, investment strategies, estate planning, tax planning, and cash management form the base. These narrow up to the crown block: the plan itself. The information contained in the pyramid can be presented from the narrow and abstract crown block to the broad and specific base blocks, or vice-versa. Does the client want a top-down presentation of facts, starting with the abstract levels of the plan and leading to the specific, supportive details? Or is it easier for the client to reach the abstract levels of the plan by building it up from the basic blocks? You know how best to present information to the individual client.

Motivator.   You also motivate the client to act. As the ideal Financial Planner, you understand the psychology of human needs for:

- Survival
- Security
- Belonging
- Love and affection
- Recognition
- Achievement
- Creativity
- Adventure

Why? Because no plan can work in and of itself. The plan is only a model of reality. To make the goals of a plan into realities, the client must follow the actions defined by the plan. One of the most frustrating things you will encounter as a Financial Planner is your client's failure to act.

How can you motivate the client to act on the plan? You know how—it's part of your job.

Watchdog. The ideal Financial Planner is a fierce watchdog for his client; this can only come from a sincere interest in the client. Being a watchdog means periodic review of the plan and ensures that plan goals still reflect the client's dreams, and that planned actions are correct for the current economic environment.

At first, you may have to encourage the client to want this watchdog activity. You may have to offer the maintenance process as a low-cost service, or as a free service for a limited period of time. The client may need time to realize the ongoing nature of Personal Financial Planning, but you can make it an easy learning curve.

As the client's watchdog, the ideal Financial Planner keeps abreast of the economic environment (investments, tax problems, estate planning considerations, etc.) via publications and professional associations. You advise the client of new possibilities at appropriate intervals or when circumstances warrant a decision or change in actions.

The Ideal Process

Recall our recipe for baking the Personal Financial Planning pie:

> Financial planning is the process of coordinating a broad range of financial services, products, and strategies. These must be consistent with the client's goals and values. The process must develop and maintain a plan of action to reach the client's personal objectives. The plan must respond to changes in goals and environment, and reflect the client's stage of life; it must also include transfer of wealth at death.

The operative word in this definition is *process*. Financial planning is not a static thing, but a process. Any process can be viewed as a series of steps. The steps do not always follow one after the other; often they overlap in time. With this in mind, we can define the ideal process in terms of six essential steps.

1. Collect data
2. Set goals
3. Analyze data
4. Create plan

5. Implement plan

6. Review plan

Step 1. Collect Data. This first step in the ideal process involves gathering all the data that will be needed in subsequent analysis and planning. It will give you and your client a picture of the current situation.

You gather data via interviews, questionnaires, or worksheets. These are designed to make the gathering of data as painless and efficient for the client as possible. Your technical training will indicate exactly what information is needed. Here are some examples:

- Present family budget
- Names of relatives, guardians, in-laws, and previous spouses
- All assets and their fair market value, including business interests and life insurance policies
- Depreciable assets and current depreciable value
- Copies of personal income tax returns for the past three years
- Copies of all wills and trust agreements
- Listing of all real estate holdings with their cost and fair market value, and deeds of trust
- Listing of securities, mutual funds, certificates of deposit (CDs), and savings and checking accounts
- Titles listing how property is held (joint, separate, or community)
- Listing of corporate benefits

Step 2. Set Goals. This step in data gathering comprises the information that isn't written down as figures on balance sheets. Rather, it is the "fantasy to dream to goal" part of the process. Data gathering and analysis show clients where they are now, but this step defines where they want to go in the future.

Often clients define goals in broad, general, or abstract terms, such as "Take care of my retirement," "Protect my spouse in the event of accident or death," "Increase spendable income by reducing income taxes." Sharpen these statements to clearly focused and attainable goals. A good criterion is measurability. Ask questions such as "How will you know when . . .?"

Decisions in these areas affect not only each client, but each client's family as well. All parties involved, especially a spouse, must attend and take an active part in setting goals. In formulating reasonable goals, you should take into account ages of the client and spouse, arrangement of family unit, life-style, and attitude toward consumption. Here your swivel head must be at its loosest to reach compromises between the clients' expectations and reasonable goals.

Often conflicts arise and compromise will be necessary for the plan to succeed. For example, the goal of a new home may vie with the building of a retirement fund. This is an expected, desirable part of the ideal process. It is through conflict that the planning process forces families to establish goal priorities and then to make firm decisions on how to reach them.

Step 3. Analyze Data. Now you have all the information about where the client is and where he wants to go. Your analysis will identify problems that must be resolved to accomplish the desired goals, and may be expressed in conventional forms, such as balance sheets and budgets.

This step of our ideal process calls on your expertise as a coordinator. You must integrate cash management, tax planning, risk management, investment planning, retirement planning, estate planning, and the client's special objectives.

The foundation for making sound short- and long-term financial decisions begins with the preparation of a balance sheet. At future meetings, new balance sheets should be prepared and then compared with the original one to monitor goals. This step in the process is critical, as it provides a feedback and revision loop for dynamic planning.

Step 4. Create Plan. This is the only product you create: the actual plan document. The plan contains a summary of all the input data and defined goals, as well as written recommendations and alternative solutions to problem areas. The plan is presented in a format and style that makes it easy for the client to comprehend. We will discuss the content of the plan in more detail when we define the ideal product.

This step in the ideal process includes plan presentation to the client. Explain all parts of the plan, providing as much detail as the client needs for full understanding and full support. During this step, you can explore various options.

Your expertise as a broad-based financial generalist will be essential here. You must be familiar with various planning strategies:

- Planned use of credit
- Periodic forced savings
- Home equity as an investment device
- Maximizing income tax deductions
- Tax shelters
- Use of life insurance and disability insurance
- Planning an emergency fund
- Maximizing use of corporate benefits
- Use of gifts to reduce taxes
- Use of wills and trusts
- Investment for long- and short-term growth

Investment strategy can be developed only after goals are set. Is a growth or income strategy needed? This choice is determined by the degree of risk the client can take, plus the client's age, income, resources, and temperament. You will also need to review the client's current investment portfolio to determine if the mix is well diversified.

Step 5. Implement Plan.   Here your skill as a coordinator comes into play again. You must coordinate and implement appropriate products and services for the client. Since implementation may spread over long periods of time, this step will be ongoing, hand in hand with the next step.

Step 6. Review Plan.   This is the maintenance and watchdog part of our ideal process. It continues as long as there is time and change in the world. Here, feedback loops enter into the planning process, so that the plan can be constantly adjusted and tuned to allow for the effects of change.

Changes can be external, in the economic environment; or internal, in the client's dreams and goals. Some changes, such as those due to stage of life, can be anticipated; but some cannot. Every plan should be reviewed once a year (regardless of complexity) and changed to meet new goals or situations.

Overall, the ideal Personal Financial Planning process results in a comprehensive overview of the client's financial picture, clearly defined priorities and objectives, recommended strategies, coordination and implementation of these strategies, and periodic updating and tracking of financial affairs to accommodate changing circumstances.

The Ideal Product

Financial planning is a service, not a product. However, if any similarity could be drawn between financial planning and a product, it would be to the actual written plan that is provided to the client.

An ideal plan reflects an integrated and holistic approach—the whole pie, baked in balance and harmony. The parts of the ideal product—the slices of the pie—include:

- Cash management
- Tax planning
- Risk management
- Investment planning
- Retirement planning
- Estate planning
- Special objectives

A section of the plan document will be devoted to each of these aspects, plus summary and action sections. Remember that your plan is a visible and enduring image of your firm. In line with what your client expects, your product should indicate that your firm delivers solid value.

The ideal product is condensed information, formatted into a presentation mode that is clear and meaningful for the client. You have to be a psychologist again. Does your client want data presented in rows of numbers, graphs, narrative text, or in a combination of these formats?

The ideal plan is personal. Use your judgment when you include computer-generated reports. Be selective about what computer reports you include. Your client expects personalized treatment, in line with your sincere interest in his financial life, so be sure that your plan document reflects this attitude.

The format and content of the plan must be personalized for each client, but the general aspects of each section can be described.

Summary.   This is a clear-cut statement of the goals which have been defined by the client and a description of what the plan will do when implemented. This is the plan's purpose, and it can help both you and your client maintain perspective when you get lost in the intricate details of financial mechanics.

The summary should also highlight the problems uncovered during the analysis step of the process, along with the recommended solutions. It provides a point of quick reference to explain the details of the subsequent sections of the plan.

Cash Management.   This section shows in detail how the client should manage cash. In particular, the client will get direction for operating the household because this section includes a revised family budget. This is the place for your analysis of:

- Current situation
- Budgeting
- Cash flow
- Debt management

This section of the plan may be presented as balance sheets with supporting schedules. It should also include the needed cash flow statements, derived from analyses of prior year expenditures.

Tax Planning.   This is a review of the client income tax situation and those planning techniques which can be employed successfully. It is derived from the work of your team's tax expert, but is summarized or expanded to meet the client's needs.

Risk Management.   Here you review scenarios on death, disability, and disasters in order to lead to a review of property, health, accident, and disability insurance. Include your comments on the levels of insurance needed to reach the client's goals. Again, while your source for this information will be one of your experts, you should adapt the information to suit the client when you prepare your product.

You may be able to boost the client's security greatly in this section by your opinion on whether potential personal property insurance claims can be adequately supported by an inventory or photographs. This section of the plan also should include your opinion on the adequacy of hospitalization and major medical coverage and of disability and life insurance coverage.

Investment Planning.   In this section you trace the development of an investment strategy that fits the client's personal investment preferences. This part of your product includes cash flow projections to determine the amount of discretionary income and a proposed investment portfolio mix to meet all of the client's goals.

This is the place for your précis of the investment expert's comments and recommendations on the client's current investment portfolio.

Retirement Planning.   Your ideal product treats this stage of life in a separate section. Retirement security is often a major goal of Personal Financial Planning. This goal touches on the client's overall belief in the planning process and on your individual ability to plan for his future. This section alone can motivate your client to act on the plan.

Deal with your expert's recommendations on maximizing all company benefits. Include detailed plans for meeting future needs. If the client is a business owner, deal with strategies for disposing closely held businesses.

Estate Planning.   This area needs discussion since the way in which the client plans the estate can significantly affect the heirs after the client's death. This section of the plan covers topics such as disposition of the estate, a review of wills and trust agreements, an examination of estate tax exposure. Your review of the various planning tools that can be used should appear in this section.

Special Objectives.   Clients' individual goals deserve a special section in the plan. More than anything else, you can motivate clients to implement your plan and buy your services as watchdog when you show them how their dreams can become attainable goals.

Action Plan.   Extract what the client must do, and when, from the plan document. You and your client will save valuable time. Since your client bought your service to have a clear plan of action, make sure this section of the plan is clear and concise. Your ideal plan details the implementation steps. Plans should provide perspective, analysis, and balance. This includes the actions needed to implement and maintain the plan.

THE REAL—WHAT IS

Use and Abuse

We now have a clear picture of the ideal service, planner, process, and product. We can use these ideals to find gaps between what the consumer wants and what is now available. Our next step is to survey the competition, the suppliers of currently available Personal Financial Planning Services. Before we look at those who are valid competition, let's eliminate those who are not.

As we have seen, the ideal service includes a detailed review of all relevant information about a client's finances and culminates in a plan of action to reach the client's personal goals and objectives. This theoretical model of Personal Financial Planning was established in the early 1980s. However, even at the end of this decade, theory and facts are widely separated.

Since Personal Financial Planning is a new field, there is ambiguity as to what Personal Financial Planning is and what a Financial Planner does. There are no restrictions on using the term Financial Planner, as compared with the controlled use of other professional designations, such as engineer or physician.

Some of the problems arising from the newness of the field are not created out of deliberate bad faith, but are part and parcel of any new discipline. However, some Financial Planners are clearly bandits, using the period of uncertainty and lack of regulation to profit in unethical or illegal ways.

Here are two pending criminal charge cases. In the first, the planner sold investors interests in gold from a Nevada mine. He claimed to be able to sell the gold to California precious metal dealers for a 120% annual return to investors. In the second, a business owner in Utah claimed to rip apart old computers for precious metal content. In both cases, these "Financial Planners" raised millions of dollars, with exorbitant finder's fees (see Weiss and Phillips in Bibliography).

Financial Planners who work with full-service financial firms are often regulated by federal agencies as registered investment advisers. However, others are unsupervised, unregulated, and unqualified. Many independent practitioners are accountable only to themselves, and use feigned objective advice merely as a sales pitch for their products. Some give free or fee advice on topics such as cash flow, budget, or financial statements; then they make unwarranted gains on commissions earned during the implementation of slanted plans.

Individual practitioners are not alone with regard to questionable practices. Large and trusted institutions also have had a mottled record. Some view Personal Financial Planning as a marketing tool for their financial products. Others have Personal Financial Planning departments that are no more than redesigned product outlets.

Also legitimate, but on the edge of ethical behavior, are single-product salespeople who use Personal Financial Planning as a buzzword to cover their sales activities with glory. Most people are not logical about service purchases. They buy the sizzle, not the steak. That is, they buy nonquantifiable experiences. Salesmen know this and can capitalize on the consumer's fears and insecurities.

Often a single-product specialist emphasizes his own area of expertise. This results in a plan that lacks direction and purpose. Obviously, we do not need to study competitors who simply use the title Financial Planner as a guise to get in the door. We can learn little from planners who use impressive computer-generated reports, showing unreasonably high rates of return needed to reach financial goals in order to scare clients into risky investments.

You cannot use Personal Financial Planning to sell a product. Anyone who knows in advance what he will propose is not a Financial Planner. Personal Financial Planning may or may not result in the recommendation of a specific product. An investment is not the means for achieving a financial goal, but simply one of several steps to be taken. Without integrating insurance protection, payment of the home mortgage, savings plans, and retirement, you do not have a holistic plan. Remember: Personal Financial Planning is a service, not a product.

There is a need and a move toward regulation and control of the Financial Planner and his activities. This comes from three sources: government, professional organizations, and the Financial Planner. We will look more closely at these in the next chapter.

Having eliminated invalid competitors, we can turn to our study of worthy opponents. Here we look at the traditional sources of financial services and products. We will examine each for strengths and weaknesses that are pertinent to our establishment as purveyors of an independent Personal Financial Planning Service.

Various marketing surveys have been conducted about the Personal Financial Planning market and the Financial Planner. From these we gain the public perception of the strengths and weaknesses of the traditional financial professionals as Financial Planners. Temper your reaction to these ideas. The public claims that no one is competent to do the job, not lawyers, stockbrokers, bankers, insurance agents, CPAs, or even CFPs. Temper your reaction by remembering that this is the public perception, and not fact. Public perception is a function of information available, and we can remedy informational deficiencies when we know what they are.

Banks and Bankers

Strengths. Banks and bankers enjoy a solid reputation in the community and have gained the public confidence in handling some aspects of our personal finances. Their image is one of honesty, objectivity, and stability.

Banks and bankers have established high levels of expertise in several areas of the financial industry. They understand the fiduciary role and offer investment advice and management experience. They also have estate planning experience and a history of dealing with wealth.

Banks have already established their branch locations. Since people generally go to a local bank at least once a week, banks have a strong local presence. Bankers know their customers and have ready access to them. The existing customer base of a bank is large.

Banks usually have strong marketing departments, with large advertising budgets. Therefore, they are able to campaign through expensive media: mail, magazines, radio, and television. Since deregulation, banks have begun to handle an increasing array of products and implementation methods.

Weaknesses. Banks as institutions, and the bankers who staff them, are seen as being too narrow in their expertise to create a balanced and holistic financial plan. Their conservative image conflicts with the risk levels desired by younger clients.

Despite their good local presence, banks generally are considered places to borrow funds or safely store assets, not places to manage them. Further, consumers are aware of the high overhead involved in large institutions such as banks, and are wary of subsidizing the banks' budgetary deficiencies.

With all the budget allowances for their marketing departments, banks have been over zealous and are often seen as coming on too strong. The public is suspect of their entry into the Personal Financial Planning arena, and the negative aspects of their "me too" philosophy have established a poor marketing record. In the final analysis, banks and bankers have limited selling experience.

The weakest point for banks entering the Personal Financial Planning market is their personnel. Traditionally low compensation in banking creates high staff turnover, eroding the element of human interaction. Those staff who do remain to offer good Personal Financial Planning Services are hampered by lack of full management support. The banker is often seen as an impotent implementor, needing the permission of numerous superiors or committees to make decisions. All these factors prevent bankers from being truly qualified planners.

Despite their rapidly broadening range of financial instruments and products, banks have had poor investment performance. Overall, their product offerings are still too limited to effect a well-balanced plan.

Law Firms and Lawyers

Strengths.   Of all professionals, lawyers have the strongest image of professional education and training. They are well respected and have a high standard of ethical conduct that is tightly regulated by their peer organizations. Lawyers also have an image of high objectivity, usually using the fee-only approach that ensures freedom from product bias.

Law is one of the areas of specialized expertise needed in Personal Financial Planning. Moreover, legal issues tend to be the broadest area of expertise, touching on all other aspects of Personal Financial Planning. Law firms have a large base of clients that can be directed to new Personal Financial Planning Services by a simple expansion of existing services.

Weaknesses.   All professionals tend to be highly specialized, but a generalized expertise of coordination is needed by the Financial Planner. Therefore, the same specialized level of expertise that distinguishes the lawyer also acts as a barrier to entry into the role of Financial Planner. Lawyers are considered too specialized to provide broad and generalized planning skills.

A lawyer's image is also one of avoiding or correcting legal problems, not one of managing finances. Lawyers lack aggressiveness, partially due to their sense of professional ethics but mainly due to their emphasis on professional expertise rather than people skills.

Law firms lack Personal Financial Planning expertise. Their area of specialization touches on all aspects of Personal Financial Planning, but this is not enough. Specifically, they lack knowledge and experience in the areas of insurance and investments.

The fee-only approach used by most law firms in Personal Financial Planning relies on a more affluent segment of the population, since only a limited number of clients can afford the higher fees generally required by this method of compensation.

Finally, lawyers' sense of professional ethics often gets in the way of marketing new services to existing clients. Lawyers are afraid to venture into marketing Personal Financial Planning Services for fear of appearing unprofessional.

CPA Firms and CPAs

Strengths. CPAs have a solid professional reputation regarding analytical ability and objectivity. Their code of ethics lends objectivity to their advice, as they cannot take commissions on product sales. They are clearly committed to confidentiality and are the most trusted financial advisers of any profession.

CPA firms have their own established areas of expertise, but they are respected primarily in the area of taxation. They are less known to the public for their well-developed data gathering skills. Due to progressive employee compensation, CPA firms are able to attract and hold top-notch personnel.

Like banks, CPA firms often have established branch locations and are able to serve clients on a local basis. In addition, CPA firms have better national coordination and expertise networking than banks. The CPA can tap a large and affluent customer base.

Weaknesses. CPAs are considered too specialized by the consumer to perform the generalist role required of the Financial Planner. Their training and attitude are too narrow and conservative to effect balanced or aggressive plans. In addition, the CPA firm is considered quite expensive—and the expense does not include implementation.

Consumers feel that CPAs are too narrowly trained for broad financial or business advice since CPAs are strong in taxes but weak in investment advice. In general, CPA firms have limited exposure and expertise in insurance planning and investment advice. Since they cannot implement and track a plan well, they have limited product knowledge.

Often the entry of a CPA firm into Personal Financial Planning is seen as one more marketing fillip. The large CPA firms have made powerful marketing entrées, but the CPA acting as a Financial Planner has limited management support.

Brokerage Firms

Strengths. These firms have the cushion of an established name and a strong capital base. In addition, they enjoy a rapidly expanding customer base. Their existing clientele are good Personal Financial Planning candidates because of their high income and net worth.

Brokerage firms have good research, or back office, capability and have the best experience with the financial products they sell. In effect, their clients have been subsidizing their product analyses for years. Of all the traditional sources, the broker has a corner on experience in implementation.

Marketing a Personal Financial Planning Service is simpler for brokerage firms than for other competitors. If the brokerage firm has successfully guided the client's investment portfolio, then it can easily expand its current services to include Personal Financial Planning. The compensation basis is usually commission, rather than fee. This, too, makes for an easy transition since the customers are already accustomed to paying broker commissions.

The customer service and sales support at brokerage firms, coupled with branch locations and broad product availability, make them a formidable competitor. However, they do have weaknesses.

Weaknesses. Stockbrokers work against a perceived conflict of interest because of product sale commissions. Often, clients are reluctant to use them as Financial Planners as a result of this bias and their narrow knowledge and experience in financial areas.

With their objectivity in question, brokers are rarely seen as trusted advisers. Personnel at brokerage firms must make a deep conversion to the human needs orientation of Personal Financial Planning. They must move from a product to a customer focus.

Since their compensation tends to have a short-term focus, brokers' plans are poorly balanced from a standpoint of time. Coupled with this, brokers lack the data-gathering skills needed to define and analyze the client's current situation.

Overall, brokerage firms give only weak management support to their new Personal Financial Planning programs. Because of this lack of support, there is a related lack of qualified planners or planning-oriented brokers.

Insurance Firms

Strengths. Insurance firms have the same marketing cushion as banks and brokerage firms: a large capital base and an existing customer base. They also have a huge marketing force already in place.

Insurance agents have good data-gathering skills and are often experienced at using computers for analysis purposes. The insurance firm enjoys a strong local presence, and local service is enhanced by the home office's product support for field planners.

Insurance firms have a unique advantage in the marketing of their Personal Financial Planning Service. The insurance agent's custom of meeting in the client's home has the psychological advantage of setting the client at ease.

Weaknesses. Insurance agents who act as Financial Planners have to overcome a strong negative image as self-serving product salespeople. The commission bias also blemishes their image of objectivity. In general, the public perceives insurance agents as having too limited an education to do Personal Financial Planning.

Insurance firms and agents have no history of being broad-based financial advisers. Even with a product rather than a customer focus, they have strong experience with only a few products and a rather fragmented understanding of the Personal Financial Planning process.

Insurance firms are fighting a weak image with training, new products, and marketing muscle. They have a long way to go to divorce their advice from their sales pitch in the consumer's mind and perception.

Converting the veteran insurance salesperson to a competent Financial Planner is not a quick process. Typically weak management commitment is reflected in a reluctance to revamp compensation for the upgraded agent. Finally, the home office has too little control over the agent to effect an integrated and smooth entrance to the Personal Financial Planning market.

Now that we have listed the strengths and weaknesses of traditional sources, let's consider competition from the perspective of compensation methods. This involves not only compensation, but also the service versus product approach.

Service Approach

Definition. The service approach offers a pure service only. This is often described in terms of compensation as "fee planning." The plan is developed for a flat fee or at an hourly rate, and is the only product of the service. There is no implementation and, consequently, no compensation except for the time spent in preparing the plan. Professionals such as lawyers and CPAs often work in this mode.

The fee-oriented planning service gathers information, analyzes it, and makes recommendations that help clients reach their goals. The Financial Planner obtains a fee regardless of whether the client implements any portion of the plan. The fee is based on the plan's complexity and depth and the time needed to collect and analyze the information.

Strengths. The service-only Financial Planner is considered free of product bias. This professional has greater objectivity since compensation is not related to the financial products that the client would purchase in implementing the plan.

The professional image of the fee-oriented planner is strong, as is his educational background. These are professionals with high standards and ethics that are regulated by their own peers. Fee planners have their own clientele which can be encouraged to buy expanded services.

The service-only Financial Planner brings strong expertise in his selected area of specialization and often has a good, broad business exposure.

Weaknesses.   Often the CPA, lawyer, or trust officer is afraid to venture into the Personal Financial Planning Service market for fear of appearing unprofessional or damaging his professional image in his primary service area. These professionals also often lack knowledge and experience in the areas of insurance and investments.

Fee planning tends to tap into a more affluent segment of the population since generally only a limited number of individuals or families can afford the required fees. For members of a professional organization, ethics codes can prohibit some marketing and advertising efforts.

Service-only Financial Planners lack aggressiveness, partially as a result of their sense of professional ethics but mainly because of their emphasis on professional expertise rather than people skills. They are experts in finance, not human nature.

Product Approach

Definition.   This approach does not refer to the single-product salesperson, but rather to the many insurance firms, investment brokers, and banks who act as multiple-product vendors. This is also called "commission planning." Not only the institution, but also the independent Financial Planner who is licensed in a number of areas may choose to receive commissions as the only form of compensation.

If the commission-only Financial Planner is a true planner, he still deals with his client's complete financial picture. He still gathers and analyzes information, and makes recommendations. Rather than direct the client to others for specific products, he sells the client any instruments for which he is licensed.

Strengths.   There is abundant motivation for the planner and client to implement the plan, as the Financial Planner's compensation depends on the client actually following his advice. Also, commission-only planners tend to offer more ongoing plan maintenance since they benefit if clients continue to partake of their financial offerings.

The product approach allows the Financial Planner to capture a wider share of the Personal Financial Planning market since his services do not have a heavy up-front investment. Clients pay for only what they actually buy.

Weaknesses. Obviously, it is difficult to remain objective when your compensation is based on clients buying a financial product that you are selling. Thus, the commission-only Financial Planner must overcome certain problems regarding objectivity. There is an ethical obligation to inform the client of commissions earned from the sale of such products, and this procedure can often impede the actual planning process.

These planners also face the problem of mastering a broad range of financial products and gaining in-depth expertise in such diverse areas as taxation and estate planning.

Service and Product Combinations

Definition. This is a compromise between fee- and commission-only services. It is the method used by full-service organizations such as American Express or Sears Financial Network and is also referred to as "fee and commission planning." Compensation is derived from fixed fees and from commissions earned during plan implementation.

Generally, the plan is prepared for a fixed fee, but the Financial Planner relies on the commissions earned from product sales to bring his compensation to a satisfactory level. Since these Financial Planners have the potential of earning commissions with each client, the set fees are usually lower than those charged by fee-only planners. Clients are not obligated to purchase products from the planner; they may go to their preferred vendors.

Strengths. This service has the advantage of being a total service. Clients can get everything they need from one source. This overcomes the feeling of having to pay twice—first for the plan and then for its implementation. In addition, the plan fee gives greater credibility to the objectivity of the fee-and-commission Financial Planner.

When exercised by a large firm, this method has the advantage of a large marketing budget and name recognition. In addition, the low plan fee allows the fee-and-commission planner a broader market share.

Weaknesses.   There is a perceived duplicity of collecting on both ends that is held by the knowledgeable client. Also, this approach tends to be less personalized and more computerized because of pressure to lower costs in the fixed fee portion of plan production. In general, the consumer has a lower perception of the expertise or specialized experience offered by institutions using this type of service.

Other Competitors

There are many competitors for the Personal Financial Planning Service market. At the beginning of this chapter I mentioned the glut of home computing and software packages that make your own client a potential competitor. Actually, the software vendor is your real competitor. Software packages can range in price from $50 to $5000, depending on their complexity and capabilities. The advantage is the low cost to the client, which is often unduly stressed. What is not stressed is that without periodic updating and sensible interpretation, the customer will not get a good plan.

There is also a new kind of low cost, simple, and generic Personal Financial Planning Service offered by larger firms in an attempt to capture the low end of the market. Here are some examples:

· Aetna Personal Financial Analysis is available via their agents, at a cost of $250 to the client.

· The Consumer Financial Institute Personal Profile and Projections Report can be purchased for $175. This service can be ordered through the mail from the Consumer Financial Institute.

· E. F. Hutton, Merrill Lynch, Prudential-Bache, and Dean Witter all offer low cost computer-generated services. The average cost of these generic plans is $200.

· At the inexpensive end of the computerized service is the Sears Personal Financial Planner. This costs $25 and is available at Sears stores.

THE GAP

The gap lies between what would ideally fill the consumer's need for a Personal Financial Planning Service and what is currently available. This gap can be filled by the independent Financial Planner. What are the strengths and weaknesses of those who are already trying to fill this gap?

Financial Planners

Strengths. Independent Financial Planners, whether individuals or small practices, appeal to the consumer because they are small. These Financial Planners have a clear customer focus and can devote individual attention to clients. Also, as professional planners they have the broad perspective needed for effective Personal Financial Planning. These Financial Planners enjoy a close client relationship.

Financial Planners are seen as having the largest product line and the best implementation currently available. They have strong data gathering and analytical capabilities. Increasingly, support services are improving for the independent Financial Planner, including software, datalink implementation, and financial networks. Independent Financial Planners have the best ability to implement their plans.

The new Personal Financial Planning Service firms are aware of the mistakes of traditional sources. By emerging with a fresh perspective and strategic marketing techniques, these new firms are benefiting from their competitors' weaknesses. The independent Financial Planner is more experienced at marketing, but is still disadvantaged. That is what this book is about.

The independent Financial Planner views financial products as products with known features, attributes, and behaviors. Because of the growing support for implementation, Financial Planners are now more flexible in designing the products to meet client needs. They can often create the exact instrument needed for an individual plan.

The Personal Financial Planning firm has management flexibility because of its small size and its total commitment to success in the Personal Financial Planning Service area. This firm's single-minded dedication to Personal Financial Planning means that it is better able to target its market. These firms generally have the zest and gusto of the entrepreneurial spirit.

Weaknesses. Personal Financial Planning is a new service; Financial Planner is a new profession. Both are troubled with image problems inherent in their newness. Certified Financial Planners (CFPs) have questionable certification and have not yet had time to overcome consumer fears about the objectivity of their advice. The term Financial Planner is still too new to have public credibility. Although rapidly growing in numbers and visibility, professional Financial Planner groups lack the reputation enjoyed by other financial professionals.

Consumers are concerned about the ability or intent of the independent Financial Planner to serve the middle-income family. The public perceives Personal Financial Planning as a wealth management service.

The independent Financial Planner has to work with a small capital base and a small client base. He is known only in his local area. With a lack of qualified planners, the new profession's image is easily tarnished.

Differentiability means standing out in the consumer's mind. By contrasting the ideal Personal Financial Planning Service with the competition's record, we see where we can differentiate our service by filling consumer needs that are not being met in the current market. Here are a few of the current gaps in service.

About the Service

The more flexible our pricing structure, the easier we can maximize value for both the client and ourselves. The client does not want to pay for a plan, and then pay again for implementation products, brokerage or other services. There is a perceived, if not real, element of paying twice or at least of paying more than is necessary. The solution is to offer a fee-and-commission based service.

Why not take the idea even one step further? Why not set a flat fee for the service and then credit the service fee with product commissions? The flat fee could be high enough to ensure our freedom from product sale bias. As further assurance of objectivity, we can have our service network licensed for multiple products of the same type.

It is not easy to recommend such a course to professionals whose own organizations have codes of ethics that prohibit the necessary fee structures. These codes will continue to evolve and change, but at an uncertain pace.

Personal Financial Planning is clearly an ongoing process of planning, monitoring, and revision. Thus, our service should emphasize the maintenance aspects of the planning process. Our competitors often fail to treat Personal Financial Planning as a process.

While the independent Financial Planner's small client base seems to be a weakness, this weakness can be turned to a strength. We should focus on a high quality, highly personalized service. When introducing Personal Financial Planning as a new service, you will find that a small client base is actually advantageous.

We noted the need for a service to provide ongoing security and interaction with a trusted financial adviser. This is a weakness evident in larger institutions that have personnel turnover problems. Adding Personal Financial Planning to your existing services will assure the client that you will be there for his tomorrows.

Consumer complaints about specialization, limited training, and lack of experience point to another gap. The client must clearly perceive you to be a generalist who is coordinating a network of expert specialists.

About the Planner

The best role for the independent Financial Planner is that of coordinating generalist with a specialty in one or more specific areas. You must be the quarterback of a team of experts. Your skill as coordinator will add objectivity and balance to your service.

To fight image problems, you must have all the knowledge, education, and credentials that you can manage. Examine the possibilities of various memberships, degrees, affiliations, and registrations.

All of the above will help to enhance your own, or your firm's, professional reputation. They will also provide you with ongoing professional knowledge that is critical to your success in this endeavor.

According to surveys of the competition, the image and character of the Financial Planner is a sensitive issue. We defined the attributes of the ideal Financial Planner at the beginning of the chapter. Review these and then rate yourself on the worksheet at the end of this chapter. Be as honest as you can. Those areas that you rate low are the weaknesses that you must strive to eliminate or reduce.

About the Process

In summary, what is needed is a comprehensive, ongoing service. This means that you must have a clear understanding of Personal Financial Planning as a continuing process. For client security you should offer a regular semiannual contact and a yearly formal review.

About the Product

Why not consider offering a multilevel product? Perhaps you could combine simple computer-generated reports with your interpretation and comments. Perhaps you could offer to implement rudimentary plans for a low fixed fee. Whatever products you create, be sure that they are living, not static.

The most valuable resource you have is your time. Graduate the level of individualized service sensibly through your products. We will examine this in more detail in the chapter that deals with the development of your products and services.

Be prepared to offer your clients a benchmarking procedure so that they can test the workability of the planning process early. Show them the feedback loops you will integrate to keep the plan flexible.

The special objectives section of the plan document can help you differentiate yourself from the competition. You are emphasizing that you handle the client on an individual basis.

Any use of a computer should support, not replace, the planning process. Many planners use automation today, and many programs have been developed just for financial planning. Avoid letting automation take over. Never let an impressive printout substitute for delivery of individualized service.

By now, other areas for differentiability are probably suggesting themselves to you.

Your Image

The list of attributes below is taken from our definition of the ideal Financial Planner. Rate your image as low, medium, or high for each attribute. Be as objective as you can. You are describing what your clients see, not what you wish them to see. If you can arrange to have several clients rate you anonymously, do so. This worksheet is of value only if it accurately depicts your image weaknesses. Then you can begin to overcome these weaknesses with the techniques discussed in the following chapters.

Image	Rating		
Trusted	L	M	H
Objective	L	M	H
Expert	L	M	H
Professional	L	M	H
Coordinator	L	M	H
Counselor	L	M	H
Educator	L	M	H
Motivator	L	M	H
Watchdog	L	M	H

3
Laws, Codes, and Ethics

THE REASONS FOR REGULATION

Financial Planning is still a new profession, and the Financial Planner as a professional is only slowly emerging. The accountant, lawyer, investment adviser, insurance agent, and real estate broker have been the established financial professionals who provided Personal Financial Planning Services in the past.

Little attention was paid to the Financial Planner when his services were restricted to a few wealthy clients. Only when the economic situation changed did Personal Financial Planning become a concern of middle- and upper-middle-income families. As the market increased, so did the incidence of problems—and attention became focused on Financial Planners.

Regulation of this new profession has become an increasingly hot issue for the public and for politicians. Indeed, there is a need for governmental, professional, and personal regulation of the Financial Planner that is analogous to the regulation for the traditional sources of financial services. To date, however, there is little or no regulation.

The market for Personal Financial Planning Services is large, and it is still far from saturated. Those who want to enter into the market successfully must use the techniques of modern strategic marketing. Although many of the sanctions regarding aggressive advertising and marketing of professional services have been eliminated, a number of guidelines remain to which the financial professional must adhere.

Codes and standards are needed from professional organizations to guide the Financial Planner in his work. These could help to answer some of the following questions: "What are the standards for preparing my financial plans?" "What reporting requirements must I meet?" "What is the appropriate approach for recommending strategies and implementing them?" "Which regulatory requirements apply to me?" "How much product knowledge do I need for plan implementation, and how can I gain this knowledge?" "What is my legal liability?"

The Financial Planner also needs to strengthen his public image as a professional. Therefore, we will examine some legal, professional, and ethical questions that concern the Financial Planner's image.

These are large and complex issues since the environment is still in a state of rapid change. This chapter presents a brief survey of the whole situation, rather than a detailed treatment of a few volatile issues. If you need more detailed answers to questions, contact your professional organization or attend a specific seminar. To simplify the following discussion, let me define what is meant by laws, codes, and ethics.

Law. Legislation passed and enforced by a governmental body, either federal or state.

Code. Rules, guidelines, or standards created by professional organizations to regulate and assist their members.

Ethic. Personally held rules to guide your professional conduct in accord with your own value system.

The reason for regulatory law is to protect the public. We have already seen several examples of investment fraud. These represent some of the dangers from which the public should be protected.

The Investment Advisers Act of 1940 is one law that was created to protect the public. This law requires investment advisers to register with the SEC, and it empowers the SEC to monitor and regulate registered professionals in the public interest.

Recently, SEC inspectors increased their inspections of investment advisers by 125 percent. They targeted those firms that are the greatest risk to investors: firms that hold client's securities and funds, firms that have custody or discretionary authority over client's assets, and firms that have financial interests in products sold to clients.

The codes of professional organizations have been designed for the same purpose as governmental laws: to protect the public. These codes also treat special professional protection and development issues and help attract new members by building and preserving the profession's image and prestige. Building the profession's image is important so that the profession can continue to attract high caliber people. The codes of a professional organization keep the profession alive, healthy, and well-groomed.

Professional organizations whose members are drawn to Personal Financial Planning fear that their professions will lose their integrity. Should the professional serve the general public or the individual client? If he serves the general public, he must be objective and independent. To serve the client effectively and economically, however, this position may not be possible to maintain.

In general, professional codes and standards also guide the practicing member in his work. In Personal Financial Planning there is a need for guidance in such areas as plan preparation, formatting for various financial statements, correct handling of fixed or commission fees, and techniques for plan implementation.

Personal ethics, just as laws and codes, are rules or guidelines for behavior. But they are our personal rules. We devise our own ethics, and only we can enforce them. The reasons behind ethical guides are personal, too. When we establish a personal ethic to protect the public, we think of our personal public—our clients.

This may expose us to conflict. For example, in the last chapter we discussed a flat fee method of compensation for our planning service. The flat fee would be credited with product commissions. This method attempts to avoid product bias and to maximize value for the client and then for us. However, many professional organizations consider such compensation unethical. The conflict comes with the decision to violate our professional organization's code and to act in accord with our personal ethics in order to attain a goal of better serving the client.

Like the codes of professional organizations, personal ethics can protect your profession by protecting your position and image as a professional. Professionals are made, not born. Further, they are largely self-made.

Two elements are necessary to be a professional: technical competence and a value system. Technical competence is necessary but never sufficient to create a professional. The value system, which is reflected in personal ethics, is deeply rooted in moral principles. A value system is the result of complex interactions of training, experience, observation of role models, and formal education. Where your professional education or experience lacks these interactions, you personally have to supply them.

Development of your personal ethics will serve to build your true image and stature as a professional. While it is possible to monitor and regulate the actions of Financial Planners, only personal ethics can control such personal attributes as objectivity, expertise, and sincerity.

Finally, your personal ethics serve to protect your practice. Your dedication to client service, to client confidentiality, and to your professional image are ways in which your ethics protect your practice.

In summary, we can say that laws, codes, and ethics represent a hierarchy of protective intention. Laws are intended to protect the public. Codes protect both the public and the profession that has created them. Personal ethics protect the public, the profession, and the practice. Now let us survey the ways in which laws, codes, and ethics affect the Financial Planner.

LEGAL SANCTIONS

At the federal government level, there is no specific law that regulates the Financial Planner. The Investment Advisers Act requires investment advisers to be registered with the SEC. But what is an investment adviser? The SEC definition of adviser is one who:

1. Provides advice or issues reports on securities
2. Engages in the business of providing such services
3. Provides such services for compensation

There are specified exemptions to this law. Lawyers, accountants, engineers, and teachers are exempt if their performance of advisory services is solely incidental to the practice of their profession. There is currently much confusion and debate as to whether the Financial Planner is an investment adviser.

One professional organization has established these test criteria for its members. First, do you represent yourself to the public as an investment adviser? Second, are your advisory services related and connected to the normal performance of your services? Finally, is your advisory fee based on the same factors as other service fees?

Actually, determining whether you fall within the framework of the Investment Advisers Act may be more involved than simply registering with the SEC. No examination is required. You register by filing Form ADV and paying the filing fee of $150. The SEC requires that you distribute a statement of disclosure that defines your practice as investment adviser; this can actually enhance the image of your service.

Other possible sources of regulation or regulatory law are:

Federal Reserve Board

Commodity Futures Trading Commission

Federal Trade Commission

Internal Revenue Service

Department of Labor

Comptroller of the Currency

Federal Deposit Insurance Corporation

Federal Savings and Loan Insurance Corporation

Federal Home Loan Bank Board

Securities Investor Protection Corporation

National Credit Union Administration

National Association of Securities Dealers

State Securities Commission

State Insurance Department

State Real Estate Board

This is an impressive list of government agencies. Since it would be disastrous to the Personal Financial Planning industry to be overregulated we should make a quick move to regulate ourselves before those agencies listed above do it for us.

At the state government level there are no regulatory laws, but there is a flurry of legislative activity. California is in the research and development stage of laws that will regulate Financial Planners as professionals. Some of the proposed legislature deals with the issues of licensing, written disclaimers, and submission of detailed written financial plans. A recent California bill, which was designed to force all Financial Planners to register as investment advisers, was stalled because bankers and CPAs are intent on being exempted from it. Oregon, Massachusetts, Maryland, and Maine also have bills pending, and are waiting to see the results of California's bill. Several states, which are listed below, now require registration of investment advisers.

Alaska	Nevada
Arkansas	New Hampshire
California	New Jersey
Connecticut	New Mexico
Delaware	New York
Florida	North Dakota
Idaho	Oregon
Illinois	Pennsylvania
Indiana	Puerto Rico
Kansas	Rhode Island
Kentucky	South Carolina
Louisiana	South Dakota
Michigan	Tennessee
Minnesota	Texas
Mississippi	Utah
Missouri	Washington
Montana	West Virginia
Nebraska	Wisconsin

At the state level, we encounter product licensing. Financial Planners must be licensed in each area from which they receive a commission. Licenses are governed by each state. They typically require the passing of examinations and sometimes the completion of course work.

PROFESSIONAL SANCTIONS

Your professional organization may be more aware of the blossoming Personal Financial Planning industry than you suspect. Most are now struggling to update their old codes in a timely and graceful manner. The focus of these revision activities is to develop codes that maintain professional ethics and image, while enabling members to pursue new business in a competitive environment. In order to accomplish this, your organization may already have appointed a special Personal Financial Planning Committee.

It is a perilous endeavor for financial professionals to integrate marketing with a professional image. Mistakes jeopardize the attributes that buyers value: objectivity and independence.

Some professional organizations do not permit contingency fees. However, some aggressive and entrepreneurial members are doing this and have threatened law suits if they are persecuted by their professional organizations on this basis.

The legal and accounting professional organizations are trying to determine to what extent they want to be involved with product implementation. This is a key decision, as implementation may entail commissions and licensing.

Most professional organizations have removed absolute bans against advertising and solicitation and have substituted new, looser rules and guidelines. The thrust of the new code is to prohibit false advertising. Dialogue and debate still swirl around the compatibility of advertising, solicitation, and professionalism. While special committees still ponder the question, an increasing number of professionals are already using media effectively to reach new clients.

The best alternative for Personal Financial Planning professionals is self-regulation. The IAFP is moving toward creation of an industry self-regulatory organization, similar to the NASD. In July, 1985, the College for Financial Planning and ICFP formed the International Board of Standards and Practices for Certified Financial Planners.

This is an independent nonprofit organization that has been established in the public interest to ensure that CFPs practice in accordance with recognized standards of conduct. Further, it ensures that they perform their work effectively, efficiently, ethically, and in the best interest of their clients and the public.

The International Board of Standards and Practices for Certified Financial Planners will also be responsible for establishing educational and testing standards for the CFP, administering the CFP examinations, and issuing the CFP designation to qualified individuals.

The IAFP wants to see a national law rather than a state-by-state patchwork of legislation. Consequently, IAFP advocates that all Financial Planners register under the Investment Advisers Act and voluntarily come under SEC scrutiny.

ETHICAL SANCTIONS

You must be sure to develop ethics that allow you to market aggressively and keep your professionalism intact since other sources of regulation will take time to become established. Before you proceed to develop and market your Personal Financial Planning Service, you must prepare the ethical bedrock on which to build. Remember our marketing goals:

1. *Ethics.* Maintain the highest possible level of ethics, code of conduct, integrity, sincerity, and professionalism.

2. *Aggression.* Capture your fair share of the Personal Financial Planning market without apology or hesitation.

By all means, secure and display your credentials—certified titles, registrations, and licenses—but know how to explain their significance. Above all, however, know your ethics and live by them. Your ethics must do three things: protect your client, protect your professionalism, and protect your practice.

Let me offer some suggestions for conduct in these three areas. When you have absorbed and reflected on this starter set of ethical ideas, develop your own guidelines on the worksheet at the end of this chapter.

Protect Your Client

- Place the client's interests above your own.
- Do your best job for each client.
- Respect client confidentiality in all your professional and marketing activities.
- Establish and abide by a written fee or compensation policy that is known and understood by your client.
- Do nothing that would cause a reasonable person to misunderstand or be deceived.

Protect Your Professionalism

- Continually maintain and improve your professional knowledge and skills.
- Establish and maintain good relationships with other professionals.
- Do not exaggerate your ability. Do not make claims unless they are based on verifiable facts.
- Do not make comparisons with other Financial Planners unless they are based on verifiable facts.

- Talk about the objective and measurable features of plan implementation. Avoid subjective evaluations and personal value judgments.
- Clearly distinguish between fact and opinion in your plans.
- Always base your recommendations on a clear understanding of the client's dreams, goals, and needs.
- Support your recommendations with research and documentation.
- Disclose all conflicts of interest to the client before performing your service.
- Use your professional memberships properly. Be factual about the criteria for membership. Be factual about your authority to represent the organization. Never use professional memberships for marketing or advertising purposes.

Protect Your Practice

- Know and obey all laws and codes that apply to you.
- Never let profit interfere with your professional qualities.
- Do not tolerate dishonesty or fraud or deceit by commission or omission.
- Improve public understanding about Personal Financial Planning. Provide information to the layperson explaining what Personal Financial Planning can offer and where it is available.
- Do not exaggerate the benefits of Personal Financial Planning. Be honest about possible gains and create realistic expectations about results.

Your Ethics

It is essential that you actually place your personal rules for conduct on paper. This process forces you to clarify and simplify your ideas. Try to use simple, direct language. Remember, these are for your eyes only. Try to express your ethics in a few rules under each of the three categories.

Protect Your Client

_____

_____

_____

_____

_____

_____

_____

_____

Protect Your Professionalism

_____

_____

_____

_____

Protect Your Practice

4

Develop Your Service

IS PERSONAL FINANCIAL PLANNING FOR YOU?

You now know that there is a market for Personal Financial Planning Services and that there are gaps between what consumers need and what they are being offered. We have reviewed some ways in which you can fill these gaps and capture a share of the market: Differentiate yourself from the competition, stand firm on your ethics, and aggressively market your services.

Now your commitment must extend beyond the purchase of this book and involve the time and money necessary to develop new skills, products and services. Before you begin, take a long, hard look at what will be required of you.

Are you willing to learn a multitude of new skills, perhaps even a whole new profession? There will always be a need for narrowly specialized financial professionals. In building a business based on personal interactions, however, you must be ready to plunge into the softer, more human side of the financial industry. You must be willing to refine and perfect your human relations skills. And you must be willing to learn and apply marketing and public relations techniques.

Most of all, it is the *human* side of Personal Financial Planning for which you must be prepared. Decide whether books, forms, and calculators appeal to you more than human interaction. There is a sharp distinction between the frontline personal relations of Personal Financial

Planning and the background support or specialist roles you have played so far.

Do you prefer to work on small, clearly defined problems or to coordinate larger efforts that solve more complex problems? When you assume the role of Financial Planner, you assume responsibility for managing a team of specialists, and for coordinating efforts to solve the complex and ongoing problems pertaining to clients' lifetime financial plans.

In this chapter we will examine the development of your new Personal Financial Planning Service. Therefore, you should take the role of the coordinator of a network of experts, the quarterback of a team. To gain an idea of the problems involved in the coordination of your enterprise, consider this equation. It shows the number of one-to-one relationships (R) that exist in a network of N members. The equation is:

$$R = (N \times (N - 1)) / 2$$

When you deal solely with your client, there are only two members of the network. So the equation predictably yields an $R = (2 \times 1) / 2 = 1$ relationship. When you expand to a network of four members, the equation shows $R = (4 \times 3) / 2 = 6$ interactions. If you develop a network of eight individuals, you will be the manager of 28 human relationships! And these are only the one-to-one relations of the network. Be well aware of the magnitude of the coordination task that you are about to assume.

While these issues seem intimidating when considered en masse, do not lose hope. There is a brighter side to the commitment you are contemplating. The skills that you need can be learned in easy stages of transition. We will look at these transitions, and the decisions involved, in this chapter.

MARKETING SCOPE AND SEGMENTATION

To discuss the development of your service sensibly, we have to make some initial assumptions about who you are. We will assume that you have an individual or small practice. Your firm already has one or more of the needed specialist skills. You will be taking the role of the Financial Planner, developing and coordinating a team of expert specialists. To develop your Personal Financial Planning Service, you need to see the whole picture in order to determine where you want to fit in and how to get there in easy stages.

While we are considering product and service development, we need to acknowledge marketing functions. In practice, you will develop your services and products hand in hand with your marketing plan. This is a primary tenet of strategic marketing. For many years we have operated under a selling philosophy that states: "If a product can be produced, it can be sold." The marketing philosophy that we will study in later chapters turns this idea around, and states: "If a product can be sold, it can be produced."

In marketing your new service, you should stress product innovation to meet customer needs rather than high-pressure sales of existing products. This is why marketing and product development go hand in hand. For now, however, we will merely dip into the marketing area for two helpful concepts.

These concepts are *scope* and *segmentation*. When developing your service, keep the target market small; the scope of your initial efforts should be limited to a small number of clients. For the independent Financial Planner, the scope will be about a dozen clients in the first year. Do not plan to profit from these first jobs. Let the first year be a thorough trial of your skills and service. Take your time on the first dozen clients. This shakedown period will prove valuable in resolving problems at a low volume when there is time to examine alternate solutions.

Strategic marketing also uses a valuable technique called segmentation. Here, the potential market is divided into smaller segments for which specific products or levels of service can be developed. We'll look at some options in this area, too.

DEVELOP YOUR ORGANIZATION

Striving for the Ideal

There are certain essential functions that must be performed for your service to operate. These can be organized in any number of ways, each with advantages and problems. The organization you develop must be capable of delivering those benefits sought by your clients. Recall our discussion of the ideal Personal Financial Planning Service, which enumerated the benefits that it provides:

- Security
- Direction
- Advice
- Expertise

- Objectivity
- Coordination
- Time
- Value

Your organization must be capable of delivering client security. This is accomplished by the ongoing conversion of client dreams to goals and goals to facts via the financial plan. To do this, your organization must foster long-term client relationships. Avoid any rigidity or dependence that will jeopardize the client/planner relationship. By expecting changes in your staff and the members of your expert team, you can minimize their impact on your client.

As quarterback of the expert team, your primary focus is on the client/ planner relationship. You are the trusted adviser who mediates the technical skills of experts. You will summarize advice, analyses, and information into appropriate directions for the client.

To deliver quality advice, you will use your expertise as well as the expertise of the team that you assemble. Keep doing what you do best as a financial professional while you acquire your new skills as a Financial Planner. This will keep you abreast of the financial environment while you learn to coordinate the planning process from a higher level.

Your organization will deliver both objectivity and coordination if you assume the role of coordinator and build a flexible support network around you. While functions performed stay the same, be flexible about who performs them—even to the point of using the client's preferred specialists.

Organization Structure

What functions are needed for your overall organization? Some are common to any practice; some are unique to the Personal Financial Planning Service. Here is a list of the major functional areas that your organization will need.

1. Administration. This function handles compliance and accounting as well as the usual payroll and office management tasks. The administration function may also embrace computer support services.

2. Marketing. There will be marketing and sales functions to perform. As well as a sound marketing plan, your sales efforts will need support services. Support services include market research, advertising, and public relations.

3. *Planning.* The actual financial planning function is at the heart of your organization. This includes data gathering, analysis, research, product monitoring and selection, and plan production. This function is supported by your expert team members, whether they are part of your firm or affiliated through a network.

4. *Implementation.* Consider implementation separate from planning for reasons that we will discuss later. This function includes implementation product analysis and selection and monitoring of the implemented plans.

5. *Product Development.* You will need to develop your products and services and then refine them in response to your evolving marketing plan. You will probably want to control this function yourself, perhaps assisted by outside consultants.

These functions and the roles of the expert team must be organized in some fashion. Two common organizational structures are available to you: the cottage structure and the specialist structure. Overall, I advocate the specialist structure, for reasons that will become obvious. Though it can be a bit confusing, remember that roles and functions are not necessarily performed by single individuals. But who does what, and in what capacity?

In the cottage organization, each staff member specializes in all the functions. Each is a complete service, and all functions are performed within the firm. In the specialist organization, the staff is specialized by function. Each staff member has one or two areas of expertise. Let's look at the strengths and weaknesses of each kind of organization. The cottage structure minimizes the fixed expenses of your service; it is also flexible and able to respond to changing market needs and client problems. However, the cottage structure allows only low levels of productivity. No economies of scale are possible. This limits the growth potential of your practice.

The specialist structure maximizes productivity and minimizes overhead requirements. Economies of scale give you a competitive edge if you organize along specialist lines. Further, considerable profit can be derived from the reputation of having specialist skills. Be careful, however, with this approach. Pay special attention to the client/planner relationship, or clients may perceive your service as being impersonal. Internal communication problems may also develop in the interactions of large specialist staffs. Finally, this organizational structure tends to have high fixed costs.

Despite weaknesses, you have advantages in organizing your service along a specialist structure. Focus on developing your new skills as a generalist and coordinator. Continue to perform the specialist function you already have, but develop a support team of experts, either within your firm or through an external network. Don't try to be the expert in all needed roles.

Start by farming out all functions except the client/planner relationship, plan analysis and presentation, and other coordination functions. This approach not only has the advantage of low capital requirements, but it bypasses the need for you to be registered or licensed if your implementation staff is in an external network. All the while, your focus remains on your relationship with your client.

At first, you will depend on others' expertise. You will have limited control of outside costs and may experience initial communication problems. These are manageable with your low start-up volume and speed. By the time you reach higher volumes of business, your expert team will be securely in place.

Outside firms are available to help with most major functions of your organization. Marketing specialists can handle marketing and promotion, advertising, and public relations functions. However, you can do much of this yourself if you follow the development of the strategic marketing plan outlined in the next two chapters.

If you use an external agency for plan implementation, you can also eliminate the need for licensing. For example, an insurance agency can provide analysis and implementation of the insurance planning. A broker can perform product analysis, provide brokerage services, and supply due diligence.

You will want to become more and more involved in the analysis and planning functions, but you can start with outside help in these areas. You can hire experts to do basic calculations only; calculations plus report production; or calculations, reports, and recommendations.

As your practice grows, you can incorporate in-house expertise as business warrants. Break-even analysis is helpful here. By hiring staff experts, you will increase production, but you will raise your break-even point. In the long term, however, profits will increase at a higher rate. By contracting with outside experts, you will increase profits, even while the break-even point stays the same. However, the new variable costs mean that your profits will increase at a lower rate.

The Expert Team

What functional roles are needed for the expert team? Any of the following functions may be performed by one or more members of your network, except for those of the planner. The planner must be a single individual in order to provide a consistent interface with the client. This is the function you reserve for yourself. Here are the skills you will need on the Financial Planning Team.

Planner. The Financial Planner handles the critical aspects of the client/planner relationship, acting as the interface between the client and the team members, and coordinating team interactions. The Financial Planner also has ultimate responsibility for plan preparation and presentation.

Planning Assistant. The planning assistant, who is analogous to the legal secretary, relieves the Financial Planner of less critical client interactions, handles routine administrative and clerical functions, and manages the office. Initially, your team may not have, or need, a planning assistant. But after the first year, when volume begins to build, this role will become essential to profitability. Your planning assistant can be developed from clerical functions to preliminary client data gathering and analysis.

Attorney. The attorney provides legal counsel where needed. He prepares legal documents, wills, contracts, and the like.

Broker. The broker provides information and advice on the selection of implementation products. He provides key services in implementing the securities and investments portions of the plan. He has the necessary licensing and registration for those products chosen.

Insurance Agent. The insurance agent can design and implement the insurance program since he has the necessary expertise and licensing.

Banker. The banker arranges the necessary long- and short-term financing. He also handles such vehicles for plan implementation as mortgages, trusts, IRAs, and CDs.

CPA. The accountant, the taxation expert of the team, also handles accounting functions for the client as necessary.

Networking the Team

As you can see, the expertise needed in Personal Financial Planning need not be all your own personal expertise. You have access to other professionals, including accountants, attorneys, and specialists in wills, pensions, and other disciplines. You combine their skills with yours as coordinator and manager. There is no harm in any or most of your expert team members being part of an external network. This arrangement provides both the expert specialists and the single human contact that your client wants.

Networking with friends generally works well. When developing an external expert team, consider using the services of local financial professionals with whom you have already established a rapport.

You can develop a network from among the professionals in your area, or you can work with one of the many resource sharing groups which have emerged in recent years:

Financial Service Corporation International (Atlanta, Georgia)

Private Ledger (San Diego, California)

Integrated Resources, Inc. (New York, New York)

Anchor Financial Services (Phoenix, Arizona)

Southmark Financial (Dallas, Texas)

Licensed Independent Network of CPA Financial Planners (Nashville, Tennessee)

Team Building Tools

To select and evaluate members of your expert team and network, create a survey form. You can mail this survey to prospective team members to determine which advisers will be willing to work with you and to give you a profile of their investment philosophies or preferences. This survey can even scout out potential competitors.

The survey form would cover such topics as: What is the nature of your practice? What do your clients expect from you regarding investment advice? Which investment alternatives do you prefer? How do your clients invest their tax-qualified plan money? What objectives interest your clients most?

Just as you keep client contact records, keep an adviser contact record. This will help you monitor the effectiveness of your network, track reciprocity of referrals, and prompt you to maintain contact with your affiliates.

Now let's consider development of the key member of the expert team—the Financial Planner, you.

DEVELOP YOURSELF AS PLANNER

Migration to New Skills

The ideal Financial Planner is a trusted, objective, expert professional. For the benefit of his client, he acts as:

- Coordinator
- Human counselor
- Educator
- Motivator
- Watchdog

You will need to develop a professional image and then perform various roles from this stance. As we look at both development tasks, remember that we are aiming for a gradual migration to new skills, not an overnight transformation into the complete and perfect Financial Planner!

Initial and continuing education will become a way of life for you. This need not be deeply technical. Be prepared for exposure to such esoteric subjects as investment evaluation, portfolio analysis, and cash flow projections. Mastery of these subjects is not as important as simply gaining an overview of what they are, how they mesh into the overall plan, and how to gain whatever additional outside expertise you need.

A formal education exposes you to the technical skills of the Financial Planner and helps to develop your professional image. Also, you will probably need education about the roles you play for your client, particularly in the areas of human relations and psychology. Finally, you will need to establish an information network to keep current in the financial scene.

Education

Three major independent study institutions offer Personal Financial Planning education and certification programs: The American College, The College for Financial Planning, and The Institute of Chartered Financial

Analysts. These are all self-study programs, ideally suited to a gradual acquisition of the skills you need.

The American College. This institution prepares and administers the curricula for ChFC and CLU diplomas and designations. For detailed course information, write to:

> The American College
> 270 Bryn Mawr Avenue
> Bryn Mawr, PA 19010

An outline follows of the ChFC and CLU courses that they offer.

ChFC. This program provides financial professionals with the broadened knowledge and skills necessary to provide comprehensive financial services to clients. The curriculum consists of 10 courses:

Financial Services: Environment and Profession

Income Taxation

Economics

Financial Statement Analysis/Individual Insurance Benefits

Employee Benefits

Investments

Wealth Accumulation Planning

Estate and Gift Tax Planning

Planning for Business Owners and Professionals

Financial and Estate Planning Applications

Local classes are organized by CLU chapters, life underwriters associations, colleges and universities, and allied professions. Informal study groups are permitted when formal classes are not available. This is designed as a self-study program, but intensive on-campus programs are available at The American College. Written examinations are held in January and June each year at over 300 examination centers.

You need no experience to enroll, but before you are awarded the ChFC designation, you must accumulate three years of experience "in activities related to the process of providing financial services" (see Droms in Bibliography).

CLU. This is a program for professionals who are directly or indirectly involved in the protection, accumulation, preservation, and distribution of the economic values of human life. The program is designed to meet the educational needs of the life and health insurance professional, provide a working knowledge of the overall financial counseling process and its various components, and enable the professional to effectively serve the financial security needs of the public. The curriculum consists of 10 courses:

Financial Services: Environment and Profession

Income Taxation

Economics

Financial Statement Analysis/Individual Insurance Benefits

Insurance Environment and Operations

Group Benefits and Social Insurance

Pensions and Other Retirement Plans

Investments

Estate and Gift Tax Planning

Planning for Business Owners and Professionals

Holders of the CLU designation can also obtain the ChFC designation by completing three additional courses from the ChFC curriculum since the requirements for experience, study, and examination are comparable in both programs.

College for Financial Planning. This college offers a professional education program leading to the professional designation CFP rather than a college degree. For more information, write to:

> College for Financial Planning
> 9725 E. Hampden Avenue
> Denver, CO 80231

CFP. This designation identifies an individual who has met the college's standards and achieved a high level of technical knowledge in personal financial management, risk management, investments, tax planning, retirement, employee benefits, and estate planning.

The curriculum is in six parts and is taken sequentially with each part concluded by a three-hour written examination. The six subjects of study are:

Introduction to Financial Planning

Risk Management

Investments

Tax Planning and Management

Employee Benefits and Retirement Planning

Estate Planning

Formal study programs are available around the country at affiliated colleges, and informal group study is encouraged. You can also do independent study using the college's textbooks and study guide. Written examinations are conducted at various sites on the second Saturday of each April, August, and December. To enroll, you will need five enrollment credits related to your work experience, other professional designations, and college degrees.

The Institute of Chartered Financial Analysts (ICFA). This institution, affiliated with the Financial Analysts Federation, was formed in 1962 as a professional organization of CFAs. The Institute provides a self-study program that leads to the CFA designation. For details, write to:

> The Institute of Chartered Financial Analysts
> Post Office Box 3668
> Charlottesville, VA 22903

CFA. This designation is available from the ICFA upon completion of the program. There are six major subject areas of examination:

Ethical and Professional Standards, Securities Law and Regulation

Financial Accounting

Economics

Techniques of Analysis—Fixed Income Securities

Techniques of Analysis—Equity Securities

Objective of Analysis—Portfolio Management

This is essentially a program of self-study and examination. Local societies of the Financial Analysts Federation sponsor small self-study groups. The Institute of Chartered Financial Analysts prepares a study guide for the course.

Three examinations of increasing complexity and depth must be taken and passed. Only one exam can be taken in a year; the exams are administered on the first Saturday in each June. Each examination is six hours in length and consists of essay and objective questions. The examinations are offered in 80 locations in North America. Overall, the program must be completed within seven years.

No experience is needed to enroll in the program or take the examinations. However, you do need three character references, a bachelor's degree or acceptable equivalent. You must establish three years' experience as a financial analyst to be awarded a charter.

You won't find it fast or easy to obtain any of these degrees or designations, but you can obtain them gradually while you continue your existing practice. This lets you develop competent skills as your service develops.

Registration

There are several professional organizations that you should consider joining in addition to your current memberships. These are described below.

International Association for Financial Planning (IAFP).

> International Association for Financial Planning
> 5775 Peachtree Dunwoody Road, NE
> Suite 120-C
> Atlanta, GA 30342

This is the largest professional organization of Financial Planners. Its purpose is to provide members with continuing education to increase their expertise, to build awareness for a unified approach to solving financial planning problems, to establish an ongoing dialogue with other industry professionals, and to maintain high ethical standards.

The IAFP conducts annual conferences and continuing education programs, maintains the Registry of Financial Planning Practitioners, and produces various publications (including the monthly magazine *Financial Planning*) and monthly newsletters. The Registry is a "record of those who have met standards identified by the IAFP as essential to the practice of complete professional financial planning" (see Droms in Bibliography).

Holding the CPA designation fulfills the education requirement for admittance to the Registry. The IAFP has also developed the "IAFP Code of Professional Ethics."

Institute of Certified Financial Planners (ICFP).

The Institute of Certified Financial Planners
3443 S. Galena
Suite 190
Denver, CO 80231-5093

This is a professional organization for CFPs. Its goals are to "establish and maintain professionalism in financial planning, to promote the continued advancement of knowledge in the financial planning field, to support programs increasing the abilities of CFPs to serve their clients, to strive for acceptance of the Certified Financial Planner as an objective professional in the field of financial planning, and as a self-governing body, to insure the integrity of the profession through enforcement of a rigorous code of ethics" (see Droms in Bibliography).

The ICFP holds national and regional conferences, offers continuing professional education, and produces various publications (including *The Journal of the Institute of Certified Financial Planners*) and a newsletter.

You may also wish to become affiliated or registered with one of the following reputable agencies:

Institute of Chartered Financial Analysts (ICFA)

National Association of Personal Financial Advisors (NAPFA)

National Association of Securities Dealers (NASD)

Securities and Exchange Commission (SEC)

Human Skills

Turn back to Worksheet 1—Your Image, located at the end of Chapter 2. Here you rated yourself on the skills needed as a Financial Planner:

· Trusted

· Objective

· Expert

· Professional

- Coordinator
- Counselor
- Educator
- Motivator
- Watchdog

How can you turn all the low ratings to high ratings? Your technical education will handle those attributes of your image as a trusted, objective, expert professional. What about coordinator and motivator? Consider attending a seminar offered for managers. This can give you the framework to identify and develop the skills you need to work with the expert team members and your clients.

What about counselor and educator? You need to develop human relations and communication skills for these attributes. Again, you may wish to attend a seminar or a continuing education course offered at a local community college.

Surprisingly, almost any course of personal development that builds your self-confidence will improve your communication skills. For example, consider the use of jargon. Technical terms, or acronyms, serve a useful purpose among professionals who know their meaning. However, they can ruin rapport with a client if used indiscriminately. When you have a high level of self-confidence, you will find yourself less dependent on a narrow technical vocabulary and more able to focus on the needs of the listener.

I recommend that you take a Toastmaster or Dale Carnegie course to improve your level of self-confidence. These can also refresh the presentation skills needed in a variety of situations, from seminars to presentations of individual Personal Financial Plans.

Your Information Network

You will have to establish a personal information network to keep you abreast of the financial environment. Good sources of information are statements made by the financial community in books, magazines, newspapers, and on television. You can use these to monitor economic trends on a short-, medium-, and long-range basis.

For short-term (day-to-day) trends, rely on newspapers, such as:

The Wall Street Journal

The New York Times

Intermediate (six-month to two-year) trends and situations are best observed in magazines:

Personal Financial Planning trade papers

Time

Newsweek

Business Week

Changing Times

Money

U.S. News and World Report

Long-term developments in the financial environment are presented in best-selling books about finance. Don't neglect the information benefits that derive from your own professional organization or others that you may choose to join. These are also valuable sources of information on new tools, procedures, and marketing techniques.

DEVELOP YOUR PROCESS

Aids in the Process Steps

Recall that the Personal Financial Planning process includes these steps:

1. Collect data
2. Set goals
3. Analyze data
4. Create plan
5. Implement plan
6. Review plan

You can develop and refine each step during your start-up period. Your first dozen plans will probably resolve most problems in your process. However, before you do a plan for your first client, do your own financial plan because clients will certainly ask if you have one. Do as many test plans as are possible to help you create a workable process.

Let me repeat, don't plan to profit from the first few jobs; take your time. Determine how many Personal Financial Planning clients you want in the first year and stick to it. Here are some ideas about practice management aids that are listed in the same order as the process steps.

Collect Data. Develop a Client Data Form as part of an introductory brochure that clients complete at home. The data collected on an introductory form will probably be the minimum needed to develop a financial statement, and you will need more specifics and details to actually create a financial plan. Rather than asking clients to supply the same data twice, however, you should transcribe the information from the preliminary forms yourself. Make sure clients knows what information you will need to conduct a detailed planning session.

You can help clients gather the needed data by giving them home preparation kits of forms and checklists. This helps clients come to the first data-gathering meeting fully prepared. Develop and use forms and checklists throughout the process, especially in later interviews. This ensures that you get the information you need during the interview. Missing information can be identified and requested later by the telephone.

Set Goals. At the end of the initial data-gathering interview, send the client home with a discussion checklist that will prepare the ground for goal-setting sessions. You can save time if the client doesn't have to work through all the fantasy/dream/goal transitions in your office.

The purpose of a discussion checklist is to initiate a dialogue between client and spouse or other key family members. This talk should help the client's family work out future plans. For example, how will they spend their time after retirement? Will they start a hobby business, travel, or stay at home and develop artistic talents? What will be their major activities, and where will these take place?

Of course, you need to consider the client's stage of life. Develop discussions on subsequent life stages when preparing for the goal-setting sessions.

Analyze Data. Set up standard methods to save yourself time and money. Either your professional education or members of your expert team will help guide you here.

Create Plan. Use a skeleton plan that you flesh out in accord with particular client situations. This can be derived from our discussion of the ideal plan or from your technical education. The trial plans that you develop for yourself and your friends or partners can be generalized back to a workable skeleton.

Implement Plan. Record the steps that you take to implement the first plans. These lists can be refined to become your standard procedure.

Review Plan. A regular semiannual contact and a yearly formal review are good planning and good business. Develop a client contact and tickler system to record the history of interactions and to prompt you for the next contact in a timely fashion.

Computers

Computer support can help boost profits and production for your process and service. At some volumes of business, it may even become essential. The key word is support. Automation can support your service, but it can never replace the Financial Planner in the planning process.

Many planners use automation today. Legions of hardware and software products are available to the Financial Planner. Avoid the traps into which many of your competitors have fallen: Never let automation drive the process or dominate the plan. Your clients expect personalized reporting, so use computer reports with judgment. Use them to help create a favorable image of your service, but never let them replace the delivery of expert advice and personal service.

Most Financial Planners believe that a computer is essential for successful practice. A computer can increase productivity and profit, create a uniform and professional image, handle volumes impossible to treat manually, and provide sophisticated management of your client base.

Computer support will probably become a valuable resource as your practice grows, but do not feel compelled to invest in hardware or software in the beginning stages. Power tools such as computers make jobs easier and faster, but they will not help if you do not know how to do the job in the first place. Hold back on computerization until you can do each job by hand.

Start with forms and calculators. There are very sophisticated and economical hand held calculators for the financial analysis area. When volumes warrant, invest in a basic hardware configuration that can be expanded as your needs grow. Start with software that handles spreadsheets and word processing.

Word processing systems are powerful office tools. They are the most efficient technology available for handling all the writing needs of an office. You can develop standard plans and letters that will increase productivity with a minimum of effort. You can develop mass mailings that remain personalized and professional. If you use care in your hardware and software selection, the word processing resource can be expanded to handle all your publishing needs.

Next, add software tools to support financial analysis. You can purchase software either function by function, or as a complete and integrated system. If your target market includes low- and middle-income clients, consider a package that generates complete basic financial plans. Finally, add software for client base management and product tracking.

Computer systems involve hardware, software, and support services. The hardware is the actual machinery that supports the software processing. You can lease time from an external processing firm, but this is not the best approach for the independent practice. I recommend that you buy a network of separate microcomputers, but one at a time—as needed. The first personal computer you buy will do most of the jobs that need to be done. Additional units can be added to the network to increase volume.

Software is the collection of programs that performs work functions on your hardware. Since the hardware and software must be compatible, you should purchase one of the leading brands. We'll take a detailed look at software uses later in this chapter.

Unless you intend to maintain and service the hardware yourself, consider the support or maintenance provisions of your vendor when purchasing. This applies to software, too. Most reputable software packages will include an annual update and telephone support service. You should also examine the user manuals and other support documentation provided with hardware and software. Many computer firms can provide training for you and your staff.

When you consider buying software, be sure that your business volume warrants it and that the purchased package will meet your needs. How can you determine what you need? First, prepare several plans manually. The calculations or functions that are tedious and repetitive are the ones for which you should seek computer support. As you work, make a list of the frequent or unthinking activities that are involved since these are the tasks that you would delegate to a junior or clerk. In many ways the computer serves as a tireless and efficient, but inexperienced, assistant.

When you shop for hardware and software, know beforehand the functions that need to be performed and the volume that must be handled. Specifically, know the volume of clients and know the volume of information that you want available in the system. Both hardware and software vendors can help you estimate volume needs.

The familiarity that you gain with hands-on experience of your own hardware and software will let you improve the quality of your planning effort, allowing for more extensive analysis. As you master this support tool, you can even perform complex hypothetical projections during client interviews or presentations to test plan alternatives.

The cost of a microcomputer is quite low, typically $3000 for a basic system that includes ample data storage and printing capabilities. Software costs range from $500 to $4000 for integrated Personal Financial Planning packages. The annual update and maintenance fees are usually less than 25 percent of the initial purchase price. Unless you are a computer expert yourself, it is advisable to buy the update and maintenance services available. Annual updates to the software package will reflect changes in the tax laws and other economic factors such as inflation and interest rates. Maintenance fees cover any problem solving help you need, or changes that you specifically request. A list of available software packages appears in Appendix B.

When you select software, be prepared to ask some key questions. Since an integrated system requires only one session of data entry to generate all reports, look for a system that integrates all the planning functions that you want to perform. You may elect to buy a base system that can be functionally expanded as your needs dictate. Also, make sure that the package you buy is a stand alone system, which needs no other software to perform its functions, or include the cost of additional software in your calculations.

Look for a system that can handle your client data base and produce your financial planning reports. Don't forget to consider graphics and financial planning text capabilities, as well as support, training, and maintenance provisions available.

Does the system allow editing of final reports? Can you print selected reports only, or must you print entire plans? What is the "what-if" capability of the system? Can projections be made under various assumptions?

There are many types of hardware that will work well for you. The secret is in the software. What can the available software do for you? Your basic needs are for problem solving and analysis, word processing, and record keeping and administration. Software systems are currently available to meet these and other needs. The following list details what today's software can do.

Office Management

· Client file access and update
· Mailing list creation and maintenance

- Product information files
- Client billing
- Payroll production

Client Base Management
- Prospect list maintenance
- Client financial status
- Portfolio mix analysis
- Investment product performance
- Client search and select on income, assets, or investments

Cash Management
- Current financial situation statements
- Objectives and assumptions summary
- Net worth statement
- Cash flow and tax estimate
- Debt ratio analysis

Tax Planning
- Tax estimate
- Tax return preparation

Risk Management
- Life insurance needs analysis
- Disability insurance needs analysis

Investment Planning
- Portfolio analysis
- Diversification projections ("what-if")

Retirement Planning
- Retirement capital needs analysis

Estate Planning
- Estate tax estimate
- Capital needs analysis

Special Goals
· Education funding needs analysis

Projections
· Retirement capital needs analysis
· Estate tax estimates
· Disability income needs
· Inflation projections
· Survivor income needs analysis
· Insurance projections

Business
· Closely held or owned business evaluation
· Incorporating feasibility study

Effect of Plan Recommendations
· Revised net worth statement
· Estate planning projection
· Revised cash flow and tax estimate
· Revised diversification projection

Support Schedules
· Descriptive material
· Estimated social security benefit buildup
· Glossary

Product Analysis
· Asset comparison charts
· Life insurance cost analysis
· Loan calculator
· Tax-deferred savings plan analysis
· Mortgage amortizations

DEVELOP YOUR PRODUCTS

The Plan Document

The most tangible result of your planning efforts is the plan document. Since it is often the only enduring experience your client has of your service, be sure the plan document looks professional. Consider the binding, paper, type, and dividers you use. Take pains to develop several good skeleton plans so that you can match the client situation to the plan document with minimum effort and maximum effect. The sections of the plan will include:

- Summary
- Cash management
- Tax planning
- Risk management
- Investment planning
- Retirement planning
- Estate planning
- Special objectives
- Action plan

Planning is an ongoing process. Each plan document is only one of a series of revised, improved, and updated documents. When you create the plan document, think of it as a living product and make sure that it can be easily modified and updated. Your understanding of the continuing planning process should be reflected throughout the text of the document. Most important, make sure that the *Action Plan* includes the scheduled reviews.

Client Data Form

Correct data is the basis of good planning. The Client Data Form is a critical aid in gathering all the information you need. Whether you gather the information in interviews or ask the client to complete forms at home, think through the process so you get all the information you need. Try to minimize the time and effort necessary for your client to gather this material. As you know, there is nothing more frustrating than being asked to continually supply the same information.

Design a data-gathering form that facilitates the transfer of the data to your planning process. This may involve integrating the form with the automated parts of your process.

Your image is represented by each form your client handles, sees, and uses. In theory, your technical education will give you an idea of the information you will need. Just balance the theory with the practice that you get during your trial runs.

When you offer the Client Data Form as part of an introductory brochure or when you ask the client to fill out the form at home, you should give a brief statement of the form's purpose to help motivate the client to provide accurate information. We often begrudge providing information when we can see no benefit for doing so.

Client Data Forms vary from one practice to another, but generally include the broad categories shown below. Notice that I have included the topic of personal risk tolerance and family goals in this list. This information should not be obtained on a take-home form, but should be gathered by the Financial Planner in interview situations with all key family members present since this kind of information can rarely be determined by the client alone. Your skills as a psychologist and adviser must help to generate real goals and needs. Often your client will state goals that he feels he is expected to have. Often your client will need help to define long-term goals in objective or measurable terms.

General Data

- Family profile
- Adviser names and addresses
- Personal and family risk tolerance, goals, and objectives

Income and Expenses

- Annual income
- Expenses (on an annual basis)

Assets and Liabilities

- Real property
- Personal property
- Credit card balances
- Loan balances
- Mortgage note balances
- Other payments due

Income Tax Information
- Copies of returns for last three years
- Tax information for current year (estimated)

Insurance Information
- Personal
- Property
- Liability
- Business

Retirement Benefits
- Employer
- Government
- Individual

Estate Planning
- Business agreements
- Divorce settlements
- Gifts
- Location and listing of all important papers
- Marital agreements
- Property ownership
- Safe deposit box
- Trusts
- Wills

Client Files

If yours is a small practice, you have the advantage of giving highly personalized treatment to a small client base. At whatever volume you reach, however, remember to offer individualized service at some fee level. As your practice grows it will be essential to groom and develop a profitable client base. In order to do this, you need to keep accurate and current client files.

Use the low volume of start-up client files to perfect the content, format, and organization of your files. Take these files through all the stages and angles of your process, either in practice or imagination. How will you store and access key information? Will all files be kept in the same location, or will support documents be stored in separate files?

Key information is best kept in a computer system for rapid access, but you will want this information in printed format for interview situations. Consider the impression you can make on your clients if each sees his file as one of only a dozen or so files that are kept at your desk. This is a tangible demonstration of personalized service.

For your client file, you will need to store and maintain the following kinds of information:

- Completed data-gathering forms
- Various planning questionnaires
- Copies of will and trust documents
- Supportive analyses from the expert team
- A copy of each plan document
- A summary of recommendations
- Tracking form and calendar of actions to be performed
- Investment portfolio reports
- Income tax returns
- Year-to-date gain and loss worksheets
- Minutes of meetings and advice given

PRODUCT LEVELING AND SEGMENTATION

Consider all your products and services. Each can be divided into smaller pieces, or performed in a variety of fashions, or offered at various levels. Why would you do this? One reason is time. Your time is your most valuable resource. You need the flexibility of product leveling and segmentation to spend your time where it is most profitable.

A product or service that involves your time in one-to-one interactions with a client will be expensive. Can you offer the same service to a large group of clients? Often you can. Perhaps a part of your service can be offered in the form of a seminar. Basic information that you give repeatedly to each client could be presented in a brochure or a cassette tape.

Your products and services can be divided into various levels or segments to match market segmentation. As an example of market segmentation, divide the target market into the following annual income segments:

- Less than $30,000
- $30,000 to $50,000
- Over $50,000

The over $50,000 segment could further be divided into these segments:

- Business owners
- Professionals
- Executives

You can see that the needs of these segments will vary substantially. You can offer a diversity of products to suit specific needs by carefully organizing and dividing your service capabilities according to your strategic marketing plan.

Using the previous example of market segmentation, consider the following. The less than $30,000 segment might not be judged to be good prospects for Personal Financial Planning. There are exceptions, however. Graduates of dental, legal, medical, or other professional schools are typically in debt, but they generally aren't for long. If you can help them establish the right habits early, they will benefit. Further, the client/planner relationship will be established with your firm.

This can be compared to gardening. You can't eat carrot seeds, but with the right preparation, nurturing, and weeding, you can grow carrots. How could you attract and "plant" these new graduates? You could develop a preplanning service or product in the form of a simple savings action plan or a low-cost skeleton plan that treats only the development of discretionary income. You could develop a series of booklets that details the initial steps toward planning for wealth, and members of this market segment could enroll as subscribers to the series. The series could include a fixed amount for your consultation time for personal advice. Such a product would spread your time over a large base of prospects and future clients.

For prospects in the $30,000 to $50,000 segment, your detailed Personal Financial Plan may be the desired product. This segment is also a good market for simple, generic, computer-generated plans that can be augmented by your analysis and recommendations. With inexpensive software packages, you can offer a plan of from 15 to 40 pages at a cost of no more than $250. Such plans can be offered as a trial product to show prospects how Personal Financial Planning can help them. The cost can be rebated to those clients who decide to buy your fully personalized plan.

For the over $50,000 segment, you might want to separate your advisory and implementation services. As well as comprehensive Personal Financial Planning, you can offer analysis and recommendations for any part of the plan.

Of course, clients can use their own specialists for many of these services. What you can offer is the coordination of two or more expert advisers. Consumers of Personal Financial Planning Services need and want this coordination.

As you develop your complete planning service, you will be developing and networking additional services for a broad market. Don't forget to emphasize your own specialist expertise! But also consider offering budgeting assistance, monthly or quarterly personal bookkeeping, cash flow monitoring, and the host of other services to which you can now provide access.

Even your first few clients will demonstrate how the planning process varies according to stage of life. You can deliberately segment the planning process so that each segmented product treats a specific need of a specific stage of life. For example, your retired clients will probably not need to plan for their children's educations. Here is a recap of the stages of life in the Personal Financial Planning process.

1. *Employed Before Marriage.* Clients are concerned only with themselves and can afford high risk levels. Time permits them to consider long-term growth. Insurance is not relevant.

2. *Married Without Children.* Insurance is relevant at this stage, but it is not a substantial factor. There are usually opportunities for savings, but the pressure to spend can necessitate careful budgeting. The client's investment strategy is more conservative.

3. *Married With Children.* Expenditures increase sharply, but there also may be a significant rise in income that makes tax planning necessary. Insurance protection becomes important, and the client may be concerned about future college costs.

4. *Children Have Left the Nest.* Your client's earning power is probably at its peak. Therefore, investment strategy should aim at building capital.

Risk aversion becomes important to the client, and life insurance needs should be reviewed.

5. Retirement. Your client may have embarked on a second career. Maintaining a comfortable income is a concern, and while your client now has greater freedom and independence, his investment strategy will avoid extremes.

You should also consider segmenting the steps of the planning process, allowing breaks between appropriate steps. You can view this segmentation in terms of how your Personal Financial Planning Service is introduced to the client.

The process actually starts when you begin to educate your client. Remember: We teach best what we need to learn most. Since you need to learn all about Personal Financial Planning, why not teach it to your prospects? Use inside or outside staff to outline the subject in an informative seminar. Invite your prospects and encourage them to bring guests.

An introductory seminar series could be presented in two three-hour sessions. It would cover such topics as:

- Goal setting
- Money management
- Income tax planning
- Tax shelters
- Insurance
- Investments
- Retirement planning
- Estate planning
- Trusts
- Wills

End the last session by distributing either your client data form or an introductory brochure that helps the client generate a simple financial statement. Interested prospects can then begin the data-gathering step. Hopefully, they will gain enough momentum (aided by your diligent follow-up) to request a goal-setting interview.

With the data collection and goal-setting steps completed, you can proceed to analyze the data and to create a plan. This could be a basic plan that completes one level of the service and that includes a recommendation about the next level of planning detail or complexity. At this point, you can offer your services in implementing the plan.

Finally, ongoing review and maintenance services can be offered. These services include the regular semiannual contact, yearly formal review, and required adjustments.

RELATED PRODUCTS

If you use the principles of leveling and segmentation wisely, you can develop your basic services and products into a flexible and profitable array. In addition, you should consider a host of related products that follow the idea of segmentation and that support your marketing efforts.

Related products that you can develop include booklets, seminars, tapes, newsletters, and brochures. Your personal time and attention are the most expensive commodities you offer, but you can also develop a wide range of variously priced products.

In the discussions that follow, remember that these products all project the image of your service. Be clear and consistent in the image that you project. A prominent logo will help to identify your products and distinguish them from your competitors. Adopt a pleasing color scheme and maintain it. Use the same quality and a consistent format for all products.

Introduction to Firm Brochure

You will need a data sheet or brochure that introduces prospects to your firm. This should show who you are and what services you offer. It should also show your qualifications, and it might include a structure chart showing your expert network.

Since consumers of Personal Financial Planning Services have become increasingly sophisticated about their purchases, you should anticipate and answer their questions with this brochure. What will the educated consumer be asking about your Personal Financial Planning Service?

Do you have a written fee policy? Show prospects that they can determine exactly what you charge, and on what basis. You need not be specific in this introductory brochure, but define the basis of your fee structure, whether fee only, commission only, or a combination. Be prepared to offer written estimates.

What credentials and experience do you have? Give the prospect an outline of your qualifications, credentials, and experience. Mention your registrations and those of your network. Register with the Better Business Bureau in your area.

What will you do for your clients? Outline the steps you will take. Specify which steps involve interviews and where the recommendations of your expert team enter the process. You will also want to stress the comprehensive nature of your service, from goal setting to implementation and monitoring.

How many companies do you represent? The educated consumer knows that versatility and objectivity are proportional to your breadth. Again, this is the ideal place to outline your network and affiliations.

Whom will I deal with on a regular basis? Define the client/planner relationship that your clients enjoy. Let prospects know that your emphasis is on personal attention and quality.

This brochure is the ideal place to summarize your product and service range. It is also the best place to establish your image of solid durability. Include a list of your community service activities or contributions. A brief corporate history can be reassuring about your permanence and experience.

Introduction to Personal Financial Planning Brochure

This is a product brochure, specifically for your Personal Financial Planning Service, that gives clients an introduction into the subject of Personal Financial Planning. This brochure should include simple data-gathering forms and financial statements. These are important for two reasons. First, prospects will actually be doing something about their futures by completing the forms. The momentum that this generates leads naturally to your services. Second, prospects can decide whether your services are needed and, if so, at what level.

The brochure should have an introductory statement about the economic situation and the problems we face. Remind prospects that even though they are achievement-oriented, they may not know how to make money from money. There are several problems to overcome in order to invest wisely, including inflationary pressures, which create artificial increases in income but real losses in purchasing power; higher tax brackets; and complex tax laws. It becomes more and more difficult to save for retirement in our complex economy. Surely, there is a proliferation of financial products, but most of us are not trained to deal with these factors.

Next, provide a list of goals we all hold, and leave space for prospects to fill in their own special goals. You can expand this area with worksheets that project the cost of reaching various goals. Common goals include owning your home, educating your children, retiring with an adequate amount of money, and settling estate considerations.

This may reinforce your prospects' anxieties about their futures, but you can allay many of their fears by showing what Personal Financial Planning can do for them. Show them the steps in the Personal Financial Planning process.

Include examples of how Personal Financial Planning helps in various cases. Since case studies are interesting and comprehensible, provide several from among these possible situations:

- Single young professionals starting out
- Young couples starting out
- Couples with a new family, looking forward to future needs
- Single parents with multiple needs
- Older couples looking forward to retirement
- Older couples, optimizing retirement
- Old couples putting an estate in order

From case studies, lead the prospect into participation by providing worksheets. These can be integrated with your basic client data form, so carefully consider their content and layout. Worksheets can include a critical records locator, a financial statement including net worth, and a calculation of cash flow.

At this point the prospect may have decided to seek the services of a Financial Planner. You can demonstrate your objectivity by providing some tips on how to shop for a Personal Financial Planning Service. Of course, your firm will meet all of the following criteria!

- Adequate credentials, experience, registration
- Available references, including satisfied clients
- Fluidity in financial strategies
- Emphasis on the client/planner relationship
- Emphasis on personalized, high quality service
- Written fee policy

One of the greatest impediments to comprehension is an undefined term. The next time that you find yourself reading without understanding, look back through the text for an unfamiliar word. Chances are good that without an understanding of this term, the material following it lost meaning for you. Therefore, include a glossary at the end of your brochure and be sure that all necessary financial terms are in this glossary. You can enlist the help of a financial novice to pinpoint the difficult terms. There is an appendix of financial planning terms at the end of this book from which you may extract when you prepare your brochure.

Fee/Service Schedule

You will need a form that shows your clients what products and services are available and what they cost. While you don't have to be specific, let the schedule show how costs are determined so that clients can exercise their sense of value.

Each service should be defined in your schedule, and the cost or fee basis should be shown. You may want to include samples of the product or service in order to allow the client to catalog shop. One way to define segmented services is to list the topics covered at each meeting or step.

Contact Records and Tickler System

Develop a simple, consistent way to log your contacts with members of your expert team and prospective or established clients. A simple sheet that is filled in manually each day, even your desk calendar, can be entered into a computer system to allow rapid searches. This is a valuable information resource for keeping regular contact with clients.

Your calendar can also log future events and periodic reviews. If this becomes cluttered, try a simple index card system. Set up dividers for each month of the year and file a separate card for each contact or action needed under the appropriate month. Before the beginning of each month, review and priorize the activities needed.

Reference List

As you serve clients, ask if they can give a good recommendation and if they are willing to be included on your reference list. Tell them the purpose and use you make of personal recommendations.

No one wants to be burdened with inquiries, so make your list extensive enough to allow rotation. Assure the client of the limited use of the list and the limited demands necessary to act as a reference.

Although written recommendations are not as persuasive as personal

discussion, keep about ten letters from your more successful or prominent clients.

Sample Plans

Prepare a sample plan document to show to prospective clients. This is
the only tangible product of your service.

The sample plan can be assembled from fictitious data or compiled
from selected case histories. You can have a binder with several case histories in each section of the plan document in order to show the prospect
how the plan might look for his special case.

Case History File

In many cases, an example will be illuminating to a client in order to
explain a strategy or situation. As you work, keep an eye on potential case
history material that can be stripped of specifics in order to create a generic case history. Remember to delete any material that would endanger
client confidentiality.

Newsletter

A periodic newsletter can be both a marketing and a client relations tool.
Newsletters will present your image to the public to help maintain client
loyalty. Like Personal Financial Planning, a newsletter is an ongoing commitment. Before you distribute the first issue, be sure you can produce
the following issues regularly and promptly. Delays or missed issues can
impact your image negatively. Plan at least a year ahead, and have some
emergency canned issues.

The format and size can vary, but an 8½-by-11 inch newsletter of from
four to eight pages is a good idea. The standard size makes it easy to store,
especially if the pages are drilled for a three-ring binder. Don't tax your
clients by sending them a twenty-page tome each month!

Your newsletter can be offered free to established clients and at a small
price to prospective clients. You could include an ongoing section of tips
for preplanning grooming. You could also prepare special issues for other
large market segments. For example, a special annual tax preparation issue could be printed for general distribution to your entire prospect list.

Newsletter articles can range from home refinancing to market timing
strategies. You can mention information about your firm, new staff, additional services or products. You can scan your file of case histories and
feature unusual or outstanding benefits that your clients have gained.

When you provide Personal Financial Planning advice, give enough to be informative and useful but not enough to eliminate the need for your services.

When you prepare your newsletter, use simple, consumer-oriented language and present information that will be of direct benefit to the reader. Describe your services and how the consumer can benefit from them. Include some do-it-yourself hints, business information, personal financial planning tips, and other tidbits as a goodwill gesture.

Make your newsletter visually attractive by including lots of white space. Keep explanations simple and use type that is large and easy to read. Material for your newsletter can be obtained from these sources:

- Wholesalers of investment products
- Marketing departments of financial services companies
- Libraries
- Financial and insurance magazines and newsletters
- Your professional organization

Bulletin Letters

Periodically, you may want to issue single-page bulletins in letter form. These are ideal for alerting groups of clients to economic changes that require attention or to new products and services. Again, develop and use a consistent image that reflects your professionalism.

Bulletins can also serve as low-cost marketing tools. They can be included in general mailings, either as information sheets or as questionnaires to help prospects determine their need for Personal Financial Planning Services.

Never hesitate to make strategic use of a postscript (P.S.) on any letter. Why? The P.S. is always read. When you want a decision to be made or an action to be taken, put your call to action here.

In word processor-generated letters, do not use the right-hand justification feature; use a ragged right-hand margin. This will preserve the hand typed image of a personal letter.

Miscellaneous Materials

A host of products can fill the gaps left by your major products. You will want a business card that reflects your desired image and shows your earned designations. You may need checklists of material for the client to bring to certain key meetings. If you use a telephone answering machine, consider producing a message that sells your new services. In the following chapters we will look at more products and techniques for selling when we begin to develop your strategic marketing plan.

Now it is time to summarize the steps and decisions involved in developing your service.

LIMITATIONS AND ALTERNATIVES

The skills and resources needed to develop a complete and coherent service seem overwhelming, and I would be surprised if you felt equal to a single-handed attack of the task. You will probably want to handle the areas of development that you feel most comfortable with and enlist the aid of a few outside professionals to handle the rest. This is a reasonable decision since it lets you focus on what only you can develop: yourself.

You have to determine which tasks you can handle and where to seek outside help. You must consider your time, your financial resources, and your firm's current resources. Let's tackle this with a decision worksheet that lists areas for development and that lets you decide who will be responsible for each. The worksheet includes some cost estimating space to help you define the financial resources you will need. Before you complete this worksheet, review your alternatives to single-handed development.

Make the best use of your existing staff before you consider hiring outside help. Make a survey of the skills and talents that your staff has. Start developing your planning assistant by assigning the preparation of some of your related products, such as brochures or newsletters.

If you gradually evolve new services and skills, you will have the time to educate not only yourself, but your support staff. There are courses available to develop planning assistants as well as planners. Look into the computer resources and skills that your secretarial staff may already possess. Be prepared to develop and augment these.

Isolate low-level resource gaps, and consider hiring additional clerical staff to help fill these gaps.

Before you start developing your service, compile a list of the marketing, planning, and implementation services in your area that can support your efforts. Where these services are not available, examine the skills and resources offered by Personal Financial Planning network services.

Finally, explore and list the resources offered by your professional associations.

WORKSHEET 3
Develop Your Service

Organization Needs	Who Is Responsible	Initial Cost	Annual Cost
Marketing	_____	_____	_____
Planning	_____	_____	_____
Implementation	_____	_____	_____
Product development	_____	_____	_____

Expert Team	Who Will Perform	Cost Basis
Planner	_____	_____
Planning assistant	_____	_____
Attorney	_____	_____
Broker	_____	_____
Insurance agent	_____	_____
Banker	_____	_____
CPA/Tax expert	_____	_____

Financial Planner	Circle	Cost
Education	ChFC CLU CFP CFA	_____
Registration	IAFP ICFP ICFA NAPFA NASD SEC	_____

Human skills	Course	Cost
· Management		
· Presentation		
· Psychology		

Information network	Name	Cost
· Newspapers		
· Magazines		
· Book allowance		

Computer Support	Description	Initial Cost	Annual Cost
Hardware			
Software			
Support			

Products	Who Will Develop	Cost
Skeleton plan document		
Client data form		
Client files		
Expert teamroster		

Leveling and Segmentation Notes

By market segment _____

_____

_____

By stage of life _____

_____

_____

By step in process _____

_____

_____

By network services _____

_____

_____

Related Products	Who Will Develop	Cost
Firm brochure	_____	_____
Personal financial planning brochure	_____	_____
Fee/service schedule	_____	_____

Contact records and tickler system _____ _____

Reference list _____ _____

Sample plans _____ _____

Case history file _____ _____

Newsletter _____ _____

Bulletin letters _____ _____

Miscellaneous products   *Name*   *Cost*

_____ _____

_____ _____

_____ _____

_____ _____

_____ _____

5

Introduction to Strategic Marketing

INTRODUCTION TO WHAT?

The next three chapters are the core of the marketing information in this book. Chapter 6 gives a step by step process for developing your strategic marketing plan. Chapter 7 presents the details of some useful techniques. This chapter is a relaxed introduction to the background you will need.

This is a great chance for you to practice swiveling your head, to learn how to adopt the perceptual framework of another person. Right now, you stand in the same relation to marketing as your client stands to Personal Financial Planning. The specialized terms of this field are unknown to you. You may have various negative feelings toward the area of marketing.

This is the same situation your client is in, and understanding his position is essential to your success. So study your own reaction to learning about marketing. Where I fail to make you comfortable in entering into this new area, you should learn, improve, and succeed with your client.

One key is to avoid jargon that is known to you, but not to your client. One of the first things I will do is define some terms that are the jargon of modern marketing. In the last chapter we talked about the selling versus the marketing philosophy. To recap, the two are:

SELLING. If a product can be produced it can be sold.

MARKETING. If a product can be sold it can be produced.

POSITION

Strategic marketing positions you midway between the consumer need and the service being marketed. Positioning tactics can seem strange at times. Sometimes consumer needs are actually created, to sell a new product.

Remember that flurry of clever television advertisements that promoted a foot deodorant? Now you and I were probably not overly concerned about our foot odor when these came out. They were designed to make us aware, make us concerned. They were intended to create a need for a new product, the foot deodorant. Fortunately, the product didn't go over too well. I think we have enough training from Madison Avenue about how malodorous and generally undesirable we are, without worrying about our feet, too! But you get the idea.

Positioning is like an axe, cleaving a space from solid wood. On one side of the wedge emerges the created or refined need in the customer. On the other side is the product or service destined to meet the need. This is what strategic marketing is about.

We do not need to create artificial needs in our clients in order to market our Personal Financial Planning Service. The need is there of its own accord. What strategic marketing can do is present us with a clear picture of these needs, help us tailor our products and services to meet these needs in an exact and satisfying way, and determine our profitability by stimulating the flow of services to that need.

Market position also takes into account the competitive environment in which you operate. It helps you design and create your image, distinct from that of your competitors. It helps you create a distinct stance and location among various needs and services.

WHY MARKET?

Marketing can make the difference between success and failure in Personal Financial Planning today. Two planners with similar services and equal credentials can experience widely divergent success. It all depends on how they use public relations, advertising, and other aspects of strategic marketing. A strategic marketing plan can make the difference between a marginal or a flourishing practice.

Ongoing mergers and acquisitions tend to decrease the number of large corporate clients. This forces the large scale financial service firms to seek more business in other market segments. As small or independent practices, we feel this as an increased pressure to compete for clients, or even retain our existing clients. Today competition in the financial services sector is fierce.

There is an influx of new products and services, a host of new entrants to the arena, and dozens of innovative new marketing approaches. In short, you must compete to survive. Part of competing well is making good use of the strategic marketing tools available to both you and your competitors.

Beyond competitive forces, there is a surge of public awareness of our critical personal economic situation. More and more people are considering the possibility of applying Personal Financial Planning to secure their financial futures. You have to let these consumers know you exist, that you are aware of their needs, and that you have services that can meet these needs.

Both existing and new clients must be made aware of your service, or, no matter how ideal it is, they will not buy it. They must know you are there, or you will fail in your professional obligation to meet the needs of the client.

If you are a new entrant to the marketplace, you have to work even harder and smarter than the entrenched firms. If you have already established your practice, but are ready to expand, strategic marketing is your best hope for reaching the growth goals you have set for yourself.

You know that Personal Financial Planning can make all of life's major transitions more manageable. It can meet the needs of the consumers. You also have a notion about developing and using brochures, seminars, and the media to reach your clients. Strategic marketing will tie all this into a workable plan.

Does the word *plan* trigger some new thoughts in your mind? It should, because all the ideas we've looked at in Personal Financial Planning also apply to planning a marketing strategy. We'll follow the parallels closely in this chapter and the next, as we work toward developing your strategic marketing plan.

There is a logical series of steps you can follow to develop and implement your strategic marketing plan. We will look at these in detail in the next chapter. This part is devoted to easing you into the water. To make sense of the currents, channel markers, and signal flags, we need some definitions.

MARKETING DEFINITIONS

The first thing I want to do is vaporize my position as a knowledgeable expert. I will do that by defining the jargon of marketing. When I use defined terms, you will know what I mean. This is how to convert jargon to dialogue.

1. *Marketing.* This is an organized, ongoing process. It clearly defines consumer needs, and the products and services that will best satisfy these needs. Further, marketing delivers the products and services to the target market that is most willing to purchase them.

Strategic marketing is often called a "direct" method, since it addresses specific consumers, rather than the general public. With strategic marketing, as opposed to public relations, you can expect measurable benefits in the size or composition of your client base, or in explicit financial returns.

2. *Advertising.* This is one of the methods used in a marketing plan. The purpose of advertising is to attract and motivate the target audience to make the purchase. Advertising in the media can be paid or free. That's right, free. We'll look at some of the free advertising available in the chapter on tactics.

3. *Public Relations.* This is a process of communication that seeks to create maximum understanding and acceptance of the mission, goals, and objectives of a person or firm.

Public relations works to improve your image, as a basis or platform for your business activities. It is indirect, but can be more effective than marketing over the long run. Compared to the rifle of marketing, public relations is more of a shotgun approach.

The place to begin with public relations is in your own house. You and your co-workers must have an experience of pride in your work that can be reflected outward. General public relations work can also be a beneficial part of a strategic marketing plan, when it reaches your target market.

4. *Direct/Indirect.* These terms are used to distinguish between marketing tactics aimed at specific or general audiences. Examples of direct marketing tactics are: seminars, cold calls, or advertising. Examples of indirect tactics are: public relations work, speech-making, news releases, or appearances on radio shows.

Direct tactics involve direct connection or contact with specific individuals. These put you in a one-to-one confrontation with potential clients. Indirect tactics put you in one-to-many situations with the general public, only some of whom are your potential clients.

5. *Strategy/Tactics.* These terms have boggled the minds of business people for so long that it is a real pleasure to clarify them here. Strategy is what you want to do. Tactics is how you will do it. The strategy of your

planning will define broad objectives. The tactics will be chosen to achieve specific goals.

6. *Scope.* The scope of your marketing effort can be measured by your budget, your goals, the size of your target audience, or the duration of your activities. All in all, scope just means how big you plan to go.

7. *Segmentation.* This is the process of dividing and subdividing a general target market into smaller, more specifically defined markets. Segmentation will prove so valuable to your marketing plan that more detail is given later in this chapter.

In simplest terms, there is no point in marketing to those who can't afford or don't need your services. Sometimes segmentation is used to find the specific market that can afford the services you want to offer. Sometimes segmentation will point out needed products and services that you can add to your offerings.

8. *Profiling.* When you have isolated a target segment, you will need to get to know the people it represents. Profiling gives you a picture of your potential client as a person. When you know the person, you can determine the real needs he has, and the best way to communicate your service potential to him.

You can profile to whatever level of detail is called for. Profiling may involve financial factors, demography, life-styles, and so forth. When you profile a market segment, you are building the information you need to determine the needs and deliver the services.

THE PSYCHOLOGY OF MARKETING A SERVICE

The first critical area of marketing psychology is in your own head. You must overcome your fears and hesitations about marketing. Remember that your competitors—the banks, brokerage houses, insurance agencies, and CPA firms—are not hesitating. A successful marketing strategy is essential to your business success. Stop the negative talk you carry on in your head about your marketing activities. Any conflicts between your concepts of marketing and professionalism will be resolved when you understand marketing.

The goal of a professional is to satisfy the needs of his clients. Marketing is a business activity directed at satisfying needs and desires in an exchange process. Marketing can thus make you more profitable and provide better service to your clients. Success means that you will meet and satisfy the needs of your clients more effectively and efficiently than your competition does.

Consumers are not logical about service purchases. They buy the sizzle, not the steak; the glitter, not the diamond. In other words, people tend to buy nonquantifiable experiences and benefits. When you market your services, you must sell the benefit gained or loss avoided. This means that you must identify the benefits and losses, especially those with emotional loads, connected to your client.

Thus, a good marketing plan will have these three characteristics:

Client orientation

Integrated effort

Profitability

Client orientation means that your marketing plan will conceive, develop, and communicate services that meet real client needs. It will be sensitive to discovering new client needs. Profiling your target market segments will prove invaluable here.

The marketing plan must result in an integrated effort. Your consumer focus must radiate back into your firm, as well as out into the market. All your business activities must be organized, directed, and accounted for by your marketing plan. All your marketing, advertising, and public relations efforts must be integrated through your marketing plan.

To be profitable, your plan must encompass accurate pricing decisions and mechanisms. Further, the plan must be monitored, and have feedback and adjustment provisions to optimize its performance.

You are probably familiar with the idea of prospect nurturing. A new client moves from the suspect to prospect to client stages over time. Your marketing plan can dovetail to a curve of prospect nurturing. For example, you can screen suspects to qualified prospects via a seminar product. Prospects can then be converted to clients through a leveled Personal Financial Planning Service.

You should keep the process of client nurturing in the back of your mind as you develop your strategic marketing plan, to make sure it allows for an appropriate development of suspects to clients.

The whole sequence of nurturing starts with suspect identification. You can identify suspects among your existing client base, purchase specific mailing lists, or develop networks with acquaintances or affinity groups. The result is a list of suspects. These are developed into prospects.

Prospect development can be accomplished by direct mail campaigns, seminar presentations, or newsletters. Prospects are screened for appropriateness, for their needs, and for their financial positions. Qualified prospects are then converted to clients.

MARKETING AS A PROCESS

A multitude of factors affect and are affected by your marketing efforts. There are external factors like the market demographics of your area, or the competitive forces you struggle against. There are internal factors like your philosophy and goals, your present size and intended growth. These have an impact on your clients, your costs, and your image. Your marketing plan will be the overall focus and control point for all these factors.

Factors that determine strategies are your budget and resources, and the target market you are aiming at. The target market and the target products and services will mutually define and refine each other as you go along. The strategies you choose will determine the tactics you use to implement them.

Implementation of the strategic marketing plan will connect the target market with your products and services. As you implement your marketing plan you will monitor the marketing effort, and adjust your plan accordingly. This monitoring also includes monitoring the target market to refine your definition of the consumer needs.

Notice that like Personal Financial Planning, marketing planning is a continuous modeling and revision process that helps you realize your goals. It needs periodic adjustment in light of the passage of time, and changes both in the environment and in your goals. It must have a built-in monitoring and feedback mechanism.

Strategic marketing is still an art, but more of a science than it was in the last decade. Today marketing is more accountable because it is more direct. Strategic marketing gets your message to a well defined target audience. It persuades your potential clients to take immediate action. It also records its performance and allows you to monitor results.

A good marketing plan will acknowledge your objectives—how much business you want to generate—along with your capacity, how much you can handle, and when additional resources will be needed.

A balanced marketing plan will use advertising and public relations in appropriate ways. Both have the common goal of gaining understanding and acceptance of you and your services by the public you want to reach. Only the techniques differ.

Your marketing plan will involve some direct selling. The needs of selected groups will be used to create a desire for your services. Advertising will help here. Paid space or time in the media is not always cost effective, but we will examine some ways to make it so. Public relations, the indirect selling part of your marketing plan, can also use the media to present information.

The use of communications media in public relations has the added advantage of third party endorsement. Consumers will unconsciously accept information from an independent third party more readily than they would from you. Public relations tactics include being interviewed on television, making speeches, preparing news releases, or producing special events.

LEVELS OF DECISION

In developing your strategic marketing plan, you will make decisions on four levels: planning, strategy, tactics, and operations.

At the planning level, you create and maintain the model used to accomplish your goals. Planning decisions include:

Goal setting

Market definition

Analysis of competition

Pricing

Budgeting

Monitoring

Such planning establishes your goals, both long- and short-term. It also defines your market position, the context or structure within which you will attack the marketplace. Positioning results from your definition of the market and analysis of the competition. In turn, your market position is reflected in the development of your services, and in your pricing decisions.

When you define the market, you find out who the customers are, what they want, and how they buy. To accomplish this, you need to develop a rudimentary marketing information system. As you develop the system, keep these criteria in mind. Your information must be:

Reliable, valid, verified

Relevant

Adequate

Timely

Useful

Cost effective

To develop your strategic marketing plan into a useful tool, monitor and evaluate the plan as it is implemented and operating. You will also want to record and evaluate consumer and client reactions to product or marketing changes you make.

At the strategic level, you will decide what needs to be done to accomplish your goals. The four major strategies are:

1) Defending your existing client base from your competition.

2) Cross selling your present clients, to move them from your present products and services to your new products and services. This depends on whether or not your present clients are qualified and desirable as consumers of your new services. The main obstacle is their inertia.

3) Expanding your customer base from present to new clients. You can either create new Personal Financial Planning Service consumers, or capture clients from your competition. Here your marketing costs will be higher than product development costs. You will need sound and tested services to offer, and your capacity to handle an expanded customer base must be carefully planned.

4) Diversifying, adding new products and services to your present ones. In this strategy, both marketing and product development costs will be the main factors. You will also need to make decisions about keeping or dropping your present clients and products or services.

Once you have decided on a strategy, you make decisions at the tactical level. The target market segment, the strategy you have chosen, and the service you want to market will all determine the appropriate tactics to use. Tactical decisions are the selection of the ways and means, the specific techniques you want to use.

Operational level decisions will help you implement the strategic marketing plan in a controlled way. These will include the specific content, vendor, medium, scope, and frequency with which you use each tactic.

Also, the operational levels determine how you will monitor and adjust the plan when it is in operation.

OUTLINE OF THE STEPS

The water seems to be getting a bit rough. There are so many things to be considered, that safe harbor begins to look appealing. Here is an outline of the sequence of steps we will take to tie this all together. The steps are presented as a sequence of steps, but in practice they will be iterative. Oops! I may have jargoned you there. Iterative means repeating a sequence of steps from crude to increasingly refined accuracy. So these steps will be taken one at a time, jumping back and forth occasionally, often repeating the whole sequence from front to back several times, until the final product is created. The steps are:

1) Set goals
2) Define market
3) Analyze competition
4) Define strategic marketing plan
5) Design products and services
6) Price products and services
7) Budget strategic marketing plan
8) Implement strategic marketing plan
9) Monitor and adjust

In the goal setting step, you take time to write out the short- and long-term goals of your practice in general. This will help keep you on track when you get into the details that follow. It is also a good way to check that your objectives and your capacity are in line. Next you define the specific goals for this strategic marketing plan. Define your goals with the qualifications and capabilities you already possess in mind. Also keep your target market in mind. You will have to stay within the interests, needs, and understanding of your target market as you develop the plan.

There are many ways to define the market you are after. You could start with an informal survey of your client needs, and how the competition is meeting them. You could study your files for potential cross selling or for clients with specific levels of wealth, higher tax brackets, undiversified investments, no retirement plan, upward mobility of profession, or potential estate tax problems.

New marketing opportunities could come from referral discussions with bank trust officers, lawyers, and other financial professionals in your area. Valuable information about your local demographics is available from marketing firms, census publications in the public library, or local government records.

The main consideration is what consumer needs exist in your service area that could be satisfied by your service? To answer this question, we will focus on two important techniques: segmentation and profiling. By now you should be able to take these terms in stride. If not, remember that all they mean is breaking the total market into manageable chunks, and getting a clear picture of the prospects in each chunk.

The objective of segmentation is twofold. First, it lets you focus and direct your marketing efforts toward a narrow range of highly desirable prospects. Second, segmentation lets you develop your products and services with the specific needs of each segment in mind.

This lets you reach the prospects more effectively, with a better understanding of their real needs, and the services that will satisfy these needs better than your competitors. You can specialize in those services most needed, and develop your own skills and the skills of your expert team in a profitable fashion.

Unfortunately, you are not the only Financial Planner hoping to serve the Personal Financial Planning needs in your area. For this reason, the strategic marketing plan includes an analysis of the competition. Research the products offered by your competitors. Contact the local banks, brokerage houses, and insurance agencies to find out what products and services they offer. Find ways to do what they do better and more economically.

Now you are ready to define your strategic marketing plan in terms of the strategies and tactics you will use. Strategic decisions will not often be simple. Usually, you will have to include strategies that are both defensive and offensive. You will probably want to cross sell existing clients as well as develop new clients. Further, you will be introducing new services and products as you and your practice develop.

With the strategies in mind, you can select the tactics that will effect them best. Some ideas on the major marketing tactics are presented in Chapter 7.

With all this information at hand, you can set about designing the products and services you want to offer. Look back to Chapter 4 for ideas here. As I said, the marketing and product development phases will go back and forth through several iterations before you reach your first final plan. Don't be discouraged by the "back to the drawing board" cycles. Expect them, and confine them to paper where it is much less expensive to correct your errors.

The keys to sensible product and service development are leveling and segmenting. Remember that each service you provide can be offered at various levels. Each part of your planning process can be offered as a separate service. This is sometimes called unbundling.

With a good idea of the services you want to offer, you can then set about pricing each, to make your practice both profitable and competitive. Pricing is an important step, so we'll go into more detail later in this chapter.

Once you know what you intend to do and how best to do it, the next step is to arrange the budget, the resources you will need to do it. Of course this can work the other way, too! Budgeting will list the capital, skills, time, and other resources you will need to implement your plan.

With all this done, it is finally time to implement the strategic marketing plan. Well, almost. Before you go all out, I suggest you perform a miniature or test implementation, with much scaled down resources. This can be part of your first year, where I suggest you limit your scope to a dozen or so clients. A test run could also be a single seminar presentation to solicit first hand information about client needs.

With information from a test marketing effort, you can refine your strategic marketing plan to its final form before full implementation. During implementation, you will have to coordinate the production of materials, the various events, and keep to the schedules you have set.

During implementation of the plan, you start to monitor and adjust it. You will want to measure the costs and the results, in order to fine tune your marketing efforts.

We will repeat these steps in greater detail in the next chapter. Before we get there, let's discuss some detailed background information on the most important steps.

SEGMENTATION

The objective of segmentation is to help identify profitable Personal Financial Planning Service customers. It lets you develop specific plans for specific segments, and develop tailored services for specific needs of target segments. Stated simply, it is a means of focusing on who you are after.

Segmentation is a way of partitioning the general market with a specific purpose in mind. Say you wanted to polish the chrome on your car. You have a good quality chrome polish and a rag. Would you apply the polish to the whole car, hoping that enough of it would get to the chrome? Or would you mentally divide the car into sections, pick ways to spot the chrome in each section, and apply the polish just to the chrome? I've had my car polished by those who follow the first method, but I think we can agree that the second method is better.

How do we break the general market into partitions? How do we spot the chrome? If our purpose is to isolate likely prospects for Personal Financial Planning Services, several useful criteria are:

Income

Net worth

Age

Occupation

Marital status

Financial product use

Attitudes and goals

Equally important are the factors that are not to be used. These are:

Family size

Race or religion

Number of earners

Geography

Housing status (own/rent)

Extremes in net worth or income

These factors are not used because they are nondiscriminating. That is, they don't separate the market into segments you want to know about. You could easily break the market into segments by family size, but this factor does not play a significant role in the purchase of Personal Financial Planning Services.

Some factors will yield segments with few prospects. It is difficult to develop valid profiles or reach sound conclusions about groups of 20 or so people. It can also be unprofitable to sell a service to such a small group. Equally futile is a segmentation factor that is of no explanatory value. For example, do not segment by the number and gender of children in a family, as this tells you nothing about the prospect's needs or buying patterns.

You can get the information you need from a marketing firm in your area, or assemble it yourself from various sources. Consider your existing client base as one source of the demographic information you need, and as a guide to segmentation factors. When segmenting, remember you can cover the low- and high-income ends of the market by leveling and segmenting your services if the volume or profitability warrants. You can choose to go after one or many segments in your marketing effort.

PROFILING

One objective of segmenting the market was to focus in on a small and specific target market. Profiling is creation of a detailed picture of the members of a segment. You profile the segments to understand who they are in terms of their needs, preferences, attitudes, and financial situation.

Profiling starts with a clear definition of the segment, usually in terms of the segmenting factors. You might want to profile each segment with a balance sheet, a summary of their demographic information, attitudes, use of financial advisors, and risk tolerances.

This information will be average or typical only. You can derive the demographic ratios for your area from your own client base. As an example, let's segment the total Personal Financial Planning market using the factors of wealth and income.

This yields three groups as follows:

Low wealth, low income

Low wealth, high income

High wealth, high income

These are critical factors, as both wealth and income determine specific planning needs. They are too general to use in actual segmentation and profiling, but these simplified ideas will show how the process works, without getting bogged down in details.

SEGMENTATION AND PROFILE EXAMPLE

Low Wealth, Low Income

We could define this segment as the mass market. While this group has a high resistance to purchasing Personal Financial Planning Services, they have real needs. They are unlikely candidates for full Personal Financial Planning, but can benefit from low cost plans aimed at developing their discretionary income. Such plans would have to be profitable in themselves, since little cross selling revenue or implementation commissions can be expected.

This is a large group of consumers, who are heavy users of credit, depository, and insurance products. They will have a high price sensitivity to our services, so price will be a key issue.

Their financial situation is more homogeneous, and they like to compare their behaviors to the norm. They do not need extensive plans, but rather planning services that are budget and education oriented. This is a good group to target for do-it-yourself and preplanning products.

Low Wealth, High Income

We could call this group the accumulators. Planning services for this group must define an investment strategy in line with risk tolerances. A high level of maintenance and monitoring is needed as accumulation shifts to protection. Investment implementation will be your main revenue, so use a commission fee structure over fixed or hourly rate structures.

This group is only somewhat price sensitive, notably at the high end of your services. Their product needs will center around tax shelters, real estate, and insurance.

High Wealth, High Income

This is the wealth market. Their key concerns are preservation and transfer of wealth. There will be intensive legal work associated with most planning activities here. Pricing as a percentage of assets becomes possible and profitable.

This group is least price sensitive, and are willing to pay large front end planning fees.

Of course, this example is simplistic, and I've anticipated some of the information on pricing we'll discuss. However, I think the example gives you a good idea of how segmentation and profiling can be powerful tools.

PRICING YOUR SERVICES

Pricing Factors

Pricing means more than profitability. It is also used to screen customers, so that you attract and develop a client base with a profitable cash flow profile. You can design and test several cash flow profiles for different hypothetical mixes of client base, and get that mix through your pricing policies.

Pricing will also determine your marketing approach and budget, your growth potential, and your bottom line profitability. Pricing decisions will affect your decision to serve specific needs, as well as the level and amount of implementation services you decide to offer.

The pricing decisions you make spring from your business philosophy. For this you need some clear definitions of your business, both the nature and the volume of business you intend to handle. Your approach to a product/service mix will also influence decisions in pricing.

The basic decision is between a pure planning service, or planning plus implementation services and products. Lower level decisions will be influenced by your target prospects' purchasing behavior and their price sensitivity.

We discussed various pricing mechanisms in earlier chapters, in an introductory way. Now it's time to examine pricing in more detail. First, let's examine two critical topics in pricing your services: conflict of interest and sensitivity.

Conflict of Interest

If you are determined to offer pure planning services, your pricing decisions will be much simpler. To a large extent, you can avoid problems with conflicts of interest. But again, I urge you to consider a full Personal Financial Planning Service, including implementation and financial product sales.

With a pure planning service, you will depend on a constant flow of new clients. This means high, ongoing marketing costs. Further, plan development is the most time intensive and costly aspect of Personal Financial Planning. Profitability in this business depends on a balanced mix of planning and implementation services. Yes, there are a host of problems and decisions to be made with a full service approach, but once these hurdles are passed you will be in top competitive form.

Your clients need implementation help, are willing to pay for implementation help, and deserve implementation help, if you intend to offer a holistic and professional service.

Studies have shown that conflict of interest issues are a deterrent only to the sale of a fee and commission plan (see Mattauch in Bibliography). Once the plan is sold, conflict of interest is not a problem, provided the client clearly sees a high quality plan addressing his personal needs, and develops trust in you as his adviser.

To minimize conflict of interest problems, separate your planning and implementation functions. Let your client implement elsewhere if he desires. Charge a planning fee that is still profitable in the event he does implement elsewhere, and produce plans of high quality.

It is helpful to disclose your biases, and even let the client participate in implementation and product selection processes. You only have to do this once or twice, to demonstrate your trustworthiness. The client is not interested in participating in all decision making processes; after all, this is one of the things he is buying your service for, to save him the time.

Price Sensitivity

Another important factor in pricing is price sensitivity. How sensitive are consumers to the plan price? What impact does the plan price have on consumer demand for plans?

At the high end of the market, few affluent customers select primarily on price. Between the selection factors of quality and price, the split goes:

quality — 45%

price   — 20%

both   — 35%

(see Mattauch in Bibliography).

High end market consumers tend to buy top-notch quality services. There is minimal sensitivity to price for the affluent market. In plain talk, you can expect little impact from increasing your prices even by 100 percent. What counts is not the plan price, but the perceived value your client gets when he buys the plan. What makes perceived value? The components are: attention to specific personal needs, professional service, and a solid plan (complete with time and change factors) that will deliver the goals.

You can expect no difference in client interest whether the initial planning session costs $100, $150, or $200. If your plan really helps your client meet a recognized need, a price difference of $100 will make no difference. Over time, your client will more than recover the plan cost in value, and he knows this.

The market is not very price sensitive to your service, but it is sensitive to your method of compensation. For the low end of the market there is an increasing awareness of and preference for fee and commission combinations. The high end prefers a fee-only pricing mechanism.

The Pricing Matrix

Here are the factors that will decide your pricing mechanism and strategy:

Service philosophy and goals

Cost of developing and delivering services

Prospect characteristics and attitudes

Client familiarity with pricing mechanism

Acceptability of fee to client

Profit yield

The decisions you must make about pricing can seem overwhelming. Will you go fee or commission or a combination? If you pass this hurdle, you still have several pricing options to decide on. Will your fee be flat or based on an hourly rate? Are commissions to be applied to the flat fee? Will you rely on actual commissions from product sales, or use a percentage basis?

There is a simple way to sort out some of this confusion. I call it a pricing matrix. It shows the basic areas of service, and the possible pricing mechanisms. By combining these, you can quickly run through all the possibilities. It's sort of like choosing "one from column A, and one from column B". The areas of service are:

Initial planning

Ongoing planning

Initial implementation

Ongoing implementation

The pricing options are:

Flat fee

Commission

Fee and commission combination

Hourly rate

Percentage fee

Performance factor

For example, for your initial planning efforts you could decide to use a flat fee. This could be coupled with an hourly rate basis for ongoing planning (yearly revisions and monitoring). You could use a pure commission basis for initial implementation, and a portfolio percentage fee for ongoing maintenance. Let's look at some of these combinations, to find out which are best in given circumstances.

Flat Fee. This is a good mechanism for some initial planning situations. Because a flat fee is a fixed, once-only mechanism, it works best in high volume production. Low flat fees for simple plans can be a good way to encourage the low end of the market to enter into financial planning. Since the fee is a known quantity, it can be clearly indicated in your written estimate. There will be no surprises for the client.

Flat fees can also be used as a retainer for ongoing planning services. Again, they are most effective for the low end of the market. To be profitable, flat fee retainers need high volume, and controllable plan revision costs.

Flat fees are also a good way to screen or qualify clients. Higher fees will screen out the merely curious. In this way, flat fees can be used to develop your client base.

The shortcoming of the mechanism is its fixed nature. Flat fees fail to take into account plan complexity, and the amount of analysis time you will need to generate the plan.

One variation of the flat fee that does allow for various plan complexities is called *unbundled pricing*. Here, your client pays for each component in the analysis step, on an as-needed basis. Thus, your prices can relate directly to the plan's complexity.

Commission: In the pure commission mechanism, the planning services are free. You rely on commissions derived from implementation as your sole remuneration. A pure commission mechanism can only be applied to initial or ongoing implementation services.

Pure commission planning can suffer from image problems. Often, this pricing mechanism is the hallmark of product-focused firms. When free financial plans are used as a sales tool they can be of poor quality, incomplete, and shallow in analysis. The focus of such plans will be on high commission products, ignoring noncommission products.

Commission-only planners must sell high commission products to break even. At a minimum, comprehensive planning and production costs are in the hundreds of dollars. Further, commission planners have substantial marketing costs. In combination, these factors create an enormous conflict of interest potential.

The commission mechanism can be used as a sincere marketing tool, when the fee plus commission mechanism is prohibited by professional or legal sanctions. To improve your chances for success with this mechanism, you must screen prospects carefully to eliminate those with low implementation needs, or excessive analysis needs.

In addition, marketing costs will have to be streamlined, and your marketing efforts must be made efficient. Since the initial planning process is free, you will need to control and limit analysis and plan production costs. Finally, to ensure ongoing profitability, you will focus on developing a long term client/planner relationship.

Fee and Commission Combination. This is the most common approach used by independent Financial Planners. The fee portion can be used to screen prospects and develop the client base mix and revenue stream. The commission portion provides the most profitable and enduring source of revenue.

Fee and commission combinations are tailor made to cover the activities of full service planners, from initial planning to ongoing implementation. The fee and commission pricing mechanism can give you an edge over those competitors who are prohibited from charging commissions directly.

In operation, the fee portion can be flat, unbundled, or an hourly rate. It usually applies to the initial planning activities, but can also cover ongoing planning in the form of an annual retainer. Commission earnings can be considered separately, or applied to reduce the fee portion.

Hourly Rate. This mechanism is most frequently used by planners with no implementation services, in a fee-only situation. The hourly rate is also a viable pricing mechanism when used in fee and commission practices. It can guarantee your ability to provide a planning service profitably, since the price is matched to the complexity (hence development costs) of the plan.

There will be no fixed bottom line cost for consumers, as it is difficult to control the variable analysis costs. Since there is no fixed bottom line cost, this method cannot be used to screen clients. If you use a minimum flat fee plus an hourly rate fee, you will retain the screening capability. For example; $75 per hour with minimum of $2,000.

The hourly rate is a good choice if your clients are used to this mode, which is usually true of professionals. It is also a good thing to do when the analysis is complex, the client needs are complex or multileveled, or counseling services are provided as needed.

It is often a good idea to use the hourly rate mechanism for initial and ongoing implementation for fee-only planning. This increases your clients' satisfaction with the value they obtain from your implementation efforts. It develops long-term client/planner relationships, and increases referral business.

The disadvantages are that the cost of your services can be too high for low volume or low income clients. The hourly rate method can leave your client uncertain of the final price of your services. This can be overcome by specifying a maximum fee in your written estimate.

Percentage Fee. Fees based on a percentage of client income or assets are a poor choice for initial or ongoing planning services. This mechanism does not take into account the complexity of the client's situation, hence is not well related to your actual costs. However, the percentage fee mechanism is another way to circumvent commissions when these are prohibited.

Percentage fees are more appropriate for implementation services. A percentage of income is the best selection for high income, low net worth clients. Otherwise, it is a poor choice, since it does not relate well to your costs. A mechanism that uses a percentage of the assets managed is often used in investment management, but a percentage of the total portfolio managed does not take into account the portfolio mix.

In the final analysis, only complicated percentage schemes are flexible enough to be profitable. Such schemes would include a percentage of both income and assets. This lets you serve both high income and high net worth clients profitably. In the ultimate complexity, the percentage fee mechanism can be based on a percentage of each asset managed, adjusted by an asset cost factor.

Performance Factor. Performance fee mechanisms provide strong incentive to the Financial Planner. This is a selling point to the client, too. It best applies to investment recommendations only.

The mechanism presents some problems for the Financial Planner. It presents conflicts of interest, since there is motivation to recommend high risk, high return products. Your implementation revenue flows will also be variable when priced on performance factors. Making sure your practice is profitable will require much time and attention.

Initial Planning. The initial planning fee can be fixed or variable. If fixed it can be free, or flat for specified services (single or unbundled). If variable it can be an hourly rate, a percentage of income, a percentage of assets, or combinations of these.

The fixed fee is best applied to low cost, high volume generic plans. These can be cost controlled to ensure profitability. Low cost plans are a good client entree to the area of Personal Financial Planning. You can arrange various levels of flat fee to screen prospects when developing your client base.

When you are operating with the fee and commission mechanism, the flat or variable fee portion applies to your initial planning efforts. The fee should be high enough to free you from conflicts of interest, and even allow your client to implement elsewhere if he chooses.

Hourly rate fees are another good choice for initial planning services. When you couple this with a fixed minimum fee, you can use the hourly rate mechanism to screen prospects. When you use a fixed maximum fee, you can include this as an incentive in your estimates. Between the minimum and maximum, the variable hourly rate will allow for various levels of planning complexity and analysis.

Ongoing Planning. This can be priced as a flat yearly retainer fee. The yearly retainer could also be a percentage of the initial plan price. In either case, flat fees for ongoing planning will only work when plan review and revision costs can be tightly controlled. Perhaps the best use of flat fee mechanisms in ongoing planning is to secure periodic reviews and reporting for the client. Detailed revisions indicated by the reviews should be priced with another mechanism, that admits of the variables involved.

Variable pricing mechanisms that work well for annual or special as-needed revisions are unbundled flat rates, and hourly rates.

Initial and Ongoing Implementation. Pure commission, fee and commission, and hourly rate mechanisms will all work for implementation services. The hourly rate can be used in lieu of implementation commissions.

In those cases where you can delimit the costs you can offer fixed fee initial implementation services as part of your planning fee. Variable rate pricing mechanisms are more appropriate to the implementation areas of service. The hourly rate is simplest, but more complicated percentage arrangements are also profitable.

Beyond the Matrix. Don't let my orderly approach to pricing stifle your creativity. You can develop and use any mechanism that works for you and your clients.

Consider a fee mechanism of 5 percent of the client's income for the first year, declining to 1 percent in the fifth year, plus 1 percent of his investment assets. This has the advantages of a fixed price for the client, plus the incentive to maintain an ongoing relationship with your firm. It would allow you to bypass commission considerations for implementation, while providing you with revenue for these services.

Pricing Summary

In summary, we can see that fee and commission pricing mechanisms are the most flexible and profitable over the range of services you can offer. The fee portion can be designed to create your implementation services market. It is this area of your work that will provide the high profit, long term, ongoing revenue you seek.

Note that ongoing services will rapidly prove more profitable than initial ones, due to the reduced cost of marketing and plan development. These costs are necessary for new clients—to build and maintain a client base—but real profit comes from maintenance services to your existing client base.

Thoroughly consider alternatives in leveling, segmenting, and unbundling your services. Workable pricing mechanisms can be found for any type of service.

Pricing is one of the toughest areas in strategic marketing. Having equipped you with the ideas you will need, I can turn back to some of the softer areas of marketing.

IMAGE AND DIFFERENTIATION

The creation of an image involves complex and artful work. You are probably well aware of the huge sums spent on the creation of a politician's image. Your image—the professional image of your firm—is just as essential to your success as is the politician's to his. Because of the restricted purpose and application of your image, its creation need not be elaborate and expensive. Often you will have the resources, skills, and intuition needed to create your own image. However, if you feel lacking in any of the prerequisites, or if you are unsure of your results, consider hiring expert help. This is the one area of your strategic marketing effort on which you cannot afford to skimp.

Differentiation means standing out in the client's mind. You can only do this if you have a clearly defined image. Your image must project your business philosophy, and appeal to the prospects you want as clients. Further, your image must distinguish you from your competitors.

The ways you find to serve your clients' real needs, and to serve them better, should be part of your image. Such an image develops over time if you provide a thorough, holistic service, with ample monitoring and follow-up.

It is not enough to create an image that differentiates you. Your image must also be presented to the public, to prospects, and to clients. What are your means of exposure? These are the tactics you will examine in developing your strategic marketing plan. They include teaching courses at a local college, carefully placed advertisements, informative *Yellow Pages* listings, volunteer work for service organizations, and the list goes on.

Public ignorance of the functions you can perform as a financial professional leads to an expectation gap. You may find a conflict between your image as reliable but conservative and the consumer's desire for creative and innovative services. Consider the plight of the CPA.

The CPA is burdened with the "green eyeshade image of accountants—the old guy writing rows of numbers into a ledger sheet and telling you what you owe in taxes" (see Bohn in Bibliography). For many years the low profile of the CPA has enhanced his image of accountability for the accuracy of his work, and the confidentiality of client information. But this same image tends to generate an air of secrecy and shyness of the limelight that must be overcome in order to market new services aggressively.

How do you change an image? To start with, develop high pride and confidence levels in the services you offer. Pride is visible and contagious. It will reflect outward through your image, changing it. A rework of your visual image can be a strong signal that your service has changed.

Your Visual Image

Remember, you never get a second chance to make a good first impression. The image of you that first reaches a potential client must be exactly what you intend. Pay close attention to the development and presentation of your image.

Your visual image should be solid and integrated. It should be built up around a simple, bold logo and color scheme. When you create a new image, be consistent in applying it. Use the same logo, colors, paper, and format in all printed materials. This will help your client recognize you as the source.

A visual image is composed of more than your correspondence, reports, and plan documents. It is created (or destroyed) by your business cards, newsletters, instruction sheets, and brochures. In short, everything you put into a prospect's or client's hands determines your image.

Your image is valuable in retaining existing clients and adding new clients, but the materials you produce and distribute will fall into many more hands than these. Such second-order effects can be useful in making a favorable impression with referral sources, and in recruiting personnel.

Overcoming Perception Gaps

Have you ever tried wearing someone else's glasses? It can be a confusing experience, but that's what I want you to do now. I'm going to ask you to put on a pair of trifocals, to split the image of your image into three images. Confused already? Let me clarify.

There are really three important perspectives of your image. First there is the image you intend to project. Second there is the image your prospect receives. Third is the image he actually retains. It is this third version of your image that counts. The retained image is colored by any preconceived ideas the prospect holds. To correct this distortion, you have to overcome perception gaps.

In addition to your new image, you have to project information that counters the perceived weaknesses of your particular profession, to fill the gaps between what the public thinks you can do for them and what you actually can do for them. To counter perceived weaknesses, you must first identify them.

In Chapter 2 we made a survey of the strengths and weaknesses of various financial professionals as Financial Planners. Perhaps you squirmed a bit when we looked at perceived weaknesses of your profession, but you must acknowledge the weaknesses before you can overcome them. In addition to our general survey, you rated your personal image on Worksheet 1. These are the starting points for changing perceived weaknesses, for making your intended image and the retained image the same.

It can be easier to consider your weaknesses if you remember that public perception is not fact. Part of your image work is correcting faults in the public perception. Public perception is a function of the information available, so it is in your interest to provide the information needed to correct erroneous perceptions, and fill gaps where information is missing.

BUDGETING

It would be nice if a few hours and a few dollars covered all your marketing needs, but they won't. By using your common sense, and a few of the hints presented in these chapters, you can get a lot for a little. But how much is enough, and how much is a little?

Unless you are well established in the field, expect to spend a large portion of your professional hours in marketing. Of the hours you devote to your Personal Financial Planning Service, from 20 to 25 percent should be spent in marketing activities: developing, implementing, and monitoring your strategic marketing plan.

How much capital will be needed? Exactly how much you will need to spend depends on your goals and scope, the efficiency of your segmentation, and the variables of your service area. As a rough guideline larger practices with several partners should be prepared to set aside one half to one percent of their overall annual budget for marketing. Smaller firms can expect to spend a higher percentage—up to five percent is reasonable.

Beyond time and capital, you will need supportive skills and expertise. You will need marketing support, whether you provide it yourself or buy it outside. Support services can take the form of marketing consultants, graphic artists, or printers. There are an increasing number of ways you can get this support. Often it is available from your professional organization, or from a Financial Planning organization like the International Association of Financial Planners. There are also independent network firms, such as the Licensed Independent Network of CPA Financial Planners.

These support sources can provide the formats for your client data forms and client letters. They can give you access to marketing workshops and seminars, to speakers and seminar leaders, or to professional telephone solicitors.

MANAGING THE MARKETING EFFORT

A client comes to you and outlines his future goals and dreams. You present the methods of Personal Financial Planning to him. He says, "Do we really have to sit down and plan all this stuff out?" I hope the next step in this scenario is that you look at him askance. If you wonder about the need to plan your marketing effort, swivel your head. Ask yourself why you think marketing is less needy of planning than your client's finances.

A Personal Financial Plan is not a final answer, neither is a strategic marketing plan. Rather, it is a model, a framework on which you plan your course of action; with which you measure your success. Only by monitoring and modifying your strategic marketing plan can you keep your goals and your reality in step.

The plan needs a feedback loop; a way to measure its success and adjustments to optimize this success. Your marketing plan needs to be specific, and it needs to be updated at least annually. This is an essential part of managing the marketing effort.

Be specific about your goals, your target market, your image and differentiation. You can express business goals in the numbers of plans, clients, or dollars you want. You can express public relations goals in terms of name recognition for your firm, or in terms of what prospective clients know about your capabilities. Any kind of goal can be made specific enough to quantify. Once quantified, it becomes measurable.

In addition to measuring your success, you must be able to determine the causes of gaps between planned and actual results. You must determine and take corrective action to close these gaps.

PUBLIC RELATIONS RELATIONSHIPS

Whether or not you intend to, you are doing public relations work every day. The question is not whether you do it, but how well you do it. Do your peers and clients know what they should about you and your profession? Newspapers and television programs accent controversial issues in Personal Financial Planning. Questions about your profession may arise in any conversation, so be prepared to answer them.

It is up to you to educate the public, to narrow the perception gaps. Think carefully about how you answer casual inquiries about your profession and services. You may be that person's only exposure to a Financial Planner. Work with the media, government, and education institutions. Be responsible for educating the business community.

The results of public relations work are hard to quantify, but the managing partners of some firms have estimated that their public relations efforts are responsible for 15 to 20 percent growth. In one case a 38 percent increase in billable hours is attributed to public relations (see Shildneck in Bibliography).

Your public relations efforts will be addressed to four groups:

Clients

Media

Government

Community

Clients: Develop an awareness of your clients' needs, in terms of the marketable services you can perform. Keep prospects and clients informed and interested by producing brochures, newsletters, and bulletins. It is important that everything the client experiences in relation to your service reflect a consistent image. This applies to your offices, your printed materials, and your appearance. Swivel your head to experience what the client experiences, and be your own worst critic.

Media: Make people in the communications media your allies. You want your name to be recognized and your voice to be heard. The media represent a vast, ready-made network that can carry your information to the market. Amazing as it seems, media people do not make up the information they disseminate. They rely on outside sources of information for their trade. Understand how to help these people do their job by providing the information they need.

Most local newspapers and cable or local television stations have expanded business news coverage. Establish yourself with them as a credible authority on Personal Financial Planning and financial issues. Prepare yourself to cover financial events before they happen, for example the latest perennial tax reforms. Invite the press to your seminars and speeches, or send them written copies. Press release all the evolutions of your firm. Consider participating in a media relations training program offered by a local public relations association or your state society.

Government: Don't hesitate to invite government officials to ribbon cuttings or office openings. Make yourself known to local officials. By working with various levels of government, you can perfect your awareness of the legal constraints under which you practice.

Community: Public relations efforts directed at your community can double as prospect generators. If people don't know you, they can't refer to you. If a prospect already knows your name, he will feel more confident in choosing your services.

There are a multiplicity of tactics that can expose you to the community of your service area. For example, you probably have professional expertise that is needed by any number of local service clubs. Voluntary contributions of time and talent will expose you to a wide variety of prospective clients.

There is no worksheet to complete at the end of this chapter. Take time to digest the background information we've just covered, then proceed to the next chapter. There you will find worksheets galore, as we create your strategic marketing plan!

6

Develop Your Strategic Marketing Plan: Getting the Client

There are many ways to market Personal Financial Planning Services, ranging from those requiring minimal resources to those requiring major capital outlays. How can you be sensible in choosing the correct methods in order to develop a strategic marketing plan that will accomplish your objectives?

You could hire the services of a marketing firm, and you may elect to do so. But much of the groundwork can be done by an informed novice. By following the steps in this chapter, you can develop your own plan and then weave in the help of experts wherever and to whatever extent you want. If you survey your capabilities at the end of the chapter, you will be surprised to find out how much of the needed resources may already be available in your own office.

While you may feel quite comfortable with calculators, computers, and telephones, you may need help in converting these service performers into service promoters. This and the next chapter are devoted to the methods or tactics of marketing.

No matter how you juggle it, you can capture only so much market share from your marketing budget. The question, then, is which marketing strategies and tactics are best suited to your existing or proposed resources?

Financial Planners are familiar with the problems of trying to help clients develop realistic expectations about their investment portfolios. Generally, clients want you to perform miracles. They want their portfolios to provide them with investment vehicles that offer all of the advantages (tax shelter, high annual yield, total liquidity, long-term growth, etc.) and none of the risks. Obviously, such investments are fantasy, but it is often difficult to explain to clients why such requirements cannot be satisfied.

The concept of marketing is not unlike the above investment scenario. The tendency is to expect major returns from minor investments, with all of the advantages and none of the risks. Therefore, in this chapter we will focus on developing realistic marketing expectations based on your resources: time, money, people, and skills. We will follow these steps in developing a strategic marketing plan:

1. Set goals
2. Define market
3. Analyze competition
4. Define strategic marketing plan
5. Design products and services
6. Price products and services
7. Budget strategic marketing plan
8. Implement strategic marketing plan
9. Monitor and adjust

There is a series of worksheets at the end of this chapter. Each step has an associated worksheet. Read through this chapter once to get an overview; then use the instructions provided for each step in order to complete the worksheets and develop your plan.

STEP 1—SET GOALS

Planning is critical and essential, but have patience. Don't worry about developing a fully detailed master plan that works exactly as you predict. On this first attempt, merely consider the plan as a tool or skill that you are developing. You must have a starting point. If you allow for trials and rethinking, you will be able to sharpen your plan to whatever degree you desire.

Stated simply, you must decide where you want to go. Therefore, when you develop your plan, you will write down what you are trying to do, how you plan to do it, how much you want to spend, what results you expect, and how you will measure success. Remember: If you don't know where you're going, it's hard to know if you're getting there.

The first step, setting goals, can be divided into two parts. First, you will define your general business philosophy and long-term goals. Second, you will define the specific goals for each year of your strategic marketing plan.

Your Business Philosophy

Setting goals will be more sensible if you do it from the context of your general business plan. Worksheet 4 can help you define this context.

First, determine your service philosophy. This is not so esoteric as it sounds. Try to state your basic reasons for offering a Personal Financial Planning Service. Note the general kind of services you want to offer, whether pure planning, a combination of planning and implementation, or mainly implementation. Do you want the bulk of your business to be in full planning or in lower-level money management programs? Will you get involved in product sales and implementation? Decide if you intend to focus on competitive pricing or higher quality services.

Next, state and quantify your business goals. I suggest that you sketch out a five-year general plan, and then prepare detailed plans one year at a time. So, state your goals over the next five years in terms of your profit, the size of your practice, and the size of your firm.

Consider your professional and personal goals for the same period. Prepare a synopsis of your preferred professional image and determine what role you want to play as a Financial Planner. Record the training, certification, and skills you expect to acquire.

You should also clearly define your intended service area and geographic market. Do this in concrete terms. If necessary, grease pencil a map to specify the limits of your service area. And if you plan to extend your service area over time, chart this growth over the same five-year period.

Finally, restate the general constraints under which you will operate. These may be the legal, professional, or ethical sanctions that we examined in Chapter 3. In addition, there may be other business or personal restrictions within which you intend to operate.

It helps to draw an organization chart of your firm, showing internal and external operations. Therefore, using your favorite format, include your organization and structure and that of your expert network. You can either diagram your financial and marketing information networks or simply compile lists of the information needed and indicate how it is supplied. As you develop your practice and your marketing program, you can add to these lists.

Strategic Marketing Plan Goals

From this point, work on just the first year of your five-year plan. You should probably do a test year first, with only a handful of clients. So this plan may actually be for your second year of operation. In any event, you will have gained much needed experience in the actual process of Personal Financial Planning to make better marketing decisions.

This part of the first step details your business goals for the first year of the strategic marketing plan. State the goals from the perspective of what you expect to accomplish. Don't be afraid of being too optimistic. As you read through these steps, you will rework much of your thinking and calculations.

How you plan to measure your success and make adjustments will depend primarily on the nature of your goals. If your goals are stated in dollars of revenue, you will measure the plan in these terms. If your goal is expressed in the number of clients or plans, you will need to monitor these things in order to manage your marketing efforts.

You must state your goals in measurable terms. If you can't measure the success or failure of your strategic marketing plan, then you can't optimize it. Without this feedback loop, your plan cannot develop into a sharpened tool. For example, you could state your goals in terms of the profit that you want to realize. Nevertheless, consider expressing your profit in terms of the revenue needed to generate it. Revenue is easier to measure than profit so that it makes a better monitoring index.

You can also state your goals in terms of your target client base. How big should it be at the end of the first year? How many new clients will be needed to attain this goal? In later iterations, you might add information about the mix you want in your client base.

If you have a clear idea of the services and products you will offer, you can state goals in terms of the quantity that you want to sell of each item.

Be sure to set your objectives with realistic goals. But use some hard questions to test how fixed your goals are. If you have a public practice, ask yourself if your client base is as large as you want it to be. Consider the kind of growth you can handle with the staffing and resources you plan. What are the limits to your growth, and who is imposing them? If you are imposing the limits, consider stretching them just a little bit more. Remember, at the planning stage, it's easy to make adjustments. Use Worksheet 5 to record your Strategic Marketing Plan goals for the first year.

STEP 2—DEFINE THE MARKET

Now that your business context and goals are defined, you must define the target market that will produce the suspects, prospects, and eventually the new clients you seek. Before you look into the general market, study your existing client base. This can be a valuable source of new business for new products and services. Perhaps even more important, your client base is a market about which you have detailed information, including financial and personal data, buying patterns, even demographic details about your service area.

If you can make the necessary statistical adjustments, your own files contain a thorough market survey of your service area. The statistical information that you need can be extracted and used as a basis for general market projections. If you have already established an expert network with local financial professionals, you can pool statistical information from several client bases for even greater accuracy.

If you turn to an outside marketing firm for help, you need to know the general profile of the market in your service area. Specifically, you need information on distribution of income, net worth, age, and professions of the general market.

Don't bolt for outside support on the first pass, though. Much of the information needed is also available in your public library in the form of census information. The Bureau of the Census does a great many kinds of studies at different levels of detail. Check the free information available from local marketing groups and the Chamber of Commerce.

On the first pass, you will not know exactly what you need to find. Don't turn to outside help until later in the planning process when you have developed some detailed target segments and services.

The second step, defining the market, is accomplished in three parts. First, you will segment the general market to determine appropriate target groups. Second, you will profile each group, specifying characteristics. Third, you will determine the Personal Financial Planning needs for each segment in which you are interested. These steps are accomplished on Worksheets 6 through 8.

Segmentation

Once you have a general idea about the demographics in your area, set about segmenting the market. This lets you target those prospects that can be profitable clients. It compares the services needed with the kind of services you intend to provide. It shows which groups can be reached accurately by specific marketing tactics.

Start with those factors that delimit the market in which you are interested, namely, income and/or net worth. For example, you could define your market as those households with over $30,000 in pretax income each year. To segment the market, use various factors to divide the whole into smaller groups. Which factors you use will depend on your purpose.

What factors are used to break a market into segments? The most useful are the following:

- Income
- Net worth
- Age
- Occupation
- Marital status

Using these factors, you could segment and integrate the market indefinitely. I know; I almost did this during my first few tries. However, the working principle of segmentation is to derive groups of people with the following characteristics:

- small enough to be able to obtain a detailed image
- large enough to have value as a market
- in need of your target services

Without knowing your final target segments and services, it can be difficult for you to segment sensibly. So be prepared to go through this process a couple of times until you get the right answers. To understand segmentation, let's work an example.

Segmentation Example

Assume that within your service area there are 7000 households with annual pretax incomes over $30,000. As a first step, segment this market by actual income.

You can use the statistical spread of your own client base or share information with a network of your peers to broaden the sample space. Again, you can go to an outside agency for this kind of information. Since this information is a marketing firm's stock in trade, it is readily available—and current.

Assume for now that there are 5000 households with income in the $30,000 to $50,000 range and 2000 households with income over $50,000 each year. Using your client base for ratio information, you could determine that average total assets and average net worth are spread as follows:

Factor/Segment	$30,000 to 50,000	Over $50,000
Average total assets	$150,000	$300,000
Average net worth	$120,000	$265,000

The purpose of segmentation is to target a small, well-defined group. These segments are still too large and general to work with, so we'll narrow them further. As a second factor, you can segment the two groups by profession. This gives meaningful information in terms of needed services, and how to reach the prospects.

Over $50,000	Percent of market	Number
Business owner	25	500
Professional	30	600
Executive	20	400
Other	25	500

The segments that develop from the over $50,000 group are clearly small enough to profile accurately. Considering the levels of service and products these segments need, they are still large enough to warrant your marketing attention.

$30,000 to 50,000	Percent of market	Number
Business owner	6	300
Professional	7	350
Executive	5	250
Tradesperson	22	1,100
Office worker	37	1,850
Other	23	1,150

Segmenting the $30,000 to $50,000 group by profession yields segments that are irregular in size. It would be difficult to design services to meet such a diversity of segments. A more meaningful way to segment the $30,000 to $50,000 group is by age.

$30,000 to 50,000	Percent of market	Number
Under 35	19	950
35 to 55	49	2,450
Over 55	32	1,600

In the $30,000 to $50,000 group, age is a more viable discriminator than occupation. It divides the group into segments that can be profiled and that warrant marketing. As we'll see later, in these brackets age is also a better indicator of financial behavior and Personal Financial Planning needs. However, in the over $50,000 group, profession offers better discrimination than age because most members of the group are over 50 years old.

Use the Worksheet 6 to delimit your general target market and to define those segments that you target. Copy the worksheet for as many segments as you want to work with. Preferably, make your first few passes on rough paper and record your "final" segments in pencil since you will have revisions. The worksheet lets you record the factors used to define each segment.

Now that you have workable segments, you should learn as much about each segment as you can. You can do this by profiling the segments.

Profiling

What can you know about a market segment, and what do you want to know? A good place to start is an averaged balance sheet, derived from your client base ratios. This would include:

- Annual income
- Assets
  - Cash or equivalents
  - Securities and annuities
  - Business interests
  - Home value
  - Other illiquid assets
  - Total

- Liabilities
  - Home-related loans
  - Personal loans
  - Investment loans
  - Total
- Net worth

Then make a brief statement about who these people are to further identify the segment. In defining who they are, include general information such as level of education, age groups, or family situations where applicable. Also define the key segmenting factors that you used to create the segment.

Next, further identify the people in your market segment by describing the nature of their wealth and assets, the level of their discretionary income, and the overall nature of their investment portfolio. This will give you clues as to what Personal Financial Planning Services they need, as well as possible areas for evaluation and optimization.

Make some notes about their financial behavior and their goals and attitudes. Determine their understanding of risk, their risk tolerance, and their use (or nonuse) of financial or other expert advice. This will indicate whether they need introductory groundwork, or whether they are already familiar with financial services and are trying to make a selection. Include a summary of their financial product buying patterns where possible.

Also summarize their life goals and general attitudes. What dreams might they want to convert to goals? Are they consumers or accumulators? What stages of life typify the people in the segment?

Select some of their key needs in the Personal Financial Planning area. You will later add to this list, but your current analysis and profiling will reveal many obvious areas for selling your services to them. Is time a big factor in their planning needs? Of the benefits listed below, what is foremost?

- Security
- Direction
- Advice
- Expertise
- Objectivity
- Coordination

· Time

· Value

Will the people in your segment seek pure planning, or will they need planning and implementation assistance? What are the prominent financial problems that face them?

Finally, make notes about the cost of delivering your services to the people in your segment. Will their situations be complex in terms of analysis time? What pricing mechanisms will they be familiar with and will they readily accept? How receptive are they to using you as their central or coordinating adviser? Read the following example of profiling, then complete a copy of Worksheet 7 for each segment you have defined.

Profiling Example

Let's continue with the example segments that we derived and profile them according to the ideas that we discussed. The derivation of average balance sheets is a straightforward exercise you can do yourself. As you read, note that the profiles below are not theoretical but are practical and real. They are culled from my own experience, and colleagues across the nation have helped me adjust them to reflect national norms.

Over $50,000 Business Owners. These are the very wealthy in Personal Financial Planning. They have ample discretionary income and need a wide range of Personal Financial Planning Services. Their company benefits usually substantially supplement their income.

This group comprises large product purchasers who often concentrate up to 50 percent of their assets in business and real estate holdings. Their assets are highly concentrated, and they hold stocks only for minimum liquidity needs, keeping the majority of their holdings in real estate. Their banking relationships are important and strong due to their illiquid holdings. Thus their bankers must become your allies.

Their generally high level of business knowledge makes them appreciate a systematic approach. Since they are already heavy users of fragmented advisory services, they are accustomed to paying experts and are comfortable with an hourly rate basis.

Business owners understand risk and expertise, are willing to take manageable risks, and show a higher risk tolerance than other groups. However, they do tend to favor investment areas where they are knowledgeable or have control. For this reason, they will focus on real rather than financial assets and will avoid products managed by others or at a distance.

The primary concern for business owners is to run their businesses. They have limited time for Personal Financial Planning for themselves. In addition, their situation is quite complex since they are faced with substantial tax liabilities. Tax sheltering is a major concern and product need for them. These people usually have large life insurance holdings, so this is a good area to investigate for optimization.

For this segment, you should use a two-pronged planning focus: one to integrate their personal and business planning and one to implement the personal portion of their financial plan. For the integration of their business and Personal Financial Plan, you will need extensive legal support on an ongoing basis as new problems emerge. Because personal and business planning are intermixed, your initial analysis costs will be higher for this group.

Business owners tend to use clusters of specialists rather than a single trusted adviser. However, you can provide coordination and overall optimization. Most often, you will not be able to replace their other advisers, so you must gain their confidence and use a team approach.

In planning for this segment, emphasize regular reviews and expect frequent consultation. Hourly rates and yearly retainers are easily accepted mechanisms here. In implementing their plans, remember that these are major purchasers, so include a commission mechanism in your pricing.

Over $50,000 Professionals. These people are the high earners in prestige professions. Their personal and business finances are often intermingled, as they are often part owners of their business. They are highly educated and, usually, narrowly specialized.

As professionals, members of this segment often feel more qualified to evaluate planning than they actually are. Even though they are well educated, they often lack planning skills. Your explanations of financial products will need to be more detailed for this group, and you may find it useful to further segment professionals by their profession: physicians or dentists, lawyers, accountants, architects, and engineers.

For members of this segment, net worth is concentrated in their business holdings. They show less understanding of investment than business owners and little understanding of risk/return trade-offs. While some have purchased investment advice or have used investment managers, they are highly risk averse, accepting minimum to moderate risks only. They are open to higher risk levels on tax shelter investments, though.

Members of this segment invest in their businesses, which are often small partnerships that have been formed with other practicing peers. Their life goals are to maintain a high income and standard of living, while building for early and comfortable retirement. They exhibit less affluent behavior than business owners.

For people in this segment, your services should reflect the goals of professionals: to improve standard of living and provide for retirement. Their major Personal Financial Planning need is for tax reduction. They pay taxes in a higher bracket than business owners because they cannot use the associated tax avoidance techniques. Generally, their estate considerations are minimal.

You will often be dealing with a two-income household, and the situation becomes more complex if this is the case. People in this group are used to seeking advice from investment advisers, but are not loyal to their advisers. They hire them and fire them as needed, so special care must be taken to develop the client/planner relationship. Of the members of this segment, doctors and dentists probably will present the toughest personal interaction problems.

Over $50,000 Executives. People in this segment form the top management levels of corporations. They have complex titles and job responsibilities. Of all segments of the over $50,000 group, these people have the largest portion of their assets in liquid investments. Corporate fringe benefits play a major role in their financial picture in the areas of retirement funds and insurance. They enjoy a high and rising income from their employment, and their affluence is due to this income, not to assets held. Often, the members of this group have common stock and retirement plans.

You have a slight advantage here. Members of this segment make limited use of planners and advisers, but this is mainly because they are unfamiliar with financial planning services. They believe time is the only constraint against doing their own Personal Financial Planning, not their ability. Once you have gained their trust and have shown them the complex nature of financial planning, they will respond to you as a trusted adviser. Some members of this group enjoy access to corporate advisers, but in general they are not heavy users of financial advisers.

Members of this group want to build wealth during their high earning years, and they need help because they have the least sophisticated investment habits. Often they seek advice, and then don't follow it. They have good risk tolerance; from substantial to moderate risks are acceptable.

Their attitudes and behaviors are shown in a high consumption orientation and a high income-to-wealth ratio. Their goals are to maintain their income after retirement and keep a comfortable standard of living while still employed. Often, they want to create an estate.

These people have a serious need for Personal Financial Planning, whether they acknowledge it or not. They want to build wealth from their high income flows, yet they are poorly equipped to make sound investment decisions. Just as the professional group, these people have high tax payments and need advice on tax avoidance strategies.

Your planning focus for this group should be on wealth accumulation, with ongoing liquid asset management. Analysis and optimization of retirement benefits is a good place to start to develop trust.

When you work with this segment, you will find no entrenched advisers to replace. You have a high potential for developing a solid client/planner relationship.

Over $50,000 Other. Members of this segment are typically in sales or sales management positions. They also include a high proportion of craftsmen and people near retirement age. You may wish to further segment this group by age or profession.

These people possess significant retirement and pension assets. They are highly liquid, and they have substantial holdings in tangibles. Their debt ratio is small.

They are heavy users of financial advisers, and they show a strong desire for a single trusted adviser. You can serve in this role if you show an understanding of their goals and orientation. They are concerned with inflation, and they have a minimum to slight risk tolerance. You will need to deal with less experienced clients here who often find financial products confusing.

This segment pays the highest taxes of the over $50,000 groups, typically up to 40 percent of annual income. It is vitally interested in tax avoidance, but lacks the needed skills to accomplish it.

Members of this segment need assistance in implementation and portfolio management, as well as advice. They need you to help them maintain their income now and at retirement, particularly through tax reduction techniques. They will also need help with estate planning and transfer of ownerships.

$30,000 to 50,000 , Under 35. This segment is composed of young professionals who have few assets beyond those needed for daily living. Their life goals still center around establishing and improving their standards of living. They are preoccupied with daily living expenses, but are interested in the rapid acquisition of wealth. As a result of this attitude and minimal family responsibilities, they tolerate very high levels of risk in investment.

For these young people, the idea of using a financial adviser is foreign, since most have never had a financial review of any kind. Overall, their concerns are for tax reduction, income protection in the form of life and disability insurance, medical protection, the future education needs of their children, and capital growth.

$30,000 to 50,000, 35 to 55. These are the middle-age people of the $30,000 to $50,000 group. They have acquired much of the assets they will need, but they feel the pinch of a worsening financial environment very acutely.

For this reason, they will take moderate risks, and as a group are the highest users of financial advisers. Yet many have never had a comprehensive financial review. They know that they are not in a position to meet their financial goals unaided, and they are generally open to buying the services of an overall Financial Planner.

Their goals are often those of people in transition. They want to improve their standard of living and keep up with inflation. College expenses are in the forefront of their concerns, but they are also concerned with adequate income for retirement.

They need overall organization and problem solving skills to get them on course and headed toward comfortable later life.

$30,000 to 50,000, Over 55. This is the elder segment of the $30,000 to $50,000 group who are near the end of their professional lives and are headed toward retirement.

Because of their age, they have little experience with financial advisers and have never had a financial review. They are conservative and will tolerate only low levels of risk.

Their goals are set from the retirement perspective. They want to secure their retirement income and meet their daily living expenses. They are also increasingly aware of their needs for estate planning and protection.

Services they want will focus on retirement, including analysis and optimization of their company fringe benefits. You can provide valuable advice on shifting the tax impact to their post-retirement years. Since children generally have left the nest, moving to a smaller home is often a concern here.

While this concludes the profiling of those segments that were derived from our example, there are two additional segments that you may decide to include in your strategic marketing plan. These are unmarried females who earn in excess of $30,000 and the mass market that earns between $15,000 and $30,000.

Over $30,000, Unmarried Females. Affluent unmarried females are a segment of special concern to Financial Planners. Most of these women are either divorced or widowed, and about 85 percent are still employed.

Members of this segment are extremely averse to risk, and their assets are concentrated in highly illiquid investments, typically, real estate, tangibles, common stock or mutual funds, and bonds. Despite tolerance for only a minimum of risk, they are heavy users of financial advisers. Generally, they rely on family or friends for their advice. They are likely to pay for a comprehensive financial review, but often from a biased source.

For women with children, child support and rearing become the main concern. For women with no children, the focus is centered on maintaining their hard-won situation and assets.

$15,000 to 30,000. Another segment of special interest is the mass market, the low end of the financial spectrum. There are over 25 million of these middle-income families. The size of this market can mean an appealing practice if you can provide low-cost services to a large enough market share. Since their Personal Financial Planning spending is low per household, they are profitable to you in high volumes only.

These people are willing to accept only a bare minimum to small risk. They are rarely astute investors and have no established investment habits. They are unaccustomed to using advisers, and their life insurance agents and lawyers are the only experts that they consult. Very few of these households have ever had a complete financial review.

These people can benefit from low-cost generic or computer-generated reports, along with sound budgeting advice. They can be groomed for discretionary income, with do-it-yourself kits and programs.

Define Segment Needs

Now that you know the segments with which you have to work, you need to focus on their specific product and service needs in order to develop your offerings in a marketable way. Sources of this information are readily available. You can start by surveying your own client base on an informal or a formal basis. Be open to all sources of feedback about real and perceived needs in the market segments, but remember to weigh them statistically to get a true picture of any segment.

You can discuss Personal Financial Planning needs with your existing clients during office visits, or you can conduct a telephone or mail survey. Surveys can be sent either to your client base or your selected market segments in order to determine what they want and need. Then you can develop your offerings to match these needs.

Surveys can be relatively inexpensive to conduct. You can include a cne- or two-page survey form with routine mailings to existing clients or do a special mailing to a list selected to represent a chosen segment. The expensive aspect of surveys is to obtain the expertise needed to create questions that will reveal the information sought; this is a good place to hire the help of a marketing consultant.

If you conduct, or plan to conduct, seminars on Personal Financial Planning, surveys are a perfect way to get the kind of information you want. A preliminary survey can help you develop the content and format of your seminars. Surveys taken after a seminar will be more detailed.

Use your information networks, too. Look for surveys conducted by financial magazines and newspapers; then adjust the figures for your service area. *Money* produces an excellent annual survey of various financial issues: *Americans and Their Money* (see Jones in Bibliography). *Money's* survey can help you segment, profile, and determine Personal Financial Planning needs; additional surveys are listed in the bibliography. Your professional organizations can lead you to additional sources of survey material.

You will want to know why people seek the services of a Financial Planner, what parts of the plan are most important to them, and what problems loom largest in their minds. Use the lists below to help you design surveys or to record results. It is better to provide a series of questions and lists of items, than to ask respondents to think of the issues. This also allows uniformity in your analysis. My experience has shown that the following list represents those items for which my clients sought advice. It is organized in decreasing order of importance.

- Tax return preparation
- Insurance optimization
- Tax planning
- Investment analysis

- Estate planning
- Personal budgeting

Additional needs that are prominent in the general market for Personal Financial Planning Services are as follows:

- Tax avoidance
- Retirement planning
- Investment strategy development
- Investment management
- General savings increase
- Saving for a house
- Saving for special goals
- Saving for education

Use Worksheet 8 to record the needs of each segment you have defined. Summarize the major needs and concerns with the intention of providing products or services that satisfy the needs.

STEP 3—ANALYZE YOUR COMPETITION

Now you must address other aspects of your market position. You are beginning to define the space between the needs in the marketplace and your ability to supply the desired services. However, you must also consider your market position with respect to your competitors.

Competitive analysis helps you answer this question. Given the gap between needs and services, why should your target market use your services to complete the exchange rather than those of your competitors?

You need to study your competition, noting strengths and weaknesses. You want to determine how to make your services more attractive to the target market and how to distinguish yourself from other competitors.

Make a copy of Worksheet 9 for each of your competitors and one for yourself. You must define your strengths and weaknesses from the same perspective as you define those of your competitors.

For each competitor, list the services and products offered. Note the areas in which the competitor has the most success, the most business. If you plan to offer similar services, make a comparative pricing evaluation.

Make your evaluation of each competitor's market position. This includes image projected, market needs that are met, and approach to price and quality. Also note relevant information about geographic area of service.

Next, perform a study and analysis of strengths and weaknesses. Refer to Chapter 2 for the general strengths and weaknesses of your competitors. Then expand on specific issues for each competitor.

STEP 4—DEFINE YOUR STRATEGIC MARKETING PLAN

By this time you have completed enough steps to define your first version of the detailed plan. You will return to this step—indeed to all the steps—many times before you have fine-tuned your plan to the point of implementation. Now, however, you know all you need to know to identify attractive marketing options, select strategies for each option, and determine the appropriate tactics.

Check Your Image

Whatever marketing options or strategies you choose, you should add one vital thing to your first strategic marketing plan—the development of the exact image you will need to achieve your desired market position. You will need a clear visual image for all your printed materials. This might include a logo, or a motto or slogan, and it is a big part of your differentiation. Unless you have public relations and graphic arts resources, use outside professionals to create and refine your image. Your image will serve you long and well, if created correctly.

Identify Attractive Options

Note the spectrum of consumer needs in your segments. Compare these needs with the coverage afforded by the competition to see where you can fit into the market.

In some cases, you will decide that your present position, business level, or services need no marketing attention. If not, don't hesitate to keep the *status quo*.

Look over your worksheets on segment profiles and needs and compare them with your analysis of the competition. Divorce your mind from the services you currently offer, and objectively note the gaps that exist. It is important to have the freedom and desire to design new services when needed, and not to be bound by services you already have.

By reviewing the information you have gathered so far, you will see where a consumer need can be met by one of your services or products, either in a way that your competitors have missed or at a more competitive price.

When you spot a possible marketing opportunity, define it in terms of the service or product that is needed and the segment for which it is intended. Make a copy of Worksheet 10 for each option you want to explore; then record the information.

Now your goals will impact on your market planning. For each option, list the strategic marketing plan goal that is met. Of course, each goal can satisfy several marketing options, and each option can satisfy multiple goals.

When doing this, restate your marketing goals in terms of the volumes needed for the proposed service or product. After all, an option must be profitable. In later iterations of this step, you may need to project revenues for each marketing option, using various pricing schemes.

When you do this, you can determine the sales volumes needed to reach your goals for each marketing option that you exercise. Essentially, you are automatically defining the monitoring factors to measure your success.

Option Example

Let us assume that your evaluation of the marketplace shows some gaps. You isolate three attractive options.

Option 1. A high quality, low cost plan for the $15,000 to 30,000 segment. No high quality, low cost plan is currently available to the low income group: the $15,000 to $30,000 segment. You do not offer such a service, but know that you could buy a software package to produce generic plans. With a minimum of analysis time, you can expand on this basic type of plan in order to create a low cost service that has the added value of your analysis and specific recommendations.

Option 2. Fragmented planning for retirement and special goals for the $30,000 to 50,000, 35 to 55 segment. Although the needs of this market are generally well met in your service area, there are specific needs for retirement planning and special goal programs. Services tailored to meet these particular needs are not offered outside of your competitors' comprehensive planning programs. By fragmenting your services, you could develop special planning packages that address only these needs at a greatly reduced price.

Option 3. Full planning and implementation for the over $50,000 medical professionals. The large numbers of medical professionals in your area could benefit from a comprehensive service designed specially for their situation. This option involves the creation of an area of specialization in your practice.

Select Strategies

Remember that your strategic decisions involve what you want to do, not how you intend to do it. So this step is simpler than it seems at first. For each marketing option that you have identified, determine the appropriate strategy. One or more strategies can apply to each option. Develop the strategy from a general to a more detailed statement. The general strategies are as follows:

- Defend your client base
- Cross sell new products and services to your clients
- Expand your customer base
- Diversify, adding new services

Some areas of your business will be doing fine, but perhaps even your base practice could use a little defensive marketing! Try to find ways to let your other marketing efforts defend and bolster your current client base and area of operation.

Remember that in cross selling you can groom and upgrade your client base, moving only qualified clients into your new service area. Clients are qualified by their desirability and the ways in which they will contribute to your client base revenue stream. A mighty river swelling. . . .

Expansion of your customer base involves either grooming new clients from suspects in the market segments or capturing clients from competitors. Neither approach is ethically superior, provided you operate from a client need perspective.

Expansion will represent the major costs in your marketing plan. For this reason, do not plan to develop a large ongoing client development or conversion program. Rather, expand your client base in stages, being careful to offer ongoing planning and implementation services to new clients.

Just as expansion of your client base requires a high marketing expenditure, so does diversification of services and products. The tactics you choose differ slightly since the thrust of diversification is usually aimed at your existing client base. Of course, you will often be following both these strategies at once.

Select the strategies that best match your goals and options. From your strategic decisions, you can select appropriate tactics to achieve each.

Matching Tactics to Strategies

Segmentation and profiling will help determine the tactics you select. The secret is to match your tactics to the audience you choose as a particular market segment.

For example, if your strategy is to cross sell to existing clients, you need to produce information about the new services. Producing a brochure or bulletin letter, sending it to your mailing list, and following up by telephone is the most economical way to create interest.

Each of the tactics listed below is defined with helpful pointers in the next chapter:

Tangible Materials
· Brochures
· Newsletters
· Bulletin letters
· Direct mail
· Tapes/videos
· Speeches
· Gifts to clients

Direct Interaction
· Networking
· Referrals
· Bird dogs
· Professional organizations
· Breakfast meetings
· Seminars
· Telephone calls
· Teaching

Trade shows

Media Techniques

· Paid advertising
· Press releases
· Television and radio shows
· Newspaper column and editorial space
· Yellow pages

Community Involvement

There is a bias to use only direct marketing tactics since these seem more pointed and more promising. However, don't ignore the very real potential of using indirect marketing tactics. Often these provide a low-cost way of generating leads.

Client reference programs, coupled with a well developed referral network and good public relations, can result in as many leads as such direct tactics as seminars, cold calls, and direct mail campaigns.

You can look ahead to Chapter 7 to familiarize yourself with the tactics described there. Once the ideas begin to flow, capture them on Worksheet 10. In subsequent passes you can narrow down to exact tactical methods.

Strategy and Tactics Example

Let's see how this concept applies to the three hypothetical options we identified earlier.

Option 1, a high quality, low cost plan for the $15,000 to $30,000 segment, would use the strategies of expanding your client base and diversifying your services. Since the profitability of this option depends on a heavy, constant flow of new clients, you will need marketing tactics that reach this segment continually, at a low cost.

You must give clients information about your new service, and then motivate them to try it. The low cost, low risk aspects of the service mean marketable benefits in consumer security and value.

These factors point to the benefits of telephone solicitation and the mailing of low cost bulletin or newsletter materials as tactics. If your budget allows, you could consider periodic advertising in local newspapers.

Option 2, retirement and special goal planning for the $30,000 to

$50,000 age 35 to 55 segment, may call for diversification, but development costs for these services will be low since they are portions of your existing overall planning service. Let us suppose that your existing client base will yield all the business you can handle for this option. If so, you must cross sell.

Information about your new service can be communicated to selected clients as a bulletin or as an item in your newsletter. The lower volume of prospects for this service may make preparation of a special brochure feasible. With your firsthand knowledge of the special needs of this group and an established relationship with them, a seminar devoted to retirement and special goals would be effective. The security, direction, and advice you will provide for your clients can help market this service.

Option 3, a full planning service for over $50,000 medical professionals may call for a strategy of expanding your customer base. A much lower volume of clients is needed to make this service profitable. Overall, your strategy will aim to secure and retain members of this segment as ongoing clients. Benefits sought by medical professionals will be the expertise, coordination, and time savings your service can provide.

Tactics used for this option should focus on professionalism. Using your referral network may not generate enough volume. This segment has a clearly defined professional infrastructure, and tactics can be chosen to make use of this. For example, you could advertise in the journals or periodicals read by members of this segment or offer your services as a speaker to their professional organizations.

STEP 5—DESIGN YOUR PRODUCTS AND SERVICES

It should be clear to you that marketing and product/service development work together. You may establish the basics of your organization, networks, and services independently of marketing considerations, but you will achieve real success only when you refine these basics in light of your strategic marketing plan.

Now that you understand the needs of your target market segments and the marketing options possible, return to Chapter 4 and refine your products and services. While your planned organization and structure probably needs no change, your strategic marketing plan may indicate the need for changes or expansion of your proposed expert team and your information network.

Since ideas about product leveling and segmentation make more sense to you, you will want to re-evaluate your decisions in these areas. The reason to fragment and level your services is to enable you to meet the specific needs of a small, clearly defined market segment.

Knowing the needs you expect to fill, you can fragment and level your services more sensibly. Your strategic marketing plan will indicate the kinds of specialized service you need to offer, but here are some fragmented services to consider:

- Tax planning
- Budgeting
- Insurance planning
- Estate planning
- Investment analysis
- Investment management
- Retirement planning
- Special goal programs

Remember to design and level your services to optimize the use of your time. Design your service to be cost-effective, affordable, and competitive. These examples of services are leveled according to the degree of your involvement:

- Do-it-yourself packages with instructions, worksheets, home computer software suggestions or products
- Computer-assisted plans with incremental pricing for expansion into areas of special interest
- A series of workshops or seminars to guide large groups through the Personal Financial Planning process
- A series of optional, independent sessions for each step of the total planning process that allows clients to determine their individual planning programs
- Full Personal Financial Planning Services

At this stage, you can also consider product and service delivery since you know your intended clients. Consider using nights or weekends for do-it-yourself workshops. Weigh the alternatives of meeting in your office, in the client's office, even in the client's home.

This step requires a marketing definition of your services, not a detailed development of the mechanics or processes of the service. Worksheet 11 will help you formulate a marketing-oriented definition.

Make a copy of the worksheet for each service that is indicated as a marketing option. Identify the service with a name, and record the segment to which it is directed. Also, to keep you on target, state the specific consumer need that each product or service will satisfy and the benefits that can be used to sell it. The balance of the worksheet pertains to the next step in our planning process: pricing products and services.

STEP 6—PRICE THE PRODUCTS AND SERVICES

Now that services are defined according to the needs of the market segments, pricing ideas must be examined. Let's review the decisions needed and consider their implications.

Your final pricing schedule will be determined by more factors than cost and desired profit margin. You will also want to match your pricing mechanism and final price to expectations of your target segments. Further, your pricing mechanism may be determined more by your future goals than by any other criteria.

Matching Price to Target Segments

To make the sale, your fee must be within the client's general expectation range. Price expectations of prospects can be determined from surveys of your client base and an analysis of the competition.

You will want to select a pricing mechanism that is readily understood by, and acceptable to, the prospective client. This is where accurate profiling of your market segments pays off.

If you want a profitable practice, don't hesitate to offer implementation-oriented services. You can ensure the value a client receives from his Personal Financial Plan only if you can see that it is correctly implemented. Clients who receive value will promote your services to others.

In the long run, implementation services are more profitable than initial and ongoing planning services. The costs of initial planning services are high. You will have major expenditures of time in the data-gathering and analysis phases and in the preparation of the first plan document. You will also spend a great deal of time in the presentation of the initial plan, as compared to its revisions.

With careful thought, your pricing mechanism can actually generate later implementation revenues, by encouraging the client to use your implementation services.

Revenue Flows

Another way to look at the issue of pricing is to focus on your long-term goals. You can design your client base and type of services to maximize your profit, and your marketing and pricing strategies can then be driven from this design basis. It is possible for you to determine the cash flows from several mixes of client and service and then to decide which to pursue. Such analyses will determine your revenue stream and show the needs for long term client/planner relationships, marketing efforts, and the overall profitability that can result.

Income/Growth Considerations

Both fee-only and commission-only pricing mechanisms can be profitable when initial and ongoing implementation services are offered. These pricing mechanisms are enhanced when services are provided to a carefully selected market segment.

A basic initial planning fee plus an implementation fee or commission mechanism can provide an ongoing base for implementation and maintenance services. This is important because, as your practice moves toward ongoing plan and portfolio maintenance, your marketing costs decline dramatically.

If you use a planning fee only, however, you will continually depend on revenues from new clients, and your marketing costs will stay high. It becomes obvious that an ongoing planning and implementation based practice is profitable. Your marketing expenses will be minimized; your referrals will be maximized. For this reason, you should consider placing your emphasis on profitable implementation services, not on initial plans.

Effects of the Plan Price

Increasing your plan price has two effects beyond increasing your immediate revenues. First, your current client base will buy less of your planning services. Second, your client base will be upgraded, with new clients willing to pay the increased price. In effect, you can use your price to create a client base that yields the revenue stream you want.

Your pricing schedule also affects the number of prospects that your marketing effort will attract and the type of client that you will secure.

The price of your initial plan thus determines what ongoing planning and initial and ongoing implementation revenues you can expect.

How to Price

It is difficult to consider all factors and effects at once when pricing services. A simpler approach is to consider variables one at a time and then to repeat the process to bring pricing to its final shape. Follow the sequence shown on Worksheet 11, but do a couple of rough draft passes before you attempt a final version.

First, determine your costs. Determine the amount of your time needed for the service by breaking the process into steps or levels. Include the average costs incurred by your expert team. Depending on the specific service or product you are pricing, estimate the additional costs of production and materials. Use whatever technique you are comfortable with to reflect overhead and background operating costs (including marketing).

Second, determine the profit margin you need for the service. This may depend on business volumes and any leveling and fragmentation of the service. You may need to calculate profit margins for a variety of market responses and define your goals or target volumes in these terms to ensure correct monitoring of your strategic marketing plan.

These steps indicate how to price each service, but they do not indicate how to arrive at the price. Since your pricing mechanism will determine bottom-line prices, this is the next step in pricing.

The first requirement of a pricing mechanism is to generate the price needed to cover costs and maintain target profit margin. Equally important, the pricing mechanism must determine prices that are appropriate and expected by the target segments.

By reviewing your segment profiles, you can ascertain which mechanisms are familiar to prospects. There may be several alternatives, each equally acceptable to prospective clients. Examine the consequences of each alternative. You may select a pricing mechanism that maximizes your profits from the ongoing planning or implementation services. Or you may elect to offer different pricing mechanisms to different members of the segment as a sales technique.

Finally, review your pricing decisions in light of their effects on your long-term growth and client base. Does your pricing encourage ongoing planning and implementation services where desirable? Are you using your price to screen prospects and to groom and evolve your client base? If not, repeat the pricing step until all considerations harmonize. When you have a good pricing plan for each product and service, continue with the next step: budgeting the strategic marketing plan.

STEP 7—BUDGET THE STRATEGIC MARKETING PLAN

Why is budgeting placed so far back in the steps for developing your strategic marketing plan? Mainly, to encourage you to dream, understand, and plan without any constraints imposed by budgetary concerns.

Often, when you clearly see what you want to do, you can find ways to accomplish things that seem beyond the scope of your available budget. In other words, the expense of your plan should not discourage you from completing the previous essential planning steps. You need this information to select profitable marketing options and appropriate strategies and tactics. Whether your budget lets you fully implement the plan, the insight you gain will be worth the effort.

Some specific cost shortcuts and time savers are mentioned at the end of this chapter and throughout the next chapter. Use these suggestions to stretch your budget to cover a good plan.

Three major resources are needed to begin your marketing effort: time, capital, and support. For support, you will need basic staff and external services in those areas of expertise not available in your firm.

Copy the budgeting worksheet (Worksheet 12) for each marketing option you have selected. Then list each tactic selected for a marketing option and estimate the costs for each. Prepare a summary-and-totals sheet when you have completed the individual worksheets.

Your Time

Your time is your most valuable resource. Therefore, keep a close watch on how it is spent to get the optimal return on your investment. As a guideline, recall the recommendation for a starting service. Whether you are starting a completely new practice in Personal Financial Planning or merely a new service area for your firm, expect to spend at least 25 percent of your hours in marketing and marketing-related efforts.

In order to determine when outside help should be hired, try to reach a fair hourly rate figure for your time. The hours budgeted in your strategic marketing plan for your own time can be delegated, when necessary, to hired contractors or to staff members with the needed skills.

Capital

There is also a guideline figure for the capital needs of your marketing effort. Set aside one-half to five percent of your annual operating expenses for marketing, depending on the size of your firm.

Remember that this is only a guideline. If you need to spend more, do so; but consider low-cost alternatives to tactics that you select. And if you can expand your marketing efforts, do so.

As you gain experience in marketing by monitoring and adjusting your strategic marketing plan, you will learn to make accurate cost/benefit studies. For now, start with a reasonable expenditure (the guideline will help here) and measure your results. If you are in doubt, hire a consultant to test the soundness of your calculations and suggest the kinds of returns you can expect, based on his knowledge of similar situations.

Support

This is the time to note your resources, using Worksheet 13. Be sure to take stock of your current marketing and public relations activities. You will later either incorporate them into the plan or discontinue their practice.

At first, you will probably be your own support staff, if not in areas of marketing expertise, then for all other parts of the job that you can do. This is more than a money saver; it will give you the hands-on experience you need to gain independence from outside help.

If you have personnel with the needed skills, then assign a full-time staff member to handle marketing, public relations, and media. Also consider hiring an outside marketing or public relations firm. The key is to have a unified approach so that your image is solid, your efforts coordinated, and your monitoring information accurate.

The marketing resources worksheet at the end of this chapter gives you the criteria to determine whether you need the help of outside experts. Briefly, you will need to have, or to hire, skills in the following areas:

- Creative thinking
- Copywriting
- Graphic arts experience and capability
- Printed material composition
- Printing experience
- Media handling experience
- Public relations skill
- Special material production skills
- Human interaction skill
- Presentation skill

Don't panic! You'd be surprised at how many of these skills are hidden in your staff. This book shows you how to develop some of these skills at a rudimentary but sufficient level, but you have several options for hiring or renting the skills you need.

Internal Marketing Department

Consider creating your own marketing department. You could contact the work/study program at a local college to hire a part-time marketing student. For example, you could hire the student half days for six months. This is ample time to launch your first year's campaign and to begin the work of monitoring and adjusting the plan. If the work relationship develops well, the graduate student can look forward to a full-time position as your marketing director.

Alternately, you can hire or promote an experienced secretary with good office skills, above-average intelligence and common sense, and an outgoing personality. This should be a salaried, full-time staff member who will be responsible for overseeing and coordinating all marketing projects.

In addition, your marketing director will place your news releases into newspapers and other publications, secure tickets to key social events, and arrange press coverage or conferences. This staff member can prepare the bulk of a newsletter, keeping its format, image, and content to consistently high quality levels. This staff person is the ideal coordinator for all activities of any outside marketing firms or contractors you use. As your confidence in him increases, the additional and more complex tasks involved in preparing and conducting seminars can be added to the list of responsibilities.

Finally, your marketing director will be the liaison between the world of marketing and Personal Financial Planning. He will foster a rewarding exchange of ideas that results in increasingly effective marketing plans and efforts.

Many of you will elect to fill this role yourself, at least for the first campaign. If and when you decide to delegate this job, remember the following points.

A marketing director must understand your business from all perspectives. He must know what Personal Financial Planning is about, what your overall business plan involves, and where marketing fits. He must be familiar with both your basic business and those areas that you may select as areas of specialization or expertise for market position.

The marketing director must work only for you. This avoids distractions and time losses. Your marketing efforts are so essential to your success that he must be a totally devoted marketing resource.

You must treat your marketing director as a professional in the marketing and public relations field. Make your attitude right—have high expectations.

Finally, your marketing director must have responsibility and authority to cover and coordinate all in-house marketing projects with all your firm's other efforts.

Public relations and marketing consultants are a financially attractive option for small firms. Often, you can arrange to barter needed services. In this event, an hourly rate equivalent of your time to place a value on services comes in handy.

External Marketing Department

If necessary, you can obtain outside marketing services at a reasonable cost, generally from $500 to $1000 per month. You may elect to hire such an agency in any event. Even a year's experience with such expertise can train you or your future marketing director in all the needed skills.

The services performed can be minimal or maximal. But even if you decide to use extensive external help, you should go through the planning exercise here. You can then provide outsiders with the information they need and check their work and results.

Decisions about hiring outside expertise are never clear-cut. You can always use a local public relations firm for limited parts of your marketing plan. Ongoing advertising and public relations jobs can be delegated in this way. For example, news releases about the evolution of your service and firm could be completed by an outside firm.

When you select an outside marketing firm, you must know your marketing strategy, your goals, and your target market: what you want, who they are, and where they are. You must be absolutely clear about the business parts of your plan.

Select an agency with good references, with a good track record for reaching your specific audience, and with whom you have a good working rapport. The image of your public relations firm should match the desired image of your firm.

How do you go about hiring an agency? You can start with names from the yellow pages, references from other professionals in your area, or recommendations from your peers. Find out, and eliminate in advance, any agency that works for your competition.

Contact half a dozen agencies to find matches in their services and your needs. Suggest a format of three meetings with members from the agency. In the first, you will inform them of your goals and give them relevant plan information, answer any general questions, and supply various contact information. In the second meeting, they will make a presentation to you on their overall services and indicate how they could meet your particular marketing goals. Finally, a third meeting will be needed to finalize details and sign letters of agreement or contracts.

The first meeting will cost you nothing but your time. Be sure to bring a list of your specific goals, including your target segments and your objectives. Answer the questions needed to develop their proposal. Include target times for any programs, fees, budgets, and expected costs. At this meeting, let each agency know that you are still shopping, but do not mention the names of the other agencies with which you are working.

The second meeting may cost you a nominal fee. Remember, the agency's staff may spend a considerable amount of time and effort to prepare a good presentation. The second meeting will indicate their flavor and should convince you of their ability to reach your goals. Notice how thorough they are. Do they address every item on your goal list? Do they show how they will meet each goal?

Don't hesitate to ask for referrals or case histories when an approach is doubtful. They should be able to estimate the media coverage you will get although there can be no guarantees on exact placements.

The second meeting should be at the agency. Get to know the agency's key people, including your ongoing contacts. Notice the quality of their equipment and staff. Successful marketing firms will invest in competent people, not expensive furniture. At this meeting, get a clear idea of how they will want to do business with you. Will you be able to reach a mutually comfortable arrangement?

You will generally have several options in securing their services. You can reach a mutual agreement on a monthly retainer or on a fee-plus-expenses basis. You can hire them on a trial basis for a fixed period, perhaps 90 days.

After you hire an agency, work often with them. You must provide them with material and feedback, both from your monitoring efforts and from any other sources. You are the only one who can tell them if their work is to your satisfaction.

STEP 8—IMPLEMENT THE STRATEGIC MARKETING PLAN

This is it! All the planning steps are done. Now you have to produce the materials, place the ads, and set and follow the public relations schedule.

I suggest a two-step strategy to implement your plan. Do a test run on a small scale to prove your planning, strategies, and tactics. With the information from this test case, refine the plan one more time and then go ahead. You can test run the plan during the first three months of the year and then fully implement the plan.

There is no worksheet for this step. You must develop and use methods that are effective for you. Whatever other tools you use, always use a marketing schedule or calendar to keep track of the chronology of each event in the campaign. You will have to coordinate several design and production tasks. Divide these activities into network preparation, material preparation, events, and fixed review points.

STEP 9—MONITOR AND ADJUST THE PLAN

Once launched, you must continue to manage the marketing effort. Just as you would monitor and adjust the Personal Financial Plan of a client, monitor and adjust your strategic marketing plan. This means that you must monitor the costs versus the benefits of the plan for each marketing option and tactic. Are the revenues being generated to reach your goals? If there are deviations, what are the causes and the cures?

Your strategic marketing plan must be a living document, just like your client's Personal Financial Plan. Rewrite your plan as often as needed to optimize it as it runs. Make adjustments in an orderly way, minimizing their impact on your prospects and clients.

You need an annual review, at least. If you do a trial run, have a thorough review at its completion. As you fully implement your plan, check results after each major stage, step, or tactic is employed.

Perform scheduled reviews for the same reasons that you review a client's plan. There is change in the outer environment, in the target segments. There is change in your goals as you build and refine your client base and as you gain experience in Personal Financial Planning and marketing. Changes must be evaluated to determine their effects on your plan.

Closing the Gaps

If you have set goals as to the number of plans or the dollar volume that you want, measure these against your results. Once you have determined a method of measuring performance, stick to it unless it is in error. When results do not match goals, you have to change your plan. What are some possible gaps between your planned and actual results?

A gap can occur between the real consumer needs and the services you offer. Check and challenge the information used to determine the needs of a problem segment. If you have misjudged the needs of a segment, you can change the services you are offering or redirect them to another segment.

It may be obvious, but it bears repeating: You cannot change the real needs of the consumer. However, consumers do not always perceive their own needs objectively. When your services meet the real needs of the consumer but do not match perceived needs, you must correct the gap by education.

Another gap can occur from poor market position. When you are in competition, you must offer strong incentives for prospects to select you over your competitor. Check your marketing image. Do prospects know that you have targeted them? Can they easily distinguish you from your competitors? What aspects of your service will make them choose you?

It is unusual to select the wrong strategy for a given marketing opportunity, but it can happen. If your marketing efforts are not expanding your customer base, again consider the possibilities of cross selling new services. More often, the strategy is correct, but the tactic chosen is ineffective. Tactics should reach, inform, and motivate your prospects. Are these things all happening? If a tactic is failing, you must either correct it or change it.

When the plan is working properly but the volumes are insufficient to generate your goal revenues, you have another gap. Prospect leads can be increased by revising tactics, using multiple tactics, or increasing your area of service. When you have enough prospects but too few clients, your problem may be in handling your prospects. We will look at this topic in a later chapter. You can also close revenue gaps by revising your pricing mechanisms and reducing your production costs.

Gaps between expected and actual results can also arise from faulty measurement methods. Here are a few more points about monitoring your strategic marketing plan.

Measuring Results

Monitoring quantified results, such as the size and composition of your client base, is relatively easy. Measuring qualitative results, such as changes to your image, is more difficult; this requires survey work. Still, it is possible to derive a wealth of information from low-cost surveys.

Besides measuring goals, monitoring can illuminate other aspects of your marketing efforts. You can easily (although perhaps painfully) measure your ability to retain existing clients. This will inform you of the need for defensive strategies. You can also monitor the effectiveness of your referral network quite easily.

Respond to these feedback loops—and be flexible. Don't simply react to the information. I have adopted a simple rule of thumb about my plans and actions. I'd hate to tell you what it cost me to develop this rule, especially the second part. The rule is this:

1. If it works, it is good.
2. If it does not work, *change it.*

Besides monitoring the progress of your marketing efforts, you will want to monitor your competition. This includes new entrants, new products, and new services. Your position in the marketplace is not a rigid pose, but a balanced stance. To keep this balance you may have to go through many subtle shifts, changing your image or pricing in view of changes in the competition.

TIPS AND TECHNIQUES

Support

No doubt you are aware of your need for marketing information. Develop your information network thoroughly, and in advance. You will find that the information is easily accessible from your files and the files of your network of experts. You can overcome any problems about confidentiality by using a statistical rendering of the information you exchange with your team.

Establish your preferred sources of information in various publications, trade papers, special reports; and use a system of abstracting and recording this information. You will find that national surveys are of value, too, once you learn to adjust for regional differences in your area of service.

Expertise

Of course, you can hire outside expertise in the marketing and production areas you need, but why not first consider low-cost alternatives. You can often find needed resources in your networks or barter advice on a technical or expert level with marketing professionals. Remember to use the full resource capabilities of your professional organization since this can prove a priceless source of creative ideas.

Things to Avoid

I hesitate to reveal how painful and difficult my own learning curve has been in marketing. Perhaps you can learn from my mistakes.

First, do not rely on your existing client base for continuing or referral business. Rather, upgrade your client base and expand on your sources of prospects. When I finally took the time to evaluate my sources of revenue, I found that only 30 percent came from my existing client base. I needed to acquire about 50 percent new client blood before my revenue stream was right.

Second, surround yourself with positive people. There are a host of people in your environment who are only too happy to point out to you why you cannot succeed. For me, this even included many of the marketing experts I consulted. Even as a novice, you can determine what works and learn how to change what does not.

Third, do not focus too narrowly on one target segment. In my first year, I spent nearly half of my marketing budget on a potentially high-return segment. While I realized good returns from this approach, I also realized astounding returns from two minor, or low-level, segments that I treated in an offhanded manner. Cover as many segments as you can in the first pass that show reasonable promise of profitable business. There will be surprises.

Fourth, use several marketing tactics. Until you have either hired or gained marketing experience, you are still taking informed guesses. Therefore, use as broad a range of techniques as you can to test the effectiveness of each. If don't shake out personal preferences and pet ideas in planning stages, your balance sheets will knock them out!

Planning Tools

When you develop your strategic marketing plan, use whatever additional tools you find valuable. The worksheets will guide you through most of the planning work, but don't hesitate to include any charts or techniques that work for you.

I find it particularly helpful to use goal-tracking charts that show my progress toward revenues projected from each year's strategic marketing plan. You can also use separate charts to record and monitor any of the marketing options you have chosen. Or you can use separate charts for each product, service, or area of revenue with which you are working.

Keep accurate notes about the production steps and timing of each tactic that you employ. These are priceless in planning, costing, and implementing the tactics in future campaigns.

Cost Reducers

Let me recap some of the business strategies that will keep your ongoing marketing costs low. Focus on building a reputation and image of high quality work. Develop and focus on ongoing planning and implementation services. Put less emphasis on the initial planning and implementation work, except as these will generate clients who need ongoing services.

Position yourself to meet real client product and service needs. This means good information networks and careful product design. Develop your referral business through high quality client servicing, extensive networking, and reciprocity of referrals.

Use the power of segmentation and profiling to zero in on the clients you need to build your optimal client base. Use the marketing tactics that are most cost-effective in order to reach your target market segments.

When you must hire expert marketing help, use freelance specialists if possible. Their fees are usually lower, and they allow a wider range of remuneration methods. Don't forget to check local colleges for student hiring programs and work/study arrangements. Additional techniques for cost reduction are presented in the next chapter.

Your Business Philosophy

Service Philosophy

_____

_____

_____

_____

_____

Business Goals

	Year 1	Year 2	Year 3	Year 4	Year 5
Profit	_____	_____	_____	_____	_____
Client Base	_____	_____	_____	_____	_____
Firm Size	_____	_____	_____	_____	_____

Personal/Professional Goals

_____

_____

_____

_____

_____

Service Area

Year 1 _____

Year 2 _____

Year 3 _____

Year 4 _____

Year 5 _____

Operating Constraints

_____

_____

_____

_____

_____

Attachments

- · Organization structure chart
- · Expert network chart
- · Financial information network chart or list
- · Marketing information network chart or list

Strategic Marketing Plan Goals

Goals for Year ____

Profits/Revenue

_____

_____

_____

Client Base Size and Mix

_____

_____

_____

Prospects/Clients Needed

_____

_____

_____

_____

Volumes of Service/Product Needed

Name _____

Volume _____

Name _____

Volume _____

Name _____

Volume _____

Name _____

Volume _____

Name _____

Volume _____

Firm Size and Staffing Needed

_____

_____

_____

_____

Market Segmentation

Segment Number ___

Segment Name _____

Segmenting Factors

Income   _____

Net worth   _____

Age   _____

Occupation   _____

Other _____ _____

Other _____ _____

Other _____ _____

Notes

_____

_____

_____

_____

_____

_____

_____

_____

Segment Profile

Segment Number ___

Segment Name _____

Description

_____

_____

_____

_____

Key Segmenting Factors _____

Wealth and Assets

_____

_____

_____

_____

Financial Behavior

_____

_____

_____

_____

Attitudes and Goals

_____

_____

_____

_____

Personal Financial Planning Needs

_____

_____

_____

_____

Benefits Sought

Security   Direction   Advice   Expertise

Objectivity   Coordination   Time   Value

Cost Factors in Serving Segment

_____

_____

_____

_____

Attachments

Averaged balance sheet

Segment Needs

Segment Number ____

Segment Name _____

Needs Checklist

____ Benefit optimization

____ Business and personal plan integration

____ Cash management

____ Debt management

____ Estate planning

____ Insurance optimization

____ Investment analysis

____ Investment management

____ Investment planning

____ Personal budgeting

____ Retirement planning

____ Risk management

____ Saving for house

____ Saving for education

____ Special goals

____ Tax avoidance

____ Tax planning

Summary of Segment Needs

_____

_____

_____

_____

_____

_____

_____

Target Products and Services

_____

_____

_____

_____

_____

_____

_____

Analysis of Competition

Competitor name _____

Services and Products

_____

_____

_____

_____

Major Business Activity

_____

_____

_____

_____

Marketing Position

_____

_____

_____

_____

Strengths

_____

_____

_____

_____

_____

Weaknesses

_____

_____

_____

_____

_____

Attachments

· Comparative pricing analysis

Strategic Marketing Plan Definition

Option Number ____

Service/Product _____

_____

Segment Number ____

Segment Name _____

Related Goal _____

_____

Quantity or Revenue Needed _____

_____

Strategy

____ Defend client base

____ Cross sell new products and services

____ Expand customer base

____ Diversify to new products/services

_____

_____

_____

_____

_____

Tactics

Product/Service Definition

Option Number ——

Service/Product ————————————————————

————————————————————————————————

Segment Number ——

Segment Name ————————————————————

Needs Met/Benefits Gained

————————————————————————————————

————————————————————————————————

————————————————————————————————

————————————————————————————————

Description of Product/Service

————————————————————————————————

————————————————————————————————

————————————————————————————————

————————————————————————————————

Pricing

Cost ————————————————————————————

————————————————————————————————

Profit _____

Mechanism _____

WORKSHEET 12
Marketing Budget

Option Number _____

Tactics List

1. _____

2. _____

3. _____

4. _____

5. _____

Your Time

	Description	*Cost*
1.	_____	_____
2.	_____	_____
3.	_____	_____
4.	_____	_____
5.	_____	_____

Capital Needed

	Description	*Cost*
1.	_____	_____
2.	_____	_____
3.	_____	_____

4. _____   _____

5. _____   _____

Support Needed

	Description	Cost

1. _____   _____

2. _____   _____

3. _____   _____

4. _____   _____

5. _____   _____

WORKSHEET 13
Your Marketing Resources

Current Marketing Efforts

_____

_____

_____

_____

_____

_____

Capital Needed/Available

_____

_____

_____

_____

_____

_____

_____

Skills Checklist

Skill	*Source*
· Creative thinking	_____
· Copywriting	_____
· Graphic arts	_____
· Printed material composition	_____
· Printing production	_____
· Media handling	_____
· Public relations	_____
· Special material production	_____
· Human interaction	_____
· Presentation	_____

Office Production Capabilities

_____

_____

_____

7

Some Marketing Tactics

This chapter is divided into four areas that cover a wide range of marketing tactics. Helpful information on each tactic is given, along with some cost-saving tips. There is an abundance of practical information here, so take your time when familiarizing yourself with each tactic.

TANGIBLE MATERIALS

Brochures

You experience your firm and its services from the inside, but what do clients experience from your firm? Since your clients spend relatively little time at your office interacting with you or your staff, they primarily experience the written material that you produce.

Brochures are a good way to communicate some types of information to prospects and clients. They can be used to provide a general introduction to your firm and services or to describe specific products and services you offer.

Brochures also project your image, thus permitting clients and prospects to experience your firm from the outside. As a marketing tactic, brochures can capture the attention of prospects and create an interest in your firm. They are an important tool.

You will probably want to prepare a brochure that introduces prospects to your firm and that identifies you and your services. Explicitly, the brochure will indicate your qualifications and define your organization. Implicitly, it will project your professional image and your firm's image as a service organization. In this brochure, anticipate and answer the questions that prospects will raise (see Chapter 4 for details).

A brochure that introduces your firm should clearly establish its image. Ensure that the visual image is correctly represented by use of your logo, color scheme, and format. Remember that a corporate history or a list of community service activities helps to establish your firm's image as solid and durable.

You can also create brochures that describe specific products and services. Your cost/benefit analyses will indicate which specific brochures are needed. For example, while producing a brochure for a once-only seminar may be prohibitive in cost, producing a brochure for a service designed specially for a target segment may be cost-effective. In one of our examples, we developed a specialized service that could be called "Personal Financial Planning for the Practicing Physician"; this service would warrant individual treatment in a special brochure.

If you create a brochure that serves to educate and interest prospects in the concept of Personal Financial Planning, be sure to discuss the particular financial problems and needs of the target segment. Show how your service can satisfy these needs and stress the benefits that the prospect will derive.

When you create any brochure, use the AIDA technique. This mnemonic reminds you that brochures must: capture the reader's Attention, then hold his Interest as he reads in order to create a Desire for your services that results in Actions taken by the reader.

Each brochure should have an attractive, direct, and clear presentation of information that reflects your professional image. Use simple, consumer-oriented language. Keep the verbal text to a minimum and use short paragraphs. Photographs and illustrations will increase the production cost of a brochure substantially, but they can be worthwhile. Your professional organizations can provide you with examples of brochures, as can your competitors!

Provide information that directly benefits the reader. You can include do-it-yourself hints, business information, and personal financial planning tips as a goodwill gesture. Give enough information to be useful and to develop interest, but don't include so much that you eliminate the need for your services.

When you investigate the production of your first brochure, you will quickly discover that length, size, number of colors, and paper quality affect costs more than quantity. Keep costs low by using single-color graphics and a single sheet creatively. A brochure can be created by folding an 8½-by-11 inch sheet into thirds and printing on both sides. Multiple-page, multiple-color brochures get costly: from $500 to $1000 per page.

The average useful life of a brochure is three to four years. Get the greatest longevity from your brochures by excluding dated material. Consider using blank spaces and pockets for additional or changing information.

One purpose of a brochure is to communicate information. Since this can happen only when the brochure is distributed, carry ample supplies of your brochures with you. Also, keep a supply of each brochure on display in your reception area.

You can use a brochure as part or all of any tactic to reach new prospects. For example, you can direct mail a brochure to a purchased mailing list that represents a target segment. Or when a cross selling strategy is called for, you can mail a brochure to clients along with routine reports or statements.

Newsletter

What are the reasons for publishing a newsletter? First, a newsletter is a low-cost way to provide uniform information to all your clients at once. This makes an excellent tactic for cross selling new services and products.

Second, a carefully prepared and produced newsletter will project the image of an integrated, professional organization. The extra effort required to produce a newsletter will reflect your dedication to high-quality services. Thus, a newsletter can serve as a general public relations tactic.

Third, regular issues can alert clients to due dates. These issues help to remind clients that they are important to you even when you are not working with them individually. This is an important tactic for maintaining client loyalty.

You have several distribution options for your newsletter. Be creative in determining your distribution so that you get the best return on invested time and money. Your newsletter mailing list can include all clients or only specific portions of your client base. You might issue on a monthly basis to active clients and on a quarterly basis to others. Make use of extra large distributions at irregular intervals; for example, tax preparation time. Newsletters can also be coupled with purchased or exchanged mailing lists for use as a client base expansion tactic.

Choose whatever format and size you need. An 8½-by-11 inch newsletter of from four to eight pages is a good guide to follow. Standard sizes keep production costs low and facilitate storage and handling.

It will save you time and effort to establish an overall format at the beginning, including the kinds of articles that you will feature regularly. This keeps you on the lookout for specific material and allows you to create canned issues in advance. The content of each issue will be determined by events in the financial world, changes in your operation, and your strategic marketing plan.

You will need sources of information for the articles and features of each issue. You can find material in the newsletters and bulletins of your professional organization. Product information and bulletins are available from wholesalers of investment products and from the marketing departments of financial services companies. Learn to rely on your information network for ideas and articles. Scan newspapers, financial magazines, and books for possible newsletter material. Think well in advance, create canned issues, and start idea folders.

Create an inviting visual image for your newsletter by using lots of white space and a type font that is large and easy to read. Add zest to your layouts with low-cost special effects such as headlines, screening, photographs, and clip art cartoons. Explore the possibilities offered by rub-off and other lettering systems. Some sources of clip art are:

Volk Corporation
Post Office Box 72
Pleasantville, NJ 08232

Dynamic Graphics, Inc.
6707 N. Sheridan Road
Peoria, IL 61614

In any writing endeavor, it is important to have a clear definition of the intended audience. Remember this as you gain valuable information about your newsletter audience during the development of your strategic marketing plan. Use client base and target segment profiles to define your audience. Then find out what kinds of information they are seeking and determine the best method of presentation.

Be careful when you choose a name for your newsletter. The name should be memorable and should project an authoritative and professional image.

I cannot overemphasize the importance of producing and distributing each issue on a regular basis. Sloppily prepared, delayed, or missed issues will do more harm to your image than having no newsletter at all. Before you publish the first issue, have the next four month's issues ready, and have a full year's issues planned.

Unless you have graphic arts experience, seriously consider hiring a designer to create the master format of your newsletter. Select a professional with experience in newsletter preparation and provide the designer with all necessary background information.

Whether you hire a graphic artist or design the master format yourself, be sure to include the essential design features. Use a letterhead that includes the name and subtitle, logo and firm name, as well as date and issue numbering information. (The subtitle should describe the purpose and audience of the newsletter.) Include an author's box that gives the newsletter's publisher, editors, contributors, frequency of publication, fee, and copyright notice.

Select two or more local printers with newsletter experience. Use multiple suppliers and printers to cover emergencies and ensure regular distribution. Discuss paper requirements with these experts and examine variations in weight, color, texture, folding, and availability in order to optimize cost and image.

There are several channels for distribution of your newsletter. The obvious channel is via the mails, but do not overlook personal contact and display options. You may want to create a newsletter mailing list that has four sections. The first section can be composed of current and past clients, and the second may contain the names of qualified prospects. The third and fourth sections can be small, high leverage lists of influential groups and press organizations.

The material costs of producing and distributing a newsletter are reasonable. Typical printing and mail preparation costs for a four page newsletter are under one dollar per copy. To keep costs low, focus on keeping your writing, editing, and layout time to a minimum; delegate as much routine preparation work as possible.

An innovative approach to reducing newsletter costs is to sell advertising space. For example, you could devote the inner four pages of an eight page newsletter to advertising. You can either charge for partial- or full-page advertisements, or barter advertising space for expert services.

The best suggestion to control cost is not to be too ambitious. Consider the newsletter's role in your strategic marketing plan and confine your expenditures to fulfilling that role. You can produce a satisfactory in-house newsletter merely using colored copier paper. Start with the minimum issue frequency (e.g., quarterly) and distribute at higher frequencies only as needed.

Your printer can provide additional cost control suggestions, such as preprinting large quantities for the color portions of newsletter forms. You will also want to evaluate paperweight in light of postage costs. If timing is not critical to distribution, use bulk or third class mail for lower rates.

Bulletin Letters

The bulletin letter is an inexpensive tactic that has many of the advantages of a newsletter. Bulletins enable you to distribute information to a large audience—only in business letter format. They can be used to cross sell, as well as to expand or defend the customer base.

Bulletins are well suited for alerting specific market segments to environmental changes and to services that can meet their needs. Before you compose a bulletin letter, however, make sure you can define your audience and your purpose in writing in a single short paragraph for each. This will help you communicate your message succinctly and effectively.

It is important that your bulletins conform to your visual image. They can be produced on your letterhead or on a specially designed bulletin form. Preprinting a large volume of bulletin forms is one way to reduce production costs.

Remember to make good use of the postscript, as it is the one part of a letter that is always read. Use the postscript to motivate prospects or clients to act. And to avoid the look of mass production, use a ragged right margin. This will preserve the hand typed image of a personal letter.

You have the same distribution and mailing list options for bulletins as for brochures and newsletters. Your mailing lists can be either designed in-house or purchased for specific target segments.

Direct Mail

Mailing your message directly to suspects and prospects is one way of being certain to reach them. Direct mail works best as a cross selling or expansion tactic. In fact, when used for expansion purposes, direct mail campaigns can show prospect to client conversion rates as high as fifty percent (see Bissett in Bibliography). Direct mail is less cost-effective for promoting seminars because the low response rates require oversaturation of the potential market.

To be cost-effective, direct mail lists must reflect your specific target segments. Since the mailing pieces you produce must compete with countless others, you should give particular care to overcome the traditionally unprofessional image of direct mailing pieces.

Mailing lists are available from a number of sources. They can be purchased from list brokers at prices ranging from \$25 to \$200 per thousand names. Often, you can purchase mailing lists from local or national publications that are organized by geographic or demographic categories.

The more closely you can match a mailing list to your target segment, the more profitable your direct mail campaign will be. Take time to consider how the geographic or demographic organization of mailing lists can be used to reach your target market. For cross selling a new service, mailing lists can be extracted from your client files according to factors you specify. Specially created lists will cost more, but the expense is returned in increased effectiveness.

Once you have a good list of intended clients or prospects, do all you can to ensure that the message is not lost. Be prepared to spend more on the creation, artwork, and production of a direct mail piece than on other printed materials. Until you have gained experience, make use of direct marketing specialists.

When I first started to cross sell my services as a Financial Planner, the most common comment I received was, "I didn't know you did that kind of work, too." The possibilities for cross selling among my existing client base seemed too good to miss. Rather than conducting several separate direct mail campaigns, I created an integrated, ongoing direct mail system.

To do this, classify clients according to those additional services or products that should be directed to their attention. When a routine piece of mail is sent to clients, add a postscript and enclose printed information that describes the specific service or product you are cross selling. Record the date when each piece of information is sent. Eventually, you will systematically present the correct information to the correct client, with no additional mailing costs.

Tapes/Videos

Audiotapes and videotapes can be used in two distinct ways. First, they are powerful tools for improving your communication skills. Second, they can represent salable products.

To gain valuable insights into your behavior and mannerisms, tape yourself in role-playing situations. Record your trial runs of plan presentations, telephone solicitations, seminar presentations, and so forth. When you review these, you can spot problem areas.

Audiotapes are a good medium for low cost planning products. They can function just like the instruction book for a do-it-yourself service, but they have a more personal, more appealing effect. When you produce a tape, work from a prepared script. Also, make an objective assessment of your speaking voice and, if necessary, use a professional reader.

Tapes can work like brochures. If you continually give an introductory talk to prospects or new clients, consider recording it. Tapes have a temporary marketing advantage over other mailable items because of their novelty. While most business people have little patience for marketing mail, few can resist the temptation to play a properly introduced five or ten minute tape. You can produce copies of a taped program of any length.

With correct preparation, your seminars can be videotaped. While there is no market for financial videos as a product yet, you could show reruns of key seminars to prospects right in your office as an educational tool.

Speeches

Public relations work will do two good things for your practice. First, it will increase your business. Second, it will force you to focus on what you do well so that you ultimately improve the quality of your services. Public speaking is a tactic with a similar twofold return. It is a vehicle that forces you to transmit your image and message to the market so that you ultimately develop your presentation skills.

Public speaking can build your morale and your reputation. It lets you demonstrate your skills to prospects, enabling you to create a favorable image. The results of this kind of public relations work spread beyond your immediate audience with a cascade effect.

Of course, you need good presentation skills and appropriate material to deliver. Neither of these items requires large expenditures of time or capital. Presentation skills can be developed in a short period of time if you practice often. Prepared speeches, interview guides, and even slide presentations are often available from your professional organization and other sources.

You will find countless opportunities to speak and write about issues in finance and Personal Financial Planning since everyone is concerned with, and interested in, these topics. Prepared speeches can also be used as outlines for news programs or radio talk shows; this kind of guide is often appreciated by interviewers.

When you start to develop your skills at this tactic, practice often. Keep an active speaking schedule as you refine your presentations and spread your image. Investigate local speakers bureaus, check with women's organizations, and contact the local Chamber of Commerce for a list of civic organizations that need speakers. Write to the program chairpeople of these organizations and volunteer your services, enclosing an outline of your speech.

When no speaking opportunities present themselves, create them. Arrange a series of breakfast meetings, perhaps every other month, with local commercial banks. Make informative presentations either on issues in your area of expertise or on topics suggested by the organizations that you address. Similar information exchange programs can be arranged with any local professional organization.

Start the preparation of any speech with a clear definition of your purpose and audience. Remember, nobody is required to listen to what you have to say. If you can offer information that your audience wants and needs, you will be well received. As you practice, be open to constructive criticism and seek professional advice on your speaking skills. Videotape yourself for later critical review.

Presentations are enhanced when you develop speaking habits that let you communicate directly with the audience. Aim for a high degree of eye contact and audience awareness. Whatever system of scripts, outlines, or note cards that you use, keep them in the background.

People absorb information most quickly through their sense of sight, then through hearing. Therefore, use visual materials and props in your presentation. You need not confine yourself to flip chart graphs or diagrams; use creative visual props, such as children's toys, household objects, and flash cards to stimulate the audience's sense of sight for key points.

When you present a speech, do not stand frozen behind the podium. Use body language to keep your audience visually stimulated and attentive. Therefore, when you use a microphone, be sure to use one that lets you move around—even if you have to supply your own.

Try to develop a speaking style that radiates confidence and enthusiasm. Take time to link your topic to the needs and concerns of the audience before you deliver the body of your material. Keep your material brief, deliver it in a topical rather than an educationsl style, and remember to thank each audience for its time and attention.

There is a memory aid for successful speaking engagements. The mnemonic is: A PIE. This reminds you of four important factors. The first is Attitude. Your attitude toward the material and the audience must be positive and enthusiastic.

The second is Preparation. You must have, and convey, a thorough knowledge of the material that you present. The material must be clearly expressed and well organized.

The third is Interest. You may want to move beyond visual innovations to keep your audience interested. Slogans, examples, and case histories are a few additional ways to engage and interest people.

The fourth is Enthusiasm. When you study human nature, you will find that we empathize with others. Use this to your advantage by projecting enthusiasm for your topic and audience; your audience will catch your enthusiasm and mirror it back.

The capital outlays for speaking presentations are minimal. In some cases, you will even be paid a speaker's fee! If you have good writing and presentation skills, you can prepare your speeches yourself. Otherwise, you may want to hire the help of a writer. Test the final version of any speech yourself in order to ensure that all technical terms and concepts are adjusted to the comprehension level of your audience.

The greatest resource expenditure will be your time. This too can be optimized by careful attention to your speaking schedule. Public speaking can be a rewarding way to turn leisure hours into productive time.

Gifts to Clients

Small useful gifts are a good tactic to keep you in the mind of a prospect. Consider some of the low cost booklets that are available; you can have your name imprinted on each copy. These have titles such as:

- Pocketax
- Social Security Benefits
- Tax Breaks for Buying or Selling a House
- Business Expense Log

Gifts like pens, calendars, memo pads, and telephone reference cards also make a good defensive tactic. They keep your name in the mind of the client, provided that they are seen and used.

DIRECT INTERACTION

Networking

Interpersonal networks are a valuable source of prospects, and your networking efforts can double as a public relations tactic. The success of this tactic depends on a basic human tendency: We prefer to do business with people we know, rather than strangers. Networking means making friends of your business allies, and business allies of your friends. Networks do not develop by themselves. You will have to create the networks you use and maintain them in an ongoing process.

In order to network, make a mailing list of everyone with whom you have ever had contact. Tell these people about the services you offer and the kind prospects you need. Often you will reap a good harvest of prospects from those people with whom you simply wanted to network. When your network is working well, members will continually send you prospect names.

Just as you would build a client base, so must you build a network. You need to make new contacts in your service area to fine tune your network. Therefore, join professional, fraternal, trade, and public service organizations and be active in those areas that bring you into contact with people.

A good networking technique is to form a "tip club" with local financial professionals. This club can meet on a monthly basis in order to exchange prospect leads. Try to limit membership to under twenty to create strong rapport among the members, and be sure to have only one representative of each profession! The club can be organized in an informal fashion or with a constitution and bylaws.

There are three rules to remember when networking. First, follow through on prospect leads. If a member of your network provides you with a prospect name and you fail to follow through, that member will be hesitant about providing more names. Remember, if you do unsatisfactory work, your network member will hear about it from the disgruntled prospect.

Second, always acknowledge and express gratitude for prospect leads from your networkers. Provide them with feedback about inappropriate leads or prospects, but let them know that you need and value their contributions.

This leads to the third rule: reciprocate. Networking works only when it is of mutual interest and benefit to all network members. Make it worthwhile in terms of reciprocity for your networkers to provide you with leads. Send business back into your network to keep it running smoothly. We'll look into methods of accounting for reciprocity in the next topic— referrals.

Referrals

Client referrals can be a major, even primary source of new clients for you. The personal recommendation of a prospect's accountant, attorney, or broker carries weight. Creating a professional referral network or improving your referral relations with local financial professionals is an essential expansion tactic.

The key to getting referrals is in giving them. Get into the habit of considering referrals when you encounter specific client problem situations. Don't hesitate to make referrals to your existing clients. This is an excellent defensive use of the tactic.

You must also show your appreciation for receiving referrals. Express your gratitude immediately by telephone, and follow with a letter. The sooner you know local professionals on a personal basis, the sooner they will make referrals to you. Again, join organizations that help you make this connection.

It is important to reciprocate on referrals in a balanced fashion. Of course, you must keep your client's interests above your needs to reciprocate. Beyond this, ensure that referrals are returned in like proportion. To maintain this balance, keep a log book of referrals.

Make a separate page in a three-ring binder for each source of referrals. At the top, record the name, address, and telephone number of the firm or person. List the names of associates and their specialties as applicable. Divide the rest of the page into two columns, one for referrals received and the other for referrals given.

For each client you refer to a source, record the date, the client name, and the specific nature of the service sought. For each prospect that is referred to you, enter the same information. This log book will tell you at a glance when your referrals are in balance.

It is a good practice to refer clients to at least two sources in each situation. Not only does this involve your client in the selection process, but it doubles your referral activities in the perception of the receiving sources.

Bird Dogs

I tried to devise a more polite term for this tactic. It's possible to think of names less harsh, but not more descriptive. Bird dogs are those business people with whom you interact who can provide you with valuable information about your business community.

Staff accountants, office supply salespeople, personnel agencies, and support service salespeople all have constant access to your competitors. Since they often have valuable information on the activities of your competition, you should cultivate their relationships and use their information so they function as an effective defensive tactic. They can warn you of a competitor's organizational or service changes before it is too late to respond.

Bird dogs can also function as an expansion tactic. For example, I have several friends in construction and related industries who keep me advised of housing projects. By knowing the size of a new subdivision and the asking price of the units being built, I can develop a strategic marketing plan for the new prospects before they have even moved into my service area.

Professional Organizations

We have already noted several tactics that profit from membership in professional organizations. Professional organizations, with their pooled membership resources and common interest, offer unique public relations capabilities. Membership is a good public relations and expansion tactic in its own right. Further, membership in professional organizations forms and maintains the interpersonal contacts necessary for your success.

Retain your professional membership in your area of expertise and add memberships for your new Personal Financial Planning activities. When you join an organization, strive to fill positions of responsibility and leadership. Focus on those activities that will maximize your business contacts.

Remember that one of the primary purposes of a professional organization is to help its members succeed. Keep abreast of the information, services, and education programs that your organizations offer. Take advantage of opportunities to develop your skills and practice.

Breakfast Meetings

A series of breakfast meetings with local financial professionals is an effective tactic for developing business allies and can be part of your networking and referral activities. Essentially, you exchange your expert information and advice for the opportunity to contact and work with the professionals you address.

Try to arrange a series of three or more meetings to strengthen the rapport that you want to create. The series can meet as often as is convenient for your audience, but try to keep it regular. Good frequencies are twice a month, monthly, and alternate months. Meetings more or less frequent than this provide either too much or too little contact.

Keep the meetings short, preferably an hour or less. Make a brief, organized presentation of the topic issue and allow time for a question-and-answer period. For topics that lie outside your area of expertise, enlist the support of members of your expert team. Be prepared to record questions that you must research and answer on your own time.

Of course, you can produce luncheon or dinner meetings, but breakfast meetings have advantages over either of these options. The most obvious advantage is that breakfast is a less expensive meal to provide. The subtle advantages lie in the timing of breakfast meetings. At the beginning of the day, your audience will be more alert, be less distracted, and have fewer crises emerge to throw your meeting schedule off than at later points in the day.

Seminars

The seminar is a tactic that focuses on direct personal contact with prospects and clients. When marketed, produced, and presented correctly, seminars can be highly cost-effective. However, they are seldom an inexpensive tactic to employ.

Seminars can be viewed from two perspectives. They can be either a service that you offer for profit or a marketing tactic that you use to generate prospects and clients. They can be used in cross selling new services and products, or as part of a prospect development cycle that expands your client base. Seminars also make an ideal test marketing tactic because of their limited scope, controllable cost, and potential for feedback.

Like brochures and public speaking, seminars convey information. And in preparing and presenting seminars, you also have the opportunity to learn more about the topics you treat.

Seminar participants must derive benefits from attending. Your attention to the purpose and audience of each seminar will ensure a valuable exchange of information. Beyond providing information that your audience needs, however, seminars are a good forum for educating prospects about your firm and its services and products.

You can rely on an effective seminar program to generate a high proportion of the new clients you need—typically up to one third of new clients. Such seminar marketing will be cost-effective only when ongoing programs allow you to spread the development costs over time. The fixed cost of developing seminar materials can range from $2000 to $4000. In addition, each program will have variable marketing and presentation costs, typically between $1000 and $2000. These arise from direct mail marketing, follow-up and reservation activities, room rental, guest speaker fees, and your own time.

Multiple-session seminar programs are more cost-effective than single-session programs because they result in a higher percentage of prospect-to-client conversions. Single-session seminar programs typically yield 20 percent closing rates, while multiple-session programs result in up to 50 percent closing rates. Prospects will be more inclined to make use of your services when they are better informed and when they have invested more of their own time in a seminar program.

When you consider using seminars as a tactic, make sure you determine your purpose first. Will the program be offered as a profitable service or as an expansion tactic? Seminars are an economical way for you to present information to multiple prospects simultaneously, but the real objective may be to get new clients into your office. Design and market your seminars to reflect your strategic marketing plan: as a needed service, as a tactic to secure and nurture prospects, as a public relations effort, or as a direct marketing program for your products and services.

When you have a clear purpose for this tactic, you should determine the audience you need to attract. What market segment do you want to reach with the seminar program? Once you have determined the segment that you want to reach, you can determine what needs must be addressed and how best to illustrate your service's answers to these needs.

Direct mail marketing is a good way to promote seminars, but be prepared for low response rates. If you can generate from a one-half percent to a one percent response, you are doing well! This means that you need an extensive mail campaign. For example, in order to secure an audience of one hundred people, you can expect to mail up to three thousand pieces.

Start the seminar marketing activities well in advance. Carefully select the date, place, and time of day to minimize conflicts with community or personal affairs. Make sure the location you choose is central to your target market segment and has ample parking space.

Be sure to include all essential information in your mailing piece. Clearly identify your firm as the presenter of the seminar; and highlight the date, time, place, and duration of the seminar. List the topics that will be covered. You can motivate prospects to attend by describing who can benefit from the seminar, and how.

Your mailing piece can be simple or elaborate, depending on your cost/ benefit analysis. You can produce a bulletin, flyer, or brochure to market your seminar. A brochure will give you additional space to describe your programs. It lets you introduce issues in Personal Financial Planning, discuss the benefits of each program, and show the advantages in using your firm. Economize by creating a brochure that describes your overall seminar program; then supplement it with bulletin cover letters that detail each session.

Make attendance convenient by including a reservation form or ticket as part of your mailing piece. If you include complementary tickets, you can extend the coverage of your mailing campaign. Mail the volumes you need for an adequate response, but don't mail more than you and your staff can follow up by phone. Follow-up is essential, both to motivate prospects and to get an accurate measure of response.

When you make follow-up calls, use a telephone script to facilitate and optimize the process. When a prospect declines to attend, ask for the names of others who might wish to attend. Try to find out if the prospect is disinterested or merely has a scheduling problem. Prospects who express real interest can be offered the option of attending a future seminar or of scheduling a convenient office appointment.

Seminar topics will be determined by your evaluation of the target segment's needs and interests. Don't try to address all the problems in one session; group the problems into related topics. Topics could include family financial planning, year-end tax planning, or budgeting. You can also develop specialized topics for narrow segments, such as financial planning for spouses or for specific professions.

There are a few simple techniques that will help you present a seminar effectively. Always stand during your presentation; this gives you a psychological advantage over a seated audience and helps you establish your authority. Familiarize yourself with the room in advance so that you can control the lighting, temperature, and public address system—not vice versa.

Review and follow the suggestions for effective public speaking discussed previously in this chapter. Use a microphone that permits mobility, and test the volume before you start the presentation. Minimize distractions in the room and in your behavior; wear low-key clothing and avoid playing with the podium equipment, your materials, or the microphone cord.

End each session with the distribution of an evaluation sheet. This mechanism will provide you with valuable feedback on your topic, the information you present, and your presentation methods. Evaluation sheets can take the form of a checklist with a rating scale of from 1 to 5 (low to high) and a combination of fill-in-the-blank questions. Ask for an evaluation of the following:

· How useful was the information?
· How effective was the presentation?

- What did you like best?
- What did you like least?
- How can the presentation be more effective?
- How concerned are you with:

    Capital Growth

    Income (present)

    Income at Retirement

    Income Tax Deferral or Reduction

    Liquidity

    Security of Your Principal

- On what would you like more information?
(List your products and services here.)

Use the evaluation form to solicit the names of others who would be interested in either this seminar or related topics. Since your seminar audience represents a cross section of your target market segment, you can survey the segment's needs for future seminars, services, and products. Use a few pertinent questions that get the information you want.

Create an effective closing for each seminar that motivates and leads the prospects to action. Ideally, the action taken will be an increased use of your services. Tell the audience what the next step is and how to make it happen. Include a request box on the evaluation form to make it easy for interested prospects to arrange for an appointment.

The average Financial Planner now presents eleven seminars per year (see Bissett in Bibliography). As I stated previously, the marketing, production, and presentation of seminars is expensive. To keep costs down, develop ongoing programs and multiple-session seminars that let you spread the development costs. Remember that multiple-session seminars will yield higher closing rates.

To save on the cost of developing seminar material, use the published seminar scripts available from your professional organization and financial planning support firms and networks. Investigate the possibilities of cosponsoring seminars with charitable organizations and local newspapers. Also, enlist time and capital support from financial product wholesalers in your area to reduce costs. Where possible, present seminars in your own office.

Telephone Calls

Before we examine the telephone as a marketing tactic, check your telephone image against the guidelines below. Public relations efforts have significant long-term marketing results. Just as you have a visual image, you also have a telephone image. Make sure that your prospects and clients experience a consistent, uniform image in all their interactions with your firm.

1. Project your personality and emotions through your voice. Your facial expressions actually affect the timbre of your voice, so behave as if prospects and clients were face-to-face with you. On the telephone, show the same courtesy, concern, and attention that you would in direct confrontation.

2. Don't put people on hold if you can avoid it.

3. Return calls within a reasonable period of time; that is, within a 24-hour period, if not the same day.

4. Always have pencil and pad in hand when you answer the telephone. When you make a call, be ready with all the materials that you will need.

The telephone can be used as both a client base expansion tool and as a defensive tactic. Your main interest may lay in expanding your market through telephone solicitation, but consider the ways in which you can use the telephone to defend your client base. Many routine maintenance services can be performed by telephone, thus saving time and money for you and your clients. Periodic calls to your clients can serve to remind them that you value their business and are protecting their interests.

Cold calls are rarely a favored tactic, yet about 30 percent of all Financial Planners use telephone solicitation. Even though it takes from 15 to 20 telephone calls to generate one client, the low costs make it a viable tactic.

Telephone solicitation involves low capital outlay, but high time costs. To be cost-effective, you must use your time efficiently. Efficiency results from selective calling lists and the careful use of references. Carefully prepared or selected calling lists can double the number of leads generated with each session of calls. Further improvements are possible when you can mention that a mutual contact has suggested that you call.

To make efficient use of your time, develop and use a telephone script. This ensures that you anticipate possible responses and cover all the necessary points. Give some initial thought to the script, and refine it as you gain experience. To keep you on target, your script should treat beginning, middle, and end situations.

Begin by introducing yourself and defining your service. Mention a mutual contact, a community involvement, or any additional references that will help the prospect identify and recognize you. State the purpose of your call. Be honest and direct: You want the chance to compete for his Personal Financial Planning business.

Move to the middle of your conversation by showing your awareness of the prospect's needs and problems. If the prospect is receptive, ask questions that will establish his value as a potential client. For example, ask if he knows his income tax bracket. If he does not know or declines to answer, ask if he paid more than a certain amount in income taxes. You can determine an attractive amount for each of your market segments.

Expand a discussion of the prospect's needs and goals in order to show what benefits he can realize with your help. Even when the prospect uses a competing adviser, your knowledge and genuine concern for his needs can make a favorable impression. Be prepared to send responsive prospects follow-up letters with your business card.

Always end your conversation by thanking the prospect for his time. Of course, the ideal next step is to arrange an appointment. When a prospect balks at a meeting, suggest sending additional printed information about your firm and areas in which he has expressed interest. Offer subscription to your newsletter or attendance at a seminar as a gradual approach to doing business together.

Teaching

Teaching a course in Personal Financial Planning has many of the advantages offered by producing a seminar. You come into direct contact with prospects and learn while you teach.

Courses offered in conjunction with community service groups are a solid public relations tactic. Your image as a community member and an expert in your field will be enhanced by your teaching activities.

Teaching has far fewer logistical and cost drawbacks than public speaking or seminar presentation. The community college, service group, or organization with which you work will handle schedules, locations, and even provide the audience. In many cases the fee that you charge can cover your expenses or result in a small profit.

The costs of this tactic arise from preparation of the material and your time. These costs can be minimized if you use the same sources and approaches for your course material as you would for a seminar or public speech. Teaching adult education courses after business hours is another way to convert leisure time to productive time.

Trade Shows

Over 7500 trade shows are held annually in this country. These shows attract audiences with specific interests and affiliations. Exhibiting at a trade show is a good expansion tactic when you can find a match of audience interests with those of a target market segment. To be cost-effective, you must have a good match because exhibition costs are high.

When you use this tactic, be clear about your purpose and audience. Do you want to get prospect leads, introduce a new service or product, or build your name recognition? Who will be attending the show, and how do they relate to your target segment?

As a guideline, multiply the number of contacts you want to achieve by $50, and budget accordingly. A simple tabletop exhibit will cost about $1500, while a modular 8-by-10 foot display panel with artwork can cost $5000. Booth rental will range from $50 to $1000, depending on the size and location of the trade show as well as on the booth itself. In addition to these fixed costs, you will need to staff the booth, provide handout materials, and pay for your travel and lodging.

When you register to exhibit at a trade show, find out what the booth rental fee includes and excludes. You may need to provide table skirting, a carpet, and chairs; these can be rented locally rather than purchased. Similarly, you can rent a display module rather than buying it outright.

Rent enough booth space to create a simple and uncluttered display. Good booth locations are those that receive high traffic, so study the floor plan and make a considered choice. When you plan the layout of your display area, create an open space with tables to the sides and back. This invites people to enter your booth.

Make your display visually attractive by organizing it around a single visual theme. Reflect your visual image in the display and in all the materials you will use and distribute. Remember that you must identify your firm and services in the time it takes a prospect to walk past your booth, typically from four to six seconds.

Market your exhibit vigorously before the show starts to make prospects aware of your presence. Extend personal and direct mail invitations, and advertise in trade journals.

When working the exhibit, be enthusiastic and energetic. Stand rather than sit. If you use additional people to staff the booth, select them with care. Make sure they understand the needs of your prospects, know your service and product capabilities, and can project the correct image. Prepare yourself and your staff with some leading questions to start visitor dialogues.

Of course, you will want to be well-groomed and neatly dressed, and you will need a large name tag. Keep your booth neat and tidy, and have ample handout supplies and business cards. Develop a simple method for capturing prospect name and address information; don't place this burden on visitors to your booth. Above all, be confident and sell yourself.

MEDIA TECHNIQUES

How to Use Media

An alternate title for this topic is "Free Advertising." This is the benefit that you can derive from an informed use of newspaper, radio, and television companies in your area.

Free media coverage offers less control and less exposure than paid advertising, but it is a solid ongoing public relations tactic. It can enhance your name recognition, add third party credibility, and reach a large market audience.

How do you get free advertising? By making contact with media people and letting them know what kind of source and resource you can be for them. Consider how you interact with valuable contacts in your own networks. If you take the time to establish a rapport and exchange of information with media people, you will become regarded as a reliable and valued contact. The media people will be sure to reciprocate your efforts.

Start by getting familiar with the newspapers and the radio and television stations in your area. Subscribe to local newspapers and use them for your specific advertising needs. Cover all of the companies in your area, not just your favorites.

Make contact with the business editors of local newspapers, television stations, and radio stations. Call to introduce yourself and express your interest in becoming a source for their information needs. Determine the kinds of news and information that would be of interest to their public and for which you have unique access. Meet with them face-to-face when you can. Name recognition is the key here, so follow up by mailing them your business card attached to a rolodex card, along with a few notes that indicate your speciality.

Stimulate the relationship by sending unsolicited items of information that their readers would enjoy: new facts about topics of current interest and comments on material they present. Make use of editorial reply letters to demonstrate your knowledge and sincere interest. When you can, send some other articles that you have had published to make them feel safe about publishing your materials.

Your professional organization may be able to provide you with lists of local media contact people. Some other sources of media contacts follow.

Bacon's Publicity Checker. This lists the business and financial editors of approximately 700 daily newspapers and is available from:

> Bacon's Publishing Company
> 14 E. Jackson Boulevard
> Chicago, IL 60604

The Broadcasting Annual. This provides similar information on most television and radio stations in the United States. Contact:

> Broadcasting Magazine
> 1735 Desales, NW
> Washington, DC 20036

Directory of Publications. This is a cross-indexed source of information on 20,000 newspapers, magazines, and college, university, and trade publications. It can be ordered from:

> Ayer Press
> West Washington Square
> Philadelphia, PA 19106

Once you have established yourself as a member of these organizations' information networks, work hard at being a good one! Be concise, reliable, and agreeable when the media calls. Even if you get no publicity this time, they too keep score and will probably repay you the next time.

Remember your allies in the media as people, too. Put them on your Christmas card list. Acknowledge their work and offer congratulations on awards they receive. Invite them to speeches, open houses, breakfast meetings, special events, and community projects with which you are involved.

When you have a specific news item about your firm, prepare a news release that follows the points discussed later in this chapter. When there is no news to release but you still want media coverage, volunteer your services as a source for expert quotes and comments on current situations. Send editors and reporters your monthly newsletter; highlight interesting items to reinforce your name recognition. Keep yourself in their minds and be readily accessible to them at home and at the office.

You can also devise ways to make news when there is none. For example, you can make a donation of books to your community library. Then have your photograph taken at the presentation and display it in your reception area. And be sure to get coverage when prominent visitors attend events that you sponsor.

Paid Advertising

Of all the possibilities for paid advertising, newspaper and *Yellow Pages* advertising are the most popular with Financial Planners. These seem to be the most cost-effective methods, but local costs and market characteristics can make a difference.

Advertising is seldom effective as a segregated tactic, so be prepared to use it in conjunction with other tactics. Use paid advertising to augment tactics that expand your customer base, cross sell new services, or promote seminars or other special events. To be effective as an isolated tactic, paid advertising must be consistent and ongoing. Remember this when you explore the costs of an advertising program.

Despite the high costs, an advertising campaign can establish your firm's name, reputation, and credibility with the mass market. It requires only a low level of personal involvement once initiated and reaches a large, diverse audience.

Unfortunately, the quality of prospect leads generated will vary greatly unless you devise a program that reaches a specific audience. The follow-up required for prospects in diverse market segments is more time intensive. There is a lower conversion rate from prospects to clients. The high initial and ongoing costs make paid advertising less cost-effective than seminar programs.

Advertising costs range from the reasonable to the near infinite. Creation of artwork and text can range from $1000 to $50,000. Typesetting and pasteup costs are more predictable but can also run into thousands of dollars. Even with these costs budgeted, media space is still a variable cost.

Media space can be purchased from local or metropolitan newspapers, news magazines, specific financial publications such as *The Wall Street Journal*, inflight magazines, and trade and professional publications. Although the cost of national coverage for radio or television advertisements is prohibitive, local radio and cable television advertising is worth considering.

Obviously, the content and format of your advertisements will depend on your purpose and the media used. In all cases, make sure that the advertisements conform to your overall professional stance and image.

Advertising that promotes your seminars or other special events should capture the prospect's attention, indicate the benefits of attending, and provide the information needed to register or attend. Ads intended to expand your customer base should be focused around an attention-getting theme or hook. They should provide the information that you want to convey and should make it easy for prospects to inquire further.

In a printed advertisement, for example, you could include a picture of a cookie jar to emphasize that financial planning isn't what it used to be. This theme of economic change can be developed to detail services offered that are needed in today's environment. Make it easy to identify your firm with the prominent use of your logo, and list your locations and telephone numbers. When you advertise to a market outside your local telephone exchange, provide a toll-free number.

To keep your creative and development costs low, use a local marketing firm. When it's time to consider broader coverage, remember that most large publications have different geographic or even demographic distributions. Use those distributions that cover your target segments.

When you consider buying television or radio time to advertise, don't get locked onto the idea of using costly prime time. When you want to change a person's attitude, present your message when that person is alone. During prime time, people often watch and listen in groups, while during off time, they usually watch alone such programs as late night movies, Saturday morning programs, or sports events. Off time advertising can be doubly effective if it helps you reach your specific target segments.

Start your advertising programs on a small, local scale. Monitor queries as a percentage of the circulation or audience reached by the medium; this is the best way to measure the effectiveness of your advertising. As a guideline, over 0.25 percent is considered a big success for a newspaper advertising campaign. Overall, a good publicity program can cost one or two percent of your sales volume. A specifically targeted advertising program can cost up to five percent of your sales volume.

Press Releases

Here are some guidelines for using press releases as a tactic for free advertising. These pointers are important since your news will compete with countless other releases. It is important for you to provide your media contacts with accurate, genuine news or information of value.

Send your press release to all members of your media mailing list. When you make a media contact, find out what the deadlines are and record this as part of your mailing list. Media people work to sharp deadlines, so distribute your release well in advance.

Keep the text of your release simple, direct, and concise. Lean toward the use of short sentences and paragraphs; use language that the average reader will understand. Type on only one side of the page and limit yourself to one or two pages. Be sure to use actual dates of events, not relative terms, as today or tomorrow.

Your text should be informally written but factual. Do not make editorial comments or offer personal opinions. Make sure you personally read the copy, and double check the facts, names, dates, titles, and addresses. When it is appropriate, include a 4-by-5 inch or 5-by-7 inch photograph.

When you write your press release, keep the specific needs of the editor or reporter in mind. If you provide no news, there is no story. Editing cuts usually start at the bottom of a submission, so make sure that the most important elements of your release are presented at the top. When you are releasing news about your firm and services or about the financial industry, format the release as a news bulletin. When you are making a comment, format the release as an interview. Don't forget the W5H formula; who, what, where, when, why, and how.

Most news services will not print or mention a telephone number. However, if you want your release to generate prospect inquiry calls, put your name and city at the beginning of your text. Even though you provide your media contacts with plenty of lead time, there is no guarantee that your release will be used when you want, or even at all.

You can improve the chances of your release being used if you write a brief cover letter. This letter should provide a summary of what the release is, and how and why you think it could be used. Make your releases attractive and complete. Your media contacts should not need to call you for additional information or clarification, but include all your telephone numbers in case they do.

Follow up on your distribution of a release with a telephone call to ensure that it was received, but do not pressure your media contacts to use it. When a media contact uses one of your releases or articles, send a thank you note but do not press for more coverage.

Cable Television and Radio Shows

Public relations work that puts your name before the prospects you seek will make a difference. However, it is difficult to measure how much a public relations effort actually contributes to success.

Because direct marketing has a specific target market segment, results are easier to quantify and monitor. Even though there is little quantitative information on the cost-effectiveness of producing your own radio or television show, many successful Financial Planners use such shows as their major ongoing public relations tactic.

If you are overwhelmed at the thought of a weekly series show, consider exploring this tactic with a single special presentation or an interview on a current topic. Consult the program directors of your local stations to explore the possibilities of appearing as a guest on a talk show.

Your appearance, show, or series must present something of interest and value to the audience. Again, your professional society may be able to provide pattern speeches or interview guidelines on various topics. These can form the basis for a special presentation show or can be used as outlines for news programs, talk shows, and interviews. Providing an outline script can motivate producers and interviewers to work with you.

Creating material for a weekly program can be relatively simple. For instance, your show could cover selected topics in Personal Financial Planning, using a moderator and panel format for discussions or talk shows. Each topic could be discussed by a specially chosen panel that was selected from among your expert team or local financial professionals with whom you work.

Production costs for local or cable shows are highly variable, but in most cases the station will be glad to help. When exploring the possibilities, try to find ways to make the program material do double or triple duty. Can you use audiotapes or videotapes of the shows as later educational products? Will local radio stations run the audio portions of taped panel or talk shows?

Be prepared to take full advantage of the exposure you can get from radio and television shows. You will probably find yourself in demand as a speaker once your show is established.

Newspaper Column and Editorial Space

Making use of editorial space in local or national newspapers is another kind of free advertising that serves as a public relations tactic. The general extension of your image, bolstered by third party credibility, will broaden and strengthen the platform from which you conduct your practice.

You can create regular appearances in your local newspapers by producing a Personal Financial Planning column. Weekly or monthly columns can précis the content of your newsletters, discuss topical financial issues, provide helpful tips, or answer specific reader enquiries in "Dear Abby" style. Discuss the possibilities with the business editors of your local newspapers.

Yellow Pages

An effective *Yellow Pages* listing and advertisement is an important part of your image and accessibility, both to clients and prospects. Consider how many times you have consulted this section of the telephone directory to find a service that you needed.

When you create a *Yellow Pages* advertisement, rely on your own experience to determine what works. Visual recognition plays an important role here, so feature your logo or slogan to help prospects identify your ad. Make sure to list all your services, highlighting your areas of specialization or expertise. Consider pooling the resources of your expert network to produce one large advertisement that gives the names of each member.

Examine the possibility of advertising in specialized directories that are produced by your local telephone company or by independent publishers.

Those mundane, dog-eared, *Yellow Pages* take on a new glimmer when you consider them as a part of your strategic marketing plan. Make sure you review all the things that you do "just as a regular part of doing business" from the marketing perspective. Are your business cards and letterhead design important in marketing your services? Does your telephone answering machine help you with cross selling?

COMMUNITY INVOLVEMENT

Public service and community involvement is a win/win situation; it helps both your community and your business. Getting involved in your community is a public relations tactic that can defend or expand your customer base. Since everyone can benefit from your involvement, don't hesitate to use it to your advantage.

Public service enhances your name recognition and image as a solid, durable member of the community. It gives you the opportunity to interact with a broad spectrum of the market in your service area while you are developing communication and presentation skills.

volunteer your skills for tax return preparation assistance programs, help sponsor community events, or donate your expertise to service organizations.

You have many of the financial skills needed by community organizations, but try to go beyond offering background help. If you join an organization, aspire to a leadership role. Work to project your image as an authority and a leader in order to develop trust in your ability.

Familiarize yourself with the organizations in your area. These will be many and varied, but will usually include:

- Hospitals
- Churches
- Parent-teacher associations
- The Chamber of Commerce
- Kiwanis, Rotary, Lions, and other service clubs
- Welcome Wagon groups
- Meals on Wheels services
- Sports associations

Learn about the activities and membership of each group and about the people they serve. Join or work with the groups that will put you in contact with your target market segments.

If your schedule will not permit the needed expenditure of time, consider contributing financially. Creating a scholarship is an excellent community service tactic. Scholarships for high school and college students need not be expensive, yet they give you abundant public relations exposure over long periods of time.

When you serve your community, project a good image. Be capable and expert in your areas of expertise but be warm and personable, too. Let your community see you as the kind of person who can be a trusted financial adviser.

Whether or not you realize it, you do public relations work each time you meet or interact with another person. Keep this in mind even in relaxed or informal situations. You may be the only exposure someone has to a Financial Planner. Let people know you are in the business of Personal Financial Planning and be prepared to discuss topical issues.

Discussing financial problems in an informal setting is always tricky. Of course, you want to be helpful and solve the problem, but you would also like to be paid for your efforts. Let people know your capabilities, but do not hesitate to cast any real problem solving efforts into a business context.

Human interaction is a vast and rapidly growing area of study. In the last two chapters we focused on how to interest prospects in buying your services. In the next chapter, we'll look at the human interactions involved in handling prospects once you have found them.

8

Deliver Your Service: Handling the Client

SELLING VERSUS MARKETING—THE KILLER GAP

In Chapter 6, when we discussed implementing and monitoring your strategic marketing plan, we looked at some of the gaps that can occur between expected and actual results. There is one gap that we didn't discuss. This gap is so critical that it warrants a chapter of its own.

What is the killer gap? It is the space between the prospect and the client. No matter how many prospects you have as a result of your marketing efforts, you will not succeed until you convert them from prospects into clients. The frustration of reaching good prospects and then losing them at the first meeting is tremendous. Hopefully, my observations and experience about handling prospects and clients in face-to-face situations can spare you some of these frustrations.

This book focuses on marketing your Personal Financial Planning Services and once you make contact with a prospect, your marketing efforts are complete. However, this book would be incomplete if it ended when the prospect walked in your door. Now you must sell your services to the prospect. This selling occurs on a personal level and requires your best human interaction efforts—people skills. Converting a prospect to a client is an intensely personal interaction. Often the conversion must take place during the difficult situation of a short initial meeting.

How do you turn prospects into clients, and new clients into long-term clients? Your marketing efforts will bring prospects to your door, but what about the final decision to buy your services? Why will a prospect choose your services over those of your competition? To be sure, there are quantitative and objective factors involved, but the factor that outweighs them all is of a personal and subjective nature. The prospect will choose a *person*, not a service, product, or firm, to entrust with his financial future. He will choose the Financial Planner whom he considers a trusted, knowledgeable, objective professional. Even though you've done all you can to project the correct image in impersonal ways, the big test takes place when you meet the prospect.

Let's find out what builds trust and what projects a favorable image during face-to-face contact with a prospect. First, we'll discuss some topics concerning prospects and clients; then we'll look at the initial meeting. The first meeting, the first impression you make on the prospect is critical. If you get it right, the rest will follow.

YOUR COMMITMENT

When I caution you to carefully consider whether Personal Financial Planning is for you, I'm not trying to discourage you. There really is a qualitative difference between most financial professions and the job of the Financial Planner. I don't want you to develop a service and design a strategic marketing plan, only to discover after your first ten clients that Personal Financial Planning requires more human interaction than you prefer.

Both human interaction and human psychology figure largely in your role as Financial Planner. Since the ultimate test of a successful financial plan is whether it results in a client's happiness, you must be prepared to deal with the full range of human emotions when you take on the job of dream mechanic.

No financial plan has value in and of itself. Value can be realized only when your client acts to implement your plan. Often, you must motivate apathetic clients to take steps that will improve their own lives. To motivate prospects to buy your services, you must understand some human motivational psychology. Your willingness to learn about and to deal with human emotion and psychology will determine your business success.

To deliver a high quality Personal Financial Planning Service, you must develop a full rapport with each and every client. Remember, to optimize a client's emotional satisfaction, you must know his motivations and dreams. Before a client will work with you in these areas, he must trust you.

An associate of mine owns an expensive foreign sports car. I overheard him talking with a friend about some repair work he was having done. He recommended his mechanic by saying, "Sure, he's expensive, but I can trust him." Sound familiar? When we buy the services of an expert, we consider objective facts such as time and cost. But when we make our decision, we decide in favor of doing business with a person whom we trust. Considerations of trust often override those of cost.

Before a prospect will let you be the mechanic of his dreams, he must trust you. Trust depends on the projected image (and the image that the prospect receives) of your objectivity. Prospects and clients must know that you put their personal interests above yours.

To convince a prospect that you are sincere and trustworthy, you must be prepared to develop a detailed knowledge of the person and his problems. To be active and effective in the fantasy/dream/goal interfaces, you must be your client's trusted adviser. To reach and serve a wide range of prospects and clients, you must be exceptionally flexible in your values and attitudes; your values and attitudes must never influence or intrude upon your client. Impossible though these goals may seem, you can reach them if you are aware and committed.

We've discussed the kinds of commitment and philosophy you need to create a high quality, professional service. We've talked about your commitment to personal ethics, to the development of a client-oriented service and organization, and to marketing efforts. Now we are at your final commitment: You must be determined to sell your services. This means that you must develop another set of skills and create the time to perform the new job of salesperson.

If you find the notion of selling to be an uncomfortable one, examine and overcome your objections. Perhaps your hesitancy simply stems from not knowing what to do or how to do it. If so, read on!

PROSPECT NURTURING

Let's look at the sequence of steps in prospect nurturing to see where human interaction and selling apply. Recall that the stages proceed from suspect to prospect, prospect to client, and client to long-term client. Once your marketing plan has culled the prospects from the suspects and brought them to your door, your sales effort will convert prospects to clients. Further, attention to the human interactions between you and your new clients will develop them into long-term clients.

You may be convinced of the prospect's need for Personal Financial

Planning, but the prospect himself must be convinced for you to make a sale. You may be aware that planning requires the combination of many professional disciplines, but unless the prospect is aware of this he may balk at the expense and effort needed. Education and salesmanship are both parts of prospect nurturing.

To develop prospects into clients you may need to educate them in order to provide them with the basis to consider your services. Ideally, this education takes place as part of your marketing program. Sometimes, the education takes place during the first meeting.

In education, it is important to let people make discoveries for themselves. We often forget what education means, but the origins of the word serve to remind us. Education comes from a Latin word *educare* that means "to draw out." Essentially, you should educate a prospect or client by leading him to make his own discoveries. Draw out what is already in his mind; don't try to pound in new ideas. Hopefully, these discoveries will cause him to choose your services.

Realize that a sale is a buying decision. Salespeople do not really sell a product or a service. Rather, they create conditions in the prospect's mind that are favorable to making a buying decision. This is what you must do when you sell your services. You must help a prospect realize that your service will meet his real needs. People are different so their needs and motivations differ, too—even with respect to the same service.

What personal needs determine the buying decision? These are as many and diverse as your prospects, but common to all is the need for empathy and rapport, based on trust. Beyond this, your task as a salesperson is to determine each prospect's specific needs and motivations. Often this has to be done in a short period of time, under conditions of pressure and strangeness. This is why your people skills must be developed to a high degree of sensitivity and accuracy.

DEVELOPING PEOPLE SKILLS

What are people skills? People skills involve the ability to "read" people, or to see beyond the content of what they present to you. You can do this through active listening and observation. The mannerisms, phrasing, facial expressions, and choice of words that prospects use are sources of valuable information.

You can use conversation to probe for real needs and attitudes, to educate, and to motivate, too. To do this, you should guide the conversation without seeming to do so. This is called strategic conversation. We will examine active observation and strategic conversation in more detail, but first let's discuss how your people skills can be sharpened.

Start with your own mind. First, recognize and change any self-defeating attitudes that you may have about selling and interacting. Then make an objective self-assessment of your people skills, noting areas of weakness and strength. Work alone or with similarly interested groups to refine your skills, expand your repertoire of techniques, and share experiences. Develop a program of self-improvement, and work at it.

What problems can you expect? Fear is a common element to most inhibitions. You may fear rejection by a prospect or client on a personal basis. When your prices and services clearly make you the best objective choice for a prospect, you may find it difficult to look for honest reasons why you lost the sale.

You may fear failure. With few exceptions, we all have what it takes to sell ourselves and to succeed. Don't let doubts stop you from trying. Remember, it is better to try the impossible and fail, than to try nothing and succeed.

You may also fear others' professional judgements when you expand your activities to include marketing and sales. There may be some romantic merit in posing as a poor but proud professional of the old school who is cloistered in a remote and dusty office. However, real merit as a professional is earned by delivering a high quality service to clients in the most effective way possible. You make the decision.

Worst of all, you may fear change, or fear stepping into unknown areas. You alone will know when you are ready to leap and how far you should leap. Unless you are prepared to accept your current level of skills and business as the pinnacle of your career, be ready for change and growth. This book should help you dispel your fear of the unknown, as we examine human interactions and selling.

You can use several tools to improve your attitude. Use creative imagery to envision how easy and exciting it will be to develop and apply these new skills. Actually picture scenarios where you handle prospects and clients effectively with your new skills.

Simply "do it," as psychologists advocate according to a technique called *desensitization*. Do it hard enough and often enough, and you will lose your discomfort. You can't grow and develop people skills by sitting in an armchair reading about them. You actually have to perform the skills to improve them and to lose your initial discomfort.

Learning and developing people skills involves trial and error. If you don't make mistakes, you can't learn. Find out what you do and don't know so that when you know what you don't know, you can learn. In practice, desensitizing yourself to human interactions and selling situations involves seeking additional opportunities to develop your skills.

Of course, there are also mechanical tools to help you develop your people skills. To be more persuasive in face-to-face communication or in groups, videotape yourself in role-playing situations. You will gain valuable insights into your behavior and mannerisms and spot problem areas of which you were unaware. And remember, think positively; you can do it!

COMMUNICATION

General Styles

Let's look more closely at face-to-face communication—talking. Think back to the last really satisfying conversation you had. What made it so successful? Whatever the obvious factors were, I'll bet there was also one underlying experience you had: a strong feeling of rapport. Good communication depends on rapport, which is a mutual feeling of empathy and understanding.

Rapport seems to develop of its own accord over a period of time. That's fine, but then how can you develop rapport with clients and prospects? You spend relatively short periods of time with your clients, the initial meeting with prospects being of even shorter duration. How can you develop rapport quickly? The surest way is to match and mirror the person with whom you are interacting. Start by matching your general communication style to that of the prospect. Communication styles fall into three categories, with two opposite types in each category.

The first category is brisk versus casual. The brisk businessperson will start talking about business with little or no incidental conversation. The casual and friendly businessperson prefers some small talk before getting to work. Match your style to the type of person. In this way, you avoid making the brisk businessperson impatient. And even more important, you avoid making the casual and friendly businessperson feel pushed.

Remember that sales activities are really meant to facilitate buying decisions. However, no one will make a buying decision under pressure. In Personal Financial Planning Services, the hard sell approach does not lead to a sale.

The second category is big picture versus detail. Does the prospect want the big picture or the details? Big picture people are those who just want information about the benefits and results, costs, and timing. Detail people demand a great deal of detail in order to feel that they are making sound decisions. Without the detail, they will not decide to buy.

In this category, you will often meet combination teams. To satisfy both elements, present the big picture first and then work down to the detail. It's a tricky balance, but with practice you can satisfy the detail person without boring the big picture partner.

The third category is leader versus follower. The issue at stake here is who is going to run, or give the impression of running, the meeting? With this category, the objective is not to match but to complement your prospect's style. Woe to novices who imagine that just because they're the financial expert, they get to run the show. Wait until they lose their first leader-type communicator!

Prepare yourself to fill either complementary role. Of course it's easy when you get to be the leader. You can anticipate how the meeting will go and keep it on track in an overt way. Less easy, but just as essential, is the ability to keep your meetings on track covertly, while playing the follower role.

To manage this, use strategic conversation to steer the meeting. Ask questions that will return the discussion to essential topics. Be prepared to mentally organize and simplify the information you get from a meandering monologue. You can gain the leading position long enough to nudge the conversation back on course by summarizing to "confirm" that you have understood; then inch forward to related topics.

These three categories of communication style are not mutually exclusive. You will meet brisk, big picture, leader types; casual, detail, follower types; and every other imaginable combination. In addition, you will encounter people who simply defy categorization and typing according to this scheme. What should you do when a prospect is neither brisk nor casual, likes to have the big picture plus supportive detail, and alternately wants to lead and be lead? For once, the answer is simple. Remember that the objective is to match the prospect's communication style in order to develop rapport. When there is no clear style to match, just relax and adopt whatever style seems appropriate and effective.

Beyond matching your general communication style to the prospect's, consider developing these additional points for your own style. To increase your credibility, talk a little bit faster. People who talk faster (up to 190 words per minute) are perceived as more trustworthy than slower speakers. Fast speakers are also seen as having honest enthusiasm. Think about people who have impressed you as experts or as enthusiasts. Didn't they talk a little fast?

To be seen as more powerful, increase your eye contact when speaking and decrease your eye contact when listening. Also increase your eye contact if you are sitting or standing at a distance.

A blend of fact and emotion will keep listeners more interested than pure fact. Mix emotions and facts for effect. This doesn't mean that you should display your own emotions, but you should discuss how people feel about things. It is important to let prospects know that you are concerned with their values and with the way they feel about their dreams and goals. But remember, businesspeople tend to respect facts and distrust emotions.

Choice of Words

While we're on the subject of verbal communication, let's talk about your choice of words. First, my pet peeve: Don't let technical ego get in the way of clear communication. In other words, don't jargonize your prospects. Be objective and honest enough to determine whether jargon is covering up areas in which you are weak or lack confidence. Remember: if you can't explain a concept from the ground up, you have no right to stand on its roof and look down on others.

Jargon is not an unqualified evil. It is a special language that is unique to a particular business. As such, it can communicate information in an abbreviated way. But jargon fails to serve you when a prospect or client doesn't know its meaning. Few of us are mature enough to admit ignorance of the meaning of a term, so you must ensure that your listeners can understand you.

The words that you choose must clearly communicate ideas to your prospect; they must also create the desired effect. Good salespeople use words to create pictures. Specific and personal words create more specific and personal pictures. For example, compare the phrases "my first car," "my first grade teacher," and "my mother," with the words "cars," "teachers," and "parents." Your prospect can more easily and vividly picture his first car or his first grade teacher than he can a general concept such as "car" or "teacher."

How extensive is your vocabulary? Do you repeat the same words over and over? Do you find yourself always groping for the word that will convey your exact shade of meaning? You don't have to be a crossword puzzle athlete to communicate effectively. In order to develop an effective vocabulary, just do more reading. Pick a subject that interests you and that will broaden your vocabulary and expose you to new ideas. Then read with a dictionary close at hand. When you hit a word that you don't know, look it up. Also, cultivate friendships with people who have extensive vocabularies. And if you have a few favorite words, list them; then check the dictionary to make sure that they convey your intended meaning.

What about your use of clichés? No, cliches are not deadly, but they lack impact. Prospects know what you are about to say so they tune out. Become aware of how you use clichés; then develop creative ways to express the same thing. If you can't be creative in expressing yourself, how can you be creative in financial planning?

Slang, like jargon, is useful only when the prospect understands it. People outside your culture and generation may not understand the slang you use. Since slang does lend a casual tone to conversations, you may want to use it to build rapport. The key is to match and mirror the slang that your prospect understands and uses.

We seem to be moving down the scale of correct word choice, so let's touch on profanity. As a Financial Planner, you understand risk and gain trade-offs. Here, the risk is simply not worth the gain. Resist the temptation to use profanity to establish rapport with a prospect, even if your prospect uses four-letter words freely. You have more subtle and effective rapport building tools from which to choose.

One subtle tool that you may wish to use is "hot and cold button" words. Just as jargon and slang words can have meanings beyond those defined in a dictionary, so can hot and cold button words. Hot and cold button words have additional unique psychological or emotional meanings for a prospect, other than the objective meanings. Hot button words are those with positive meanings; cold button words have negative meanings.

Suppose you find that a prospect reacts positively to the term "businesslike." You can use this hot button word to create a favorable impression of how Personal Financial Planning will handle his personal affairs "in a more businesslike fashion." Or suppose you find that a prospect has a cold button reaction to the word "fragmented." Use the word to warn of the possible dangers of an "uncoordinated, fragmented approach" to his personal finances.

You can discover a prospect's hot and cold button words by active observation. Look for facial expressions, modes of delivery, and body language that reveal his positive or negative reaction to certain words or phrases.

When your business success depends on talking with people, it is important to know how your voice sounds to them. Therefore, use a tape recorder to determine how pleasing your voice sounds to others, and solicit feedback from friends and coworkers. Try to correct extremes and develop a varied and interesting medium. Don't let your voice be monotone, lacking in contrast. Learn to vary your speaking pace for effect; avoid a continuous slow drone or a rapid staccato. Similarly, learn to use the range of volume and pitch that will keep your listener interested. If you have strongly developed some poor speaking habits, however, you may need the help of a diction or voice instructor to correct them.

Client Focus

You are offering an ideal service when you focus on client goals, risk tolerance, and needs. Beyond your ability to attain ideals, however, your success depends on how well you can customize and optimize for each client. To do this, you need to determine the real client needs and to develop products and services that meet these needs. This is the premise behind the marketing philosophy.

Clients expect Personal Financial Planning to be tailored to their objective (numeric) and subjective (feeling/personal) needs. You can convey a client focus with your choice of words. Use client-centered words such as "you" and "your" rather than planner-centered words such as "me," "we," and "our firm." Using client-centered words shows your interest in the prospect or client and helps to promote trust and rapport.

Examples, Cases, and Analogies

When you want to convey information that will influence a prospect's decision, you can present facts from several different angles. You can do this by using examples, case histories, and analogies.

To influence a prospect, use examples that support abstract or statistical data. Case histories that illustrate the ideas you want to convey are more believable than bare facts. Analogies help to convey and establish ideas that may be new, by explaining the ideas in familiar terms. Analogies can be drawn from any common life experience. Here are a few of my favorites.

The analogy of a sea cruise can demonstrate ideas about risk tolerance. Does the prospect prefer to steer a steady course, sailing only on clear nights? Or is the prospect ready to sail uncharted waters, willing to navigate through fog?

The roles played by a client and his Financial Planner are analogous to the jobs performed by an airplane pilot and his navigator. The pilot determines where he wants to go and controls the aircraft during its flight. The navigator uses expert skills to plot a course that will lead to the destination. He advises the pilot how to compensate for changing weather conditions, cargo weights, and fuel consumption.

The analogy of an orange and its juice can be applied to the client's investments. No matter how you squeeze an orange, there is only so much juice. Similarly, no matter how you "squeeze" portfolio investments, there is only so much "juice" to be gained.

Practice your examples, cases, and analogies by explaining Personal Financial Planning concepts to some novices. By studying how Personal Financial Planning elements and tactics work, you may find other parallels that can help in your explanations.

Visual Materials

To make presentations work, match your style to the prospect's preferred comprehension mode. Some people prefer columns of figures; some prefer charts, graphs, or pictographs. Over time, you will easily discover the best way to present visual information to a client, but your initial meeting with a prospect does not allow a leisurely exploration in communication. To use effective visual materials in an initial presentation meeting, you must prepare in advance, and then make a few trial and error experiments.

Your first decision must be whether to use visual materials to support or communicate your message. Fortunately, prospects offer strong verbal clues about the way they think and learn. Visually oriented prospects use visual words to communicate, such as "I see what you mean," "I can picture that," or "Let's focus on that perspective."

Your next decision must be what kind of visual presentation will work best. Will tables of figures work, or will a simple pie chart be more effective? Again, verbal clues can alert you to the level of detail that a prospect needs. Figure out whether the listener is a big picture person or a detail person. Remember the image of the financial plan as a pyramid. Will you present information from the detail level up to the conclusion, or work from a conclusion down to the supporting detail?

Determining the best type of visual devices for an individual prospect requires more trial and error. This is where advance preparation pays off. Have the same information prepared in a variety of visual formats. Make one or two tests using possible formats; then stick with what works best.

Don't underestimate the value of simple images to show complex relationships. The pyramid, the pie chart, box diagrams, and bar charts all have a strong impact in their simplicity.

Classify and Partition

When a prospect has difficulty with a new idea, it may be because the idea is too big and complex to comprehend at once or because masses of detail are lacking a simple, unifying idea. You can see that some method of making ideas bigger or smaller is needed. The tools for this job are classification and partitioning.

Partitioning means taking a concept and breaking it into component parts. These parts are smaller and easier to grasp than the complicated whole. Use your partitioning knife to slice an idea into manageable chunks along the most sensible lines.

Using this technique, you can discuss investment planning by partitioning it according to the portfolio mix. What parts of the portfolio provide wealth accumulation, and what parts provide protection against inflation? Alternately, you can partition investment planning according to time. What should happen during the peak earning years, when the children leave home, and after retirement?

Classification is a way of grouping several separate ideas into one whole, by virtue of a shared feature or characteristic. For example, we can classify life, disability, and property insurance considerations into the subject of risk management.

Use classification and partitioning to match the size of a concept to the prospect's comprehension ability. With a little practice, you can become quite fluid at these techniques. The better you can match and mirror the prospect, the better your rapport will become.

MATCHING FOR EMPATHY AND RAPPORT

Match and Mirror

Successful Personal Financial Planning depends on a mesh of your services with the prospect's needs. This means that you must have empathy, rapport, understanding, and compassion for and with your prospects and clients. Relating to your client is paramount to success. As the dream mechanic, your job is to map the plan to the heart, and to map the heart to the plan.

Good salespeople don't sell the service or product to the prospect; they sell themselves to the prospect. Then the prospect can take their trusted advice about purchase decisions. People don't trust a service; they trust other people. Once you gain a prospect's trust, he will buy almost anything from you if there is a valid need.

Trust is the client's belief in your competence to complete the task at hand. To get a client's trust, you first need rapport. The word rapport comes from the French, meaning "to bring back." To establish rapport, you must reach out to understand the prospect's personality, problems, and needs. You "bring this understanding back" to your position, and then show the prospect that you do understand. Essentially, you match and mirror the prospect or client in your human interactions with him.

You will make several kinds of matching decisions as you practice. It is important to match clients with other essential members of your expert team; you must also consider matching when you make referrals. Suppose your client is the fabled little old lady from Pasadena. When she needs an attorney, do you send her to the young hipster, heavy with gold chains and a shirt opened to the navel; or to the fatherly, silver-haired veteran in a three-piece suit?

Alas, matching personalities is not always so clear-cut and obvious. You have even less freedom when matching the personality of a prospect to that of the Financial Planner. After all, there is only one of you . . . Or is there? Multipartner practices offer an advantage here.

When you strive to match a prospect, what matches can you find? There are the obvious ones of age, background, philosophy, religion, and orientation. Learning to match these will help you understand the prospect's real needs and desires. There is another match that helps rapport tremendously—that of a shared experience. You can have no better experience in common with the prospect than the one on which he is embarking.

It is imperative that you do your own Personal Financial Plan first. An astute prospect will ask if you have one and will make his own evaluation of how well it seems to be working for you. Beyond making a good impression, subjecting yourself to a rigorous planning process will be a valuable way to consider the consumer's perspective.

Matching and mirroring for rapport works on all levels. After you have made the best match you can on obvious points, what are the details that need attention? There are some mechanical techniques that will facilitate the establishment of rapport and the consequent development of trust. Avoid sitting across a desk or table; this frames a confrontation rather than a communion. Rather, sit at a small round table, preferably within two feet, when seated, of the key decision makers.

Start with appropriate synchronizing conversation. Discuss a mutual friend or common interest for a minute or two. Now extend your prospect matching and mirroring efforts into the physical plane. Try to synchronize physical moves with the prospect, such as head nods, breathing, and gestures. It is possible to generate a high degree of rapport and trust in a very short period of time with sympathetic body language. Do not slavishly mimic the prospect, but wait five or ten seconds and then casually mirror some aspects of the posture and gestures that you observe. Valid candidate gestures for mirroring are leg crossing, leaning forward or backward, smiling, and arm folding.

Mirroring works with verbal communications, too. This means that you must be able to listen to the content of the prospect's communications and simultaneously observe the form of communication being used. Mirroring applies to gross forms, as general communication style or choice of words; and to subtle forms, as volume, speed of talking, and pauses for emphasis.

You can use mirroring both to follow and to lead a prospect since once rapport is established, the prospect will unconsciously start to mirror you back. For example, once you establish rapport by mirroring posture, breathing, and communication forms, you can build enthusiasm in the prospect by creating it in yourself. Get in sync; then lean forward and speak more rapidly—with intensity. The client will be swept up in the enthusiasm and actually experience it himself. If the prospect is not following your lead, then you haven't established enough rapport yet. Go back to the passive mirroring role, and work up again.

Typing Personality

To help you match and mirror a prospect or client, you can distinguish various types of personality. Creating rapport and trust depends on your understanding of the prospect's personal makeup. To be sure, this depends on the prospect's background. People raised in the Midwest have a different way of thinking from those raised in New England or the West Coast. Your prospect is a function of where he came from, and how he came.

But your prospect is now at your office door. How can you best match this unique personality? How can you keep all the personalities, communication styles, attitudes and preferences in mind when dealing with a multitude of clients? How can you swivel your head from meeting to meeting, without losing your balance and getting dizzy?

I have developed a simple method of classifying the personality of each prospect and client that I meet. I note this classification on the client folder, and can refresh myself with an outline of the personality type before a meeting or conversation. This gives me a starting block for my matching process.

The classification system is derived from a method used in Jungian psychology, called the Myers-Briggs Type Indicator. The technique lets you place a prospect or client personality within four key categories, and then determine which of two types they are within each area. Thus, there are sixteen basic personalities within which you can roughly classify each prospect or client. The four key categories are: basic energy flow, mode of perception, mode of judgment, and life-style.

Let's start with the basic energy flow category. This category indicates in which way the energy of the personality is directed, whether outward or inward. The types are extroverted and introverted, which I code with the letters E and I. The extroverted type relates more easily to the outer world of actions, objects, and persons than to the inner world of ideas. Conversely, the introverted type relates more easily to the inner world of ideas than to the outer world of actions, objects, and persons.

The mode of perception category considers how the person prefers to obtain new information, whether from the outside or from the inside. The types are called sensing, coded by S, and intuitive, coded by I. The sensing type prefers working with known facts more than possibilities and relationships. The intuitive type prefers looking for possibilities and relationships over working with known facts.

In the mode of judgment category, the types are thinking and feeling, T and F; this category indicates how personalities prefer to base or make decisions. The thinking type bases judgments on impersonal analysis and logic more than on values. The feeling type bases judgments more on personal values than on impersonal analysis and logic.

Finally, the general life-style category has two types of personalities: determined or flexible, D or F. The determined type prefers a planned, decided, orderly way of life rather than a flexible, spontaneous way of life. The flexible type prefers a flexible, spontaneous way of life over a planned, decided, orderly way of life.

The point is not to label and box clients, but to make a personality sketch that quickly lets you relate to the person with whom you are about to interact. For example, when I see the notation ISTF on a client's folder, I am reminded that the client is introverted rather than extroverted, sensing rather than intuitive, thinking rather than feeling, and flexible rather than determined. In terms of this client, I will have to spend extra time probing to reach his real internal world; extra effort is necessary to reach the introvert. Since the client learns by sensing from the outer world, I will present ideas and facts in their raw form, rather than working by analogy or case studies as are needed by the intuitive type. My client makes judgments based on his thinking, rather than his feelings. Therefore, decisions will be based on objective, quantified information; I won't have to sell the benefits of a plan or strategy based on the client's emotional satisfaction. Satisfaction is still the ultimate goal, but the facts will be enough to make decisions. Finally, I know my client's life-style is flexible rather than determined and fixed. This means that proposed changes to the plan will not need much cushioning.

Personality typing gives you a framework against which you can understand and record the workings of the people with whom you interact. However, it is only a measuring framework. To apply it, you have to actively observe the personality at hand.

Active Listening and Observation

Let's look more closely at the people skills you need to fully perceive and understand a prospect or client: active listening and observation. Remember that you must be able to penetrate beyond a prospect's appearance in order to arrive at a true understanding of his situation, problems, and needs.

Strategic conversation is not always an active process. In fact, when it works well, it is much more passive than active. A perceptive and receptive mind requires the passivity of listening rather than speaking. But don't get relaxed yet! Strategic conversation doesn't involve passive listening; it involves active listening.

While you listen, you must convey your sincere interest to the prospect. In effect, you are interviewing your prospect to find out what he needs from your service. Once you have a clear picture of his needs, you can use them to generate interest in what your service can offer.

Again, the point is to match and mirror. Active listening and observation are your tools to determine the personality that you must match. They are also your tools to uncover the real needs and motivations behind those that the prospect presents to you.

Why would a prospect be deceitful to his Financial Planner? Your prospect is probably not deceiving you intentionally, but as a result of complex psychological factors. Perhaps you have not established enough rapport and trust, and the prospect is still hesitant to reveal his financial particulars. Perhaps he feels intimidated at dealing with a professional expert. Often, a prospect is concerned with the very real human need to be accepted and liked. Acting from this need, he will say the things that he thinks you want to hear, rather than speaking what he feels.

You must learn to be a good listener and to remember that some questions do not need answers. Learn to consider why a question is being asked to understand the thinking behind it. Don't rush with a technical answer until you know the real reason for the query.

When you ask questions and are answered, learn to listen not only to the content of the answer, but also to the form of the answer. Also look for the answer you get from body language, stance, phrasing, and emphasis. For instance, when I was talking to a couple recently, I asked about their retirement dreams. The husband talked at length in an obviously sincere and enthusiastic manner, while the wife silently shook her head, even rolling her eyes at one point. Obviously, they had not communicated well about retirement plans. A client or prospect can say "yes" with his mouth, and yet be shouting "no" in body language.

To actively listen, focus your attention on the prospect. Hold yourself in readiness for as much eye contact as the prospect wants. Do not think about possible answers to questions, or what you will say next. Rather, imagine that immediately after the speaker stops, you will be asked to repeat or paraphrase what was said. This technique keeps you from getting distracted by your own internal dialogues.

Remember the value of silence and offer your clients a listening space. When you ask probing questions, wait for the first and the second answer. An active listener is sometimes more in control of the situation than the speaker.

What causes poor listening? You may find yourself distracted by the prospect's appearance, mannerisms, or speech. You may have to contend with external distractions in the form of noise, temperature, light, or movement. You may let other ideas crowd your mind or react emotionally when the prospect's views differ from yours.

To improve your active listening skill, learn to look at the prospect's face as he speaks. If you find direct eye contact uncomfortable, focus on the space between the eyes. Looking at a prospect encourages him to keep talking because it shows him that you are interested, concerned, and attentive. Also, make an effort to sit up and be alert. Your posture not only affects how your mind works, but it communicates your interest to a prospect.

Remember that no matter how many times you may have heard similar problems, you have never heard this unique individual's problems. Let the prospect complete his thoughts, at his own pace. As an active listener, you must keep the conversation on track. Keep an open mind and make sure that your body language shows this openness. This means that you should uncross your legs, unfold your arms, and lean toward the prospect.

As you listen, give signals that show you are attentive. Smile and nod at appropriate points. When a monologue gets too long to keep track of the details, ask for a pause while you repeat key points, then ask the prospect to continue.

To actively observe, you have to learn to watch the obvious things while you also watch and analyze the subtle things. You may find it helpful to use a short checklist at first to develop the split attention you need.

For example, when you are meeting a prospect, memorize his name first. What do you estimate his age to be? Compare his height with yours. What can you notice about his clothing and hairstyle? Study the sound of his voice, and his choice of words and vocabulary.

Another source of information about a prospect comes from his body language. This is a complete field of study in itself. Rather than trying to give you a hopelessly simplistic summary, I refer you to Julius Fast's *Body Language* and Henry Calero's *How to Read a Person Like a Book*. However, let me add the caution that not every body motion means what you think or want it to mean. When a prospect rubs his forehead, it could mean that he is in deep thought about a buying decision—or it could mean that you are giving him a headache. A few useful signals follow.

In conversation, watch the facial expressions of your prospect. A tense expression or a miniature grimace can mean that you have hit an area needing further discussion. Stop talking and solicit more information: "I seem to have hit a sensitive point. Would you care to comment?"

Folded arms, crossed legs, and leaning away from you indicate a defensive frame of mind. Are you rushing the prospect, or are you directing him to decisions beyond his comfort zone or risk tolerance? Conversely, unfolded arms, uncrossed legs, and leaning toward you shows relaxation and trust, the things you want. This can indicate an acceptance of your proposals and a readiness to close. Steepling, or a folding of the hands with the index fingers left extended, can mean deep thought and a potential buying decision. Cupping the chin or rubbing the brow can mean the same.

Remember to use your own body language to mirror for rapport or to give encouragement when the prospect is volunteering information. Use nods, smiles, and eye contact. When the client volunteers information, don't send disapproving signals with your face or body; he will then stop. You must be open-minded enough to accept the information value of what a prospect says, and then make your own value judgements later.

Remember to respect the prospect's physical comfort zone; that is, how close or far you stand from him. In the United States, the comfort zone is arm's length. Don't stand closer or you will make the prospect uncomfortable. Don't stand too far apart, or you will seem distant and cold. Experiment with the physical comfort zone, and learn to use it effectively.

If you want to go even farther in the process of mirroring, read into the field of neuro-linguistic programming. All the works of Bandler and Grinder are interesting to read, but their *Frogs Into Princes* deals with mirroring and subliminal signals. They even outline techniques that can help determine the thinking style of a personality.

One interesting and useful aspect of this field is the discovery that the direction in which we turn our eyes when thinking indicates our mode of thought. For example, if a person looks to the upper left, he is constructing a visual image; if he looks to the upper right, he is recalling a visual image. Middle positions indicate audible constructs or memories, while lower eye positions indicate tactile or kinesthetic thinking.

YOUR PERSONAL IMAGE

Why should a prospect choose your services over those of your competitors? Rapport and trust are critical, and these depend on the personal image you project. Recall the attributes needed for the ideal Financial Planner. You want to project the image of a trusted, knowledgeable, objective professional. Let's review this image as it applies to human interactions on a personal level.

It is one thing to project an image in your marketing efforts, but you must also be able to project this image in person. The most effective way to enhance a favorable image is to let the client discover how great you are on his own. Don't hide your light under a bushel, a file folder, or anything else. Prominently display your credentials, which are indicators of your experience, exposure, and expertise, along with letters of thanks and commendation. Also be prepared to display your attributes personally. If you disclose your product or commission biases, you may lose a profitable sale once or twice. However, your clients' gradual trust in your objectivity will be worth one or two minor losses. It is more profitable to build a high quality ongoing service than to maximize profit at every opportunity.

Rather than be an inapproachable expert who is locked into fixed truths, show prospects your expert and professional *approach* to new problems. Be ready to say "I don't know." Be ready to be amazed at your own ignorance and intrigued with the problems that a prospect raises. Share your enthusiasm for finding the answers, solving the problems. Expertise doesn't mean always having the right answers, but it does mean being able to find them. In conversations and planning discussions, you can demonstrate expertise not only by offering information, but also by asking pertinent questions.

If investment advisors are so knowledgeable about investments, then why aren't they rich? If you want to project your image as a competent Financial Planner, be prepared to look the part of success even if you are not currently living the part. You may have to make judicious expenditures to ensure the appropriate image. Be sure that you project a solid, consistent image of personal success in your clothes and grooming, the decor and location of your office, and even the year and model of automobile you drive.

THE ENVIRONMENT

Your office creates the environment for meetings and human interactions, and you have to feel good about your environment to project good feelings. While it is not always possible to control every aspect of the environment, make sound decisions about those things you can control.

Choose an office location and decor to create an environment that will help your human interactions, as well as your daily work. Then take the time to look carefully at your office or meeting room from the perspective of a prospect. What does your prospect see when he enters the room? What mood, feeling, and style do your office space and decor create? Match these to the kind of prospect you want to attract, so that both you and your prospect are comfortable.

When you are sitting at your desk or meeting table, how are you framed? What does the prospect see behind you? Avoid distractions such as busy window scenes. Arrange your work area to frame yourself in a fashion that reinforces your image of trust, expertise, and competence.

Take visual image identification as far as you can. Match or complement the color scheme and logo used in your printed materials to your office decor. Don't hesitate to have your logo or slogan displayed in large format in your reception room.

Evaluate your office furnishings and consider possible alternatives to working across a desk. Use a round table or a corner bench with an available coffee table to set clients more at ease. Overall, keep furnishings functional and logistically sound. Arrange two or three optional meeting or working spaces in your office, and use the one best suited to the prospect with whom you are working.

Practice seating arrangements with friends or partners. Stage mock meetings to see that things can flow smoothly and take into account the effect of backgrounds in each work location. Give some thought to the psychological effects of colors. For example, blues give a feeling of power and strength, whereas browns project masculinity. Other factors that influence human interactions are temperature, background noise or music, and lighting. Make sure these work for you, not against you.

You have most control over the meeting environment when it is your own office, but there may be occasions when you decide to deliver your services at another site. The alternatives are your office, the client's office, at either's home, or in a neutral place. Consider the advantages of these sites, both in terms of environment and ease of accessibility. In your own office, you are clearly in charge, but it is harder to end meetings without appearing to throw the prospect out. At a client's office he will be more comfortable, and you can end the meeting by leaving when you wish.

MOTIVATION

It is important to motivate the buyer of your services to make a buying decision. Remember that in selling a service, you must sell the benefits gained and the losses avoided. Since the benefits and losses associated with a prospect's personal finances are emotionally charged issues, you must move away from the arena of objective facts and into the field of human needs and motivations.

You must also be able to motivate a client to follow the plan once it is approved. How can you compel people to follow the advice you give? You can't compel them, but you can motivate them. Develop a clear understanding of the overt, objective motivations and the covert, subjective motivations that brought the prospect or client to you, and work with these.

What motivated the prospect to seek your services? Is he interested in reducing his tax burden, building or protecting wealth, or taking care of his family? If you can find out what motivates a prospect, you can even refer to your service by appropriate names in discussions. Rather than providing a Personal Financial Planning service, you could provide a tax avoidance planning, wealth accumulation, or family financial planning service. Let the client know that you understand his needs and can provide for them.

Look behind the overt needs to discover the personal or psychological needs that support them. Is the prospect looking at issues of survival or security, comfort or achievement, power or love, adventure or . . . ? When you understand both overt and psychological levels of need, you can correctly motivate a prospect with the potential that your service has to meet his needs.

If you deal with a particularly apathetic prospect, you can mention

your choicest horror stories to motivate him. Have various other motivational materials ready for use during the initial meeting. You will determine what works well for you, but consider using articles, quotes, even
compound interest tables to motivate a prospect to take action.

When a meeting ends, do something to motivate the prospect to act on
the next step. Do this by giving him a tangible reminder of the meeting,
such as a brochure or a data collection form.

SELLING YOUR SERVICE

When the prospect walks through your door, you become a salesperson.
Face it. What can get in the way of selling your service? The unfamiliarity
of the selling situation, the consequences of failure, or the potential for
embarrassment can all weaken your initiative, but they can be overcome
by doing. So do it.

Every product salesperson knows some basic rules. These can help you
even in selling a service. First, never talk to someone who isn't listening.
Find out why he isn't. Get him listening; then proceed.

Second, try to reason behind the appearances. Ask yourself, "What
does he really mean by that?" Probe to the underlying issues, and deal
with them.

Third, show a prospect *different* ways, not *better* ways. The prospect
has been doing his best to manage his finances, and he deserves your
respect.

Fourth, answer the prospect's benefit questions:

· How do I benefit?
· When do I benefit?
· How much can I benefit?

This is the age of abundant information. Prospects and clients are saturated with information from many sources. So make sure they know
what you can do for them. Yes, you told them in your brochures and
newsletters. You told them throughout your marketing campaign. But tell
them once again, face-to-face to make sure that it has registered.

Make sure clients and prospects know that you are not too busy to help
them. We have a bad habit of telling people how busy we are. Sure we are,
but aside from your family and your partners, no one should hear about
it. Being too busy can discourage prospects and stop referrals.

THE INITIAL MEETING

Setting the Stage

The first meeting you have with a prospect is a critical moment. Therefore, it deserves your best attention and treatment, including adequate preparation. To help you prepare for the first meeting, use the 3P technique that follows, to match the prospect's concerns.

- Who is the Person you will meet?
- What are his Problems and concerns?
- What Payoffs can you deliver by solving the problems?

When you make an appointment for a meeting, use every source of information available to learn what you can about the person you will meet. What are his personal goals, dreams, and interests? Review what you know about his communication style, his personality type. Begin to adapt yourself to match and mirror the prospect when you meet.

Find out what his problems are and decide which concerns you should address. You have gone to great lengths to create a profile of each prospect in developing your marketing plan. Using this information as a basis, add the specific needs and problems that the prospect mentions in conversation.

Finally, consider the payoffs involved if you can solve the prospect's problems. Be prepared to present these as benefits gained and losses avoided. Payoffs have to be expressed in both objective and subjective terms to make an impression on your prospect. Don't stop at the dollars, but work the payoffs back to the emotional and psychological impact that your solutions can have.

Treat the first meeting as a writing task, too. Make sure you can state the purpose of the meeting and define the prospect in terms of how knowledgeable he is. Make sure that you match your presentation to the comprehension level of the prospect.

Take some time to plan your approach and sketch out a tentative agenda. Think about the seating arrangements, the environmental factors. When the prospect walks in the door, look for clues that will help you select from among alternate approaches. Use your active observation skills to read the prospect's clothing, mannerisms, vocabulary, and communication style.

Meet where you will have the prospect's undivided attention. There should be no interruptions from people or phones. Whenever possible, arrange to have all key decision makers at the meeting. Spouses, children, and parents may all be needed. This helps to give you an understanding of your prospect's real needs and motivations. It also ensures that the key people all get the same message and information. If the prospect has to reconstruct the meeting for a missing decision maker, both he and you will suffer.

That First Impression

When the prospect first sees you, your first impression is made. This impression had better be the one that you intended to make because you won't get another chance to make it. Make sure you can remember the prospect's name. If you have to take a special course to do it, then take the course. There is no way to compensate for getting the prospect's name wrong or for fumbling to recall his wife's name. I guess it's obvious that I've had some painful moments with names. Beyond this obvious courtesy, what other factors make a good first impression?

Surprisingly, height is the first thing most people notice about you. In general, the taller you are, the better. You can't control your height, but most of the other factors that make a good first impression are controllable.

I wish I'd never discovered the next one; it's weight. Being trim helps the first impression. Since I realized this, I have been more serious about controlling my weight. You should be, too.

Glasses can help to make a favorable first impression. People who wear them are perceived as being more intelligent and industrious. I won't go so far as to recommend that you get glasses if you have perfect vision. However, if you wear glasses and are thinking about contact lenses to improve your appearance, you may want to think again.

Whether you look out from behind glasses or not, eye contact is the next most critical factor in first impressions. Eye contact shows your interest and sincerity and enhances your credibility. Don't press your prospect for more eye contact than he is comfortable with since that would be self-defeating. Rather, be ready to offer as much eye contact as he wants. Respect the prospect's personal space during the first meeting, too. Remember the arm's length rule, and be neither too close nor too distant.

The next most important element in creating a good first impression is your handshake. Get feedback from your friends about your handshake. It should be firm, but not overbearing.

At the first meeting, try to project a relaxed feeling. With experience, you will be relaxed when meeting new prospects, but you may find that it helps to take a few deep breaths before opening the door. If you know some relaxation or stress reduction techniques, all the better. Practice them before the first meeting.

Be prepared to smile when you meet a prospect. This is a great door opener. Try it out! If you are not in the habit of smiling at strangers, consider changing your habit. A smile is a great way to make a first impression because it shows that you are accepting and friendly. A smile can mark the beginning of a fruitful client/planner relationship.

You have already been exposed to the next most critical factor in first impressions—your choice of words. Be specific rather than generalized or abstract. Avoid jargon that is unknown to your prospect. Use client-centered words rather than planner-centered words.

The next factor is the amount of talking that you do. Too little will make people suspicious, too much will make you seem domineering, aggressive, and insensitive to others' needs. Try to do less than 60 percent of the talking. I know it is hard to measure, but at least strive for a balance between how much you and the prospect talk.

The final key to making a good first impression is the environment of the meeting place. The prospect will receive subliminal input from your environment, and it will reflect on you. If the environment is noisy, crowded, or hot, your image suffers. So optimize the environment.

Prospect Involvement

Keep the prospect involved in the process of the initial meeting. The new generation of Personal Financial Planning clients are trained to be assertive, responsible partners in the planning process. This puts you in the role of the expert partner, not the leader.

You can effectively control the meeting without seeming brusque or overbearing by steering the conversation. Use your strategic conversation skills to steer the conversation from its introductory phase to topics in Personal Financial Planning. This will benefit rapport and trust more than a direct approach, but it means that your skills must be in top form.

Part of your work will be to determine the prospect's dreams, comfort levels, and risk tolerance. You can solicit this information by providing test scenarios. Walking through some possible futures is a good way to keep the prospect involved and to gain the information that you need.

The more that a client participates in the Personal Financial Planning process, the better. This gives him additional motivation to implement the plan.

Presentation as Matching

When you present your service capabilities to a prospect, view the presentation as a matching process. Rather than laying out your one-hundred-and-twenty-seven service levels and options, look for matches between the prospect's needs and your services.

The first step is to identify the prospect's real needs. Sometimes these will be volunteered. Sometimes you have to probe with a line of questions. Be gentle, though. Sense the level of rapport and trust you have established and do not go past the prospect's comfort zone.

When you ask probing questions, make sure that you are matching and mirroring the prospect. Choose your communication style and words carefully. Use your active listening and observation skills in order to get all information offered through all channels. Make sure you take enough time to develop a full and detailed list of each problem and concern.

If you have a photographic memory, great! Use it. If not, make notes. Don't use an impressive notebook, but a common scratch pad. Make point form notes of key points, not the whole conversation. If you make a lengthy note, avoid long silences by commenting on what you are recording. Repeat quantitative notes to confirm their correctness.

To conduct the initial meeting as a matching process, treat each problem, concern, or area or interest according to the following sequence.

First, state the problem you will discuss to confirm that it is a valid area of concern and that you have understood the problem correctly from the prospect's perspective. Don't be tactless or overly critical when discussing a prospect's problem and don't make your own value judgments. Keep the problem to a simple objective statement of the gap between what is and what the prospect would like. Problems can always be expressed as a discrepancy between what is and what should be.

Phrase your statement of the problem to elicit a response from the prospect. For example: "John, as I understand it, one of your concerns is that you may not be getting the kind of advice and help you need to keep your income taxes to the minimum. Is that correct?."

Next, describe your ability to help resolve the problem. Since you are still trying to build credibility and trust, avoid making any wild claims or promises, even if they are factually based. Avoid making statements in the form of claims, such as "We have the best tax advisers in the state." If the prospect hears a claim, he will withhold his decision until he can verify it.

In place of claims, make factual statements about your capabilities. For example, "I rely on the expert consulting services of Bill Saver. He has a total of 27 years experience in tax planning and tax avoidance, working for people in your situation." A few sample strategies can be discussed to show your willingness and knowledge, but avoid going into too much detail. The prospect will get lost, and you need only find matches on which you can agree.

Next, state the benefits that the prospect can expect from your solutions. Facts and figures will provide credibility, but the prospect is really interested in the benefits that can accrue to him. Motivate him by describing the benefits he can derive by letting you solve his problems.

The next step is to provide evidence that will support the benefits you describe. The prospect may have followed your first three steps, and may be convinced that you can help him. He may, however, have a residual doubt. It may all seem too easy, too good to be true. This is a natural enough thought process for an astute prospect to go through. In this step, you must provide additional proof or assurance to cement his conviction that you can help.

There are several ways to do this. One is to summarize a case history example from your client files, using the form of a short story. This is where your preparation for the meeting can pay off. Consider visual evidence, too, such as graphic or tabular presentations of supportive facts. If you can do it quickly, you may roughly calculate some of the dollar benefits the prospect can realize. Be careful, though, that you can deliver what you promise.

The last part of this five-step matching process is to confirm the benefits with the prospect. There are two reasons for this step. First, you will want to confirm that you are on target and that the problem and the benefits of the solution are of real concern to the prospect. Second, you should get the prospect used to saying yes, to agreeing with you. When it comes time to close the sale, agreement will be all the more natural.

Get the prospect to confirm the benefits with a simple question. Continuing with our tax avoidance example, you could say "That's the kind of reduction in taxes you want, isn't it?" Don't use the confirmation step for each problem or point, or it will become obvious and boring to the prospect. Use it periodically, especially for key areas of prospect concern or need.

Handling Objections

It is natural for a prospect to resist buying your services. Buying the service of a Financial Planner is a major decision, and people's natural inclination is to avoid major decisions when possible. This means that you can expect the prospect to raise objections. You should be prepared to handle them. In fact, you should actively work to uncover any objections the prospect has since these will help to get to the heart of the matter: the real needs of the prospect.

Don't look at objections negatively, as a personal affront or insult. It may be hard enough to develop a reasonable answer, without letting a negative attitude get in your way. View objections as the prospect's way of saying, "Give me more information to help me make this decision." Let's look at two aspects of answering objections: when to answer them and how to answer them.

The ideal time to answer objections is immediately after they are raised. There are exceptions to this rule though. Sometimes you will want to answer an objection before it is even raised. If you are fairly certain that an objection is in the prospect's mind, you may be wise to dispose of it early in the meeting. This frees the prospect from thinking about his objection and lets him focus on what you are saying. Also, a prospect will not defend an objection brought up by you as fiercely as he will defend objections that he raises himself.

Alternately, you may want to defer your response to an objection until a later time. There are two reasons for this. First, you may not have the right answer. Never guess at answers to objections. State frankly that you do not know and that you will get the answer later; then make sure that you do. Second, answering an objection may require too great a diversion or too long an interruption of the flow of the conversation. At times like this, tactfully ask to address the objection later in the meeting.

There is a formula, or routine, that you can use for answering most objections. Of course, it may not work well for all types of objection. It is made up of some common rules about communication and interaction. Try it out. When you are comfortable with the steps involved, adapt it to fit your style and the situations that arise.

The routine involves the following six steps:

1. Stop talking and listen

2. Clarify where needed

3. Probe for the deeper meaning

4. Acknowledge the objection

5. Answer the real question

6. Confirm your answer

The first step seems obvious, but don't overlook it. The objection is the prospect's way of asking for more information and of showing you deeper needs or uncovered problems. If you miss this opportunity to gain information from a prospect, you will miss a valuable opportunity to build rapport and trust. This is the time to exercise your active listening skills.

The second step helps focus the objection in both your mind and in the mind of the prospect. Sometimes an objection will be so clearly stated that you can bypass this step and begin your answer. At other times, the prospect may simply be dealing with unclear feelings of reluctance or dissatisfaction and may voice several unrelated objections or hopelessly jumble his ideas. To keep you both on track, clarify the objections first. Repeat the points you heard, and rephrase or summarize where needed. Ask for confirmation that you have understood the objection clearly.

Sometimes the prospect will tell you what's really bothering him. More often, he will raise an objection that is superficial and does not reach the core of his discomfort. In such cases, you will have to probe for the real objection.

Once you feel you have reached the real or underlying objection, acknowledge it. Acknowledgment of an objection, no matter how trivial it may seem to you, is a way of showing your respect for the prospect's right to voice his concerns. Your prospect will appreciate this and carefully listen to your answer, so it is important.

Next, answer the objection and the real concern that you may have discovered behind the objection. There are several ways to answer objections. You can use the boomerang method to turn the objection into a reason why the prospect should use your services. You can clarify issues of which the prospect has a poor understanding. You can simply admit valid objections and seek ways to overcome them.

Finally, confirm your answer. Get assurance that your answer has satisfied the prospect's objection. If the prospect is satisfied, you can continue. If not, you have more work to do, either probing deeper for his real reasons for objection or further clarifying the issue.

Closing

When you have made your presentation and answered the prospect's objections, you are ready to close the deal. Closing is a formality that seals the buying decision already made by the prospect. To successfully reach an agreement, you have to know when to close, how to close, and above all, you have to try to close.

The time to close is when the prospect is ready to buy. You cannot determine the right time to close by the length of the meeting or the absence of objections. You know when the prospect is ready to buy by observing buying signals in his behavior.

Buying signals will rarely be obvious; you must learn to spot them. The prospect may probe for your detailed answer to a key concern or may talk about his present adviser's shortcomings. He may ask questions about your fee structure or the timing of service delivery. He may make favorable comments on your presentation or indicate how you should handle certain problems.

If buying signals are not clear but you think you may be close to reaching an agreement, try a trial close to test the waters. The trial close is usually framed as a question. Whereas a real close requests a decision, the trial close requests an opinion. A real close might be, "How soon can we start working on this?" A trial close would be, "How do you feel about working together on this?"

Outcomes from the trial close will be negative, indifferent, or positive. If the responses are negative or indifferent, you have more work to do handling objections with answers. When the response is positive, proceed with the closing.

Since closing means that the prospect wants you to do something for him, you must take action as a result of the close. Make the prospect comfortable with his decision by confirming its soundness and then discuss the timing of the first service event. If possible, get your new client started immediately with data forms that he will complete at home. Schedule the first working meeting. If this is not possible, secure a future commitment.

When signatures are required, get a pen in the client's hand first, perhaps to complete a simple information form. Sit beside the client rather than across from him in order to eliminate the process of handing papers across the table. Use soft commands, such as "Sign here to indicate your approval."

START NOW

A final piece of resistance that you can expect to encounter is the client's hesitation to start soon. Even when he has decided to buy your services, you may have to motivate him to act in a timely fashion. We all procrastinate about tackling a new project, and Personal Financial Planning is no exception.

Motivate your new client with the benefits that he can realize by getting started soon. The effects of compounding, unusual investment opportunities, or seasonal lulls in the client's business are all good motivators. You can also motivate him with the losses to be avoided, including the loss of a single night's sleep.

9
The Big Picture

This chapter is a summary and recapitulation of the miles that we've covered. It is not easy to create a single big picture of the evolution you are contemplating. To keep our vision focused, let's examine the same scene from several different perspectives. First, let's look at your environment and summarize the things of which you should be aware. Next, let's look at the decisions that confront you on three important fronts:

· Ethical decisions
· Service decisions
· Marketing decisions

Finally, let's sketch a sequence of events for the orderly development of a Personal Financial Planning Service. We'll look at an easy introductory first year, a more intense second year, and then the years ahead.

You will find a point form list, a snapshot, of each perspective following its discussion. Use these as checklists and idea generators.

THE ENVIRONMENT

Be aware of the economic environment around you. You need this awareness in order to understand the needs of your prospects and clients and to perform your planning tasks sensibly.

The key issues to watch are taxation, inflation, and the increase of economic complexity. These determine the consumer's financial needs and impact on his emotional needs, all of which are needs that you must understand and satisfy.

To market your services effectively, you also need to develop an awareness of the marketplace. National surveys have value as general indicators. However, unless you are marketing your service nationally, you need to develop a feeling for your local market.

Study the market in your service area to determine the size and situation of various consumer groups. Create your own demographic summary by using the information available in your client files, from marketing firms, and from other sources we have discussed. Use this summary to segment and profile the market in order to define your target groups of prospects.

Who else stands with you and the consumer in the marketplace? Competition abounds, both amateur and professional, ethical and piratical. Part of your marketing effort must be to study and surpass your valid competitors. Part of your professional obligation is to fill the gaps between consumer needs and professional services, gaps that are currently plugged by unqualified, self-proclaimed Financial Planners.

The laws and codes that could regulate the Personal Financial Planning industry are still being formulated. Currently, the only constraints in your environment are the ethical rules you impose on yourself. However, be aware of legislative developments at federal and state levels and the evolution of professional codes that will impact on your practice.

Finally, keep pace with the technological environment; the computer age is here. Financial Planners who make sound decisions about computer support and information networks will have a distinct competitive edge. Here is a snapshot of the environment in which you will operate.

Environment Awareness

Economy

Taxation
Inflation
Complexity

Consumer Needs

Financial
Emotional

Local Market

Values

Demographics

Competition

Regulation

Technology

ETHICAL DECISIONS

If you want to succeed in the highly competitive environment of Personal Financial Planning Services, you must use modern strategic marketing methods. Sanctions against some aspects of marketing exist in many professional codes of ethics. Clearly, these codes no longer serve their purpose when they expose our clients to fraud and undue risk. This can mean some hard decisions, but they must be made.

The laws and codes that could protect the consumer are being formulated. Until these are in place, only your personal code of ethics serves. Your ethics must allow you to compete for prospects with a valid, qualified, professional service. Your ethics must protect your client, your professionalism, and your practice. The snapshot:

Ethical Decisions

Government Laws

Professional Codes

Personal Ethics

Client Protection

Professional Protection

Practice Protection

SERVICE DECISIONS

You have many decisions to make about your Personal Financial Planning practice. First, you must determine the fundamental nature of the services you intend to provide. Will your services be pure planning, planning plus implementation, or perhaps even pure product? Remember that for the independent Financial Planner, the most needed and most profitable service combines planning and implementation.

Whatever services you decide to offer, you still need the support of a smooth running organization. The functions needed are as follows:

· Administration

· Marketing

· Planning

· Implementation

· Product development

But how should these functions be organized and structured? Of the two possible structures, cottage or specialist, the specialist structure is best suited to a Personal Financial Planning Service. When you develop your organizational structure, avoid any rigidity that will endanger the client/planner relationship.

Clearly, some of these functions can be external to your firm. You must decide which will be internal and which will be contracted to external agencies. Be sure to retain control of the client/planner relationship, the final analysis and presentation of the plan, and the coordinating functions of the Financial Planner. Beyond this, you should start with several external experts and then acquire or hire to internalize expert skills as time and experience indicate.

An important decision is whether your implementation services will be internal or external. Remember that with external implementors, you can avoid problems in registration or licensing.

You need to assemble an expert team to perform planning and implementation functions. The following members are needed:

· Planner

· Planning assistant

· Attorney

· Broker

· Insurance agent

· Banker

· CPA

Again, you have options and decisions to make about how the expert team is structured and organized. A flexible team can be developed by using a network approach. This network can be organized with local independent financial professionals or with a specialized Personal Financial Planning Service support organization.

Organizational decisions are not enough; you must also decide what role you will play as the Financial Planner. I have used the images of the dream mechanic and the quarterback to define the ideal Financial Planner. These images convey the skills you will need to act as a human adviser and as a high-level coordinator.

The skills you will need as Financial Planner are all essential; you must merely decide the level at which you will perform them. You can undertake the role of a complete Financial Planner, performing all expert functions. You can act in a purely coordinating capacity, guiding the efforts of experts on your team. Or you can act as overall coordinator, while supplying those special expert skills you already possess.

The role you define or anticipate will determine the technical education and credentials you need. Decisions about your role and the nature of your service will determine which affiliation, registration, and licensing options you select. Your technical education will establish your qualifications, but you will also need to maintain your acquired skills with a program of ongoing education and a financial information network.

You have decisions to make about your role as a Financial Planner and about the process of Personal Financial Planning. Initially, you may elect to follow the idealized six-step process that we examined earlier. As your technical education and work experience progress, you may decide to develop a specialized version of the planning process.

I suggest that you keep computer support to a minimum until you are thoroughly familiar with your planning process. Then you can make sound decisions about what parts to automate and how to develop the computer support system that will best serve you.

We have already touched on decisions about the nature of the products and services you will offer. Other decisions will be required in your first year of practice, including decisions of a marketing nature. Develop the capability to offer a comprehensive planning service, but also consider how this service can be segmented to appeal to specific groups of prospects. Is your valuable time distributed most profitably among the services you offer? What other products will be needed to support your new planning services?

Here is the snapshot I promised of the service decisions that you must make. Don't let the size of this list overwhelm you since these decisions need not be made now or tomorrow. Rather, you will face them in the due course of creating and operating your Personal Financial Planning Service. Knowing what the decisions are will simplify the process.

Internal Decisions

Service

   Pure planning
   Planning and implementation
   Pure product

Organization

   Functions
     Administration
     Marketing
     Planning
     Implementation
     Product development
   Structure
     Cottage
     Specialist
     Internal functions
     External functions
   Implementation
     Internal
     External
     Registration and Licensing
   Expert Team
     Functions
       Planner
       Planning assistant
       Attorney
       Broker
       Insurance agent
       Banker
       CPA
     Structure
     Networking

Planner

   Role
     Full planner
     Coordinator
     Coordinator and specialist
   Education and credentials
   Affiliations, registration, and licensing
   Financial information network

Process

  Ideal
  Specialized/customized
  Automated/manual

Products and services

  Nature
  Leveling and segmentation
    Market segments
    Stages of life
    Steps in process
  Related Products

MARKETING DECISIONS

This final group of decisions should be easier to make, now that you have some marketing knowledge. Of course, you need to decide what your marketing and business goals are. These can be framed most sensibly in the context of your general business philosophy, which is determined by the decisions we've just examined.

What about your marketing department? Create a marketing department, even if this is no more than a department of your mind. Eventually the marketing job may become big enough to warrant a fully dedicated staff member. Your marketing director must make decisions about when and how to use the expert help available.

Think of the marketing function in the same way as you considered your expert team. The skills you need can be either internal or external. Whatever your decision, you need to determine reliable sources of marketing information.

Your marketing information network will supply you with the facts you need to adopt an effective position. You must decide which consumer needs to serve and how to differentiate yourself from your competitors. For each marketing option you decide to exercise, you must select appropriate strategies and tactics. As you create your strategic marketing plan, you must consider your products and services.

To distinguish yourself from the competition, you need to make decisions about your image. These can be classified as decisions about your firm's image, your personal image, and the visual image that your marketing materials convey.

You can simplify decisions about pricing your services by using a matrix to examine possible alternatives. Remember the matrix that we used to consider pricing options for initial and ongoing planning and implementation services. The services were checked against the various pricing mechanisms to determine the advantages and weaknesses of each combination. The same approach will help you price any special services you choose to offer.

When pricing your services, expect to work through several iterations until all factors are in balance. Your pricing mechanism should match the expectations of your target segment, but it must also generate the right revenue flow from your intended client base. Remember to use the screening effects of pricing to attract the clients you want.

What clients do you want? More decisions! Just as you would segment and profile the market, you can also segment and profile your target client base. Knowing the financial and personal profile of your desired clients will help you determine what market segments to pursue.

Here is the last list of decisions, the snapshot from the marketing perspective.

Marketing decisions

   Goals

      Business philosophy
      Strategic marketing plan goals

   Marketing department

      Hired help
      Internal
      External
      Marketing information network

   Position

      Target segments
      Competitive stance

   Marketing options

      Strategies
      Tactics
      Products and services

   Image

      Firm
      Personal
      Visual

Pricing products and services

    Planning fees
      Initial
      Ongoing
      Special services
    Implementation fees
      Initial
      Ongoing
      Special services
    Pricing mechanisms
      Flat fee
      Commission
      Fee and commission
      Hourly rate
      Percentage fee
      Performance factor
    Client base revenue flows
    Income/growth considerations
    Effects of plan price

Customers

    Market segments
    Client base

THE FIRST YEAR

One of the benefits that a client wants to gain from your Personal Financial Planning Service is direction. This is so important that I suggested the addition of a special "Action" section to the plan document. Perhaps you can better appreciate this need for direction in light of your own situation now. We've discussed the development and marketing of your Personal Financial Planning Service in such detail that you may be confused about what to do. Well relax. I have taken my own advice and included an "Action" section. Here is an outline of what to do in the first year.

Use the first year to get better acquainted with Personal Financial Planning. Continue to rely on your original practice for your livelihood as you gradually develop new services and skills. Start in the role of overall coordinator and tailor your education to provide you with the overview needed.

During the first year, develop one or two marketable services. Don't be overly concerned with perfecting or marketing your initial offerings. These only need to provide you with a working experience of Personal Financial Planning.

Consider how many clients you want, and then stick to that number. About a dozen clients will fully occupy your time as a Financial Planner during your first year.

You should consider and experiment with various organizational structures. Rather than hiring additional staff, farm out your needs for expert services and retain control of the coordinating role. This lets you focus on the client/planner relationship and on the overall Personal Financial Planning process.

Begin to acquire the technical skills you need by making use of self-study programs so that you can proceed at your own optimal pace. Focus on getting an overview rather than technical detail. Devote the majority of your learning time to developing management, presentation, and human relations skills. When you select a program of self-study, choose one that will lead to an accredited designation, such as ChFC, CFP, or CFA.

Join one or more of the Personal Financial Planning professional organizations. These will connect you with valuable support functions and sources of information.

Make an objective evaluation of your weaknesses in the area of human relations skills, and then design a program to correct them. This cannot be done overnight, so prepare for more ongoing education. Attend seminars on management, human relations, and presentation skills offered by your professional organization.

Take time during the first year to establish your information networks, both financial and marketing. Sample the available newspapers and magazines, and subscribe to several. You have made a good start with this book, but continue to expand your library on Personal Financial Planning. Spend some time developing your sources of marketing information.

Eventually, you may want to offer a complete and comprehensive service that is literally under one roof. However, for the first year, I suggest that you create your expert team by networking with local financial professionals.

When you begin to shape your organization, you may want to rely on external implementation services to avoid registration and licensing. Otherwise, registration and licensing requirements will become a priority during your first year.

Develop your planning process by starting with the six-step ideal defined in Chapter 2. You will have problems and questions as you produce your first plans, so start with your own plan. Develop plans for your partners, coworkers, family, and friends to iron out most of the problems before you accept your first paying client.

Use your initial plans to develop the process aids you will need for later plans. Develop and refine your client data form and checklist of documents that the client needs to bring to the first meeting. Create discussion checklists to prepare clients for the goal-setting step. Define your standard analysis tools and methods and familiarize yourself with the information needs of your expert team members. Extract a general skeleton plan document that you can flesh out.

Implement your own plan first. Use this and all implementations to create and refine checklists of the essential timing and steps. Develop a workable contact record and tickler system to remind you of critical implementation and review dates.

You may be anxious to plunge into automation of the process, but wait until you know what computer support you really need. Start with printed forms and hand held calculators. Add computer hardware and software to your process only when you understand the functions they will perform and only when they are cost justified. Start with word processing; then add financial calculation, generic plan, and client base management functions. I recommend that you develop your own hardware system, based on an expandable network of personal computers. Stick with the industry leaders to ensure compatibility and upgrading of hardware and software.

When you are ready to serve your first paying clients, take your time with their plans. Don't expect to profit from your first few financial planning engagements.

For the first year, you will need to develop some workable products and services. As you gain experience and develop a marketing plan, you will revise them extensively—so don't try to perfect them yet. Also, you will need to create a professional looking plan document and a complete client data form. And you will need to determine the content of your client files.

Even with a relaxed approach to marketing, you may need some basic marketing materials. Pay attention to the visual image that these project, but keep production costs as low as possible. Again, you will rework these extensively when you develop your strategic marketing plan during the second year of your practice.

As a basic marketing kit, you will need a brochure, newsletter, or bulletin letter that informs prospects of your service capabilities. You will also need a fee schedule or form to create written estimates. As soon as possible, begin to accumulate references from satisfied clients.

Near the end of the first year, review your experience and start to explore the leveling and segmenting of your services. Consider ways to profitably deploy your most valuable resource: your time. Your experience during this year will also give you some ideas about the market segments that, with further leveling and segmenting, you could provide with specialized services.

At the end of the first year, you will have enough experience to begin to design your target client base. This will encourage you to develop a detailed strategic marketing plan. Before we go into the details of the second year, here is a checklist of activities for the first year.

First year

> Set scope
>
> Test organization structures
>
> Get education
>
>> Technical skills
>>> Certification
>>> Memberships, affiliations
>> Human relations skills
>
> Establish networks
>
>> Financial information
>> Marketing information
>
> Create expert team
>
> Develop service firm
>
>> Internal or external implementation
>> Registration and licensing
>
> Develop planning process
>
>> First plans
>> Process aids and techniques
>> First clients
>> Computerization
>
> Develop products and services
>
>> Plan document
>> Client data form
>> Client files
>> Contact record and tickler system

Create marketing materials

Brochure
Newsletter/bulletin letters
Fee/service schedules
Reference list

Explore product leveling and segmentation

Explore client base design

THE SECOND YEAR

Now it's time to get serious about developing and marketing a profitable service. The focal point for this is your strategic marketing plan. Success depends on marketing, so create a marketing department. This is a formal way of committing the resources needed, whether the department is internal or external to your firm.

The experience you gained in the first year will indicate what additional training you need as a Financial Planner. How much technical education you want will depend on the role you intend to play as planner.

Now you need to perfect your people skills in order to motivate and convert prospects and new clients in the nurturing process. We had a quick look at this critical area in Chapter 8, but a quick look is not enough. Be prepared to spend whatever time and effort that it takes to overcome your weaknesses.

At the start of the second year, develop your first strategic marketing plan. Review Chapters 5 through 7; then work through Chapter 6, step-by-step. Remember, the planning process is ongoing. Your plan should be continuously reviewed, revised, and refined. Sketch out a five-year plan; then detail year one.

Set your goals in the context of your general business philosophy. Define the market by segmenting and profiling until you can clearly focus on the consumer needs you will meet. Analyze your competition and determine your marketing position.

Define the strategic marketing plan by identifying attractive marketing options; then select the strategies you will use. Remember the four basic strategies: to defend your client base, to cross sell existing services, to expand your client base, and to diversify with new services. Choose appropriate tactics for each marketing option. Try as many different tactics as your budget will allow to gain experience with them.

The marketing philosophy calls for the design and development of products and services that can be marketed. During the second year, be prepared to scrap the services that you offered in the first year. Let your strategic marketing plan dictate what you will now offer.

Price your new services so that they cover your costs and yield the profit margin necessary to reach your goals. Choose a pricing mechanism that is acceptable to the prospects you want to reach, but that also helps to develop your client base mix.

Develop your strategic marketing plan, following the sequence of steps that we've established. Leave budgeting as the last step before implementation in order to free yourself from constraints while you plan. When you do budget the marketing effort, allocate the time, capital, and support you will need to reach your goals.

Implement your first strategic marketing plan in two stages. Start with a test run that covers the first quarter of your second year. After the test, make one more review and fine-tune the plan. Then, implement it for the remainder of the year.

Monitor and adjust your marketing effort from now on, just as faithfully as you would monitor and adjust your own Personal Financial Plan.

During the second year, finalize the design of your client base. This effort goes hand in hand with your development of the strategic marketing plan. Your goals for this year should include making any desired changes to your client base.

By the end of your second year you should be exhausted but happy. Here is a checklist that will guarantee both!

Second year

Create marketing department

Internal
External

Get additional planner training

Technical Skills
People Skills

Develop strategic marketing plan

Five-year plan
Year one detail
Set goals
Business philosophy
Strategic marketing plan goals
Define market
Segment

        Profile
        Define client needs
     Analyze competition
     Define strategic marketing plan
        Check image
        Identify marketing options
        Select strategies
        Select tactics
     Design products and services
     Price products and services
        Cost to produce
        Profit margin required
        Pricing mechanism
     Budget strategic marketing plan
        Time
        Capital
        Support
     Implement strategic marketing plan
        Test run
        Full run
     Monitor and adjust
Design and develop client base

  Fine-tune design
  Full evolution effort

THE YEARS TO COME

The need for Personal Financial Planning is real and enduring. However, neither the economic environment nor the consumer's dreams and goals are static. Change is the only constant. No matter how successful your second year was, you must continue to monitor and adapt to change.

By the end of the second year, you will have a thorough exposure to Personal Financial Planning and to marketing your service. Continue to use and refine your strategic marketing plan in light of your experience and changes in the environment and the consumers.

Focus on developing and maintaining the client base and mix that you want. Remember that implementation and ongoing planning services are more profitable than initial planning. Offer initial planning services to develop your client base, but don't depend on them for revenue.

In the years ahead, keep growing and evolving, both professionally and personally. Make Personal Financial Planning your vehicle for development. It is a rewarding enterprise, and the rewards go far beyond financial gains.

Professional ethics and modern marketing are not incompatible. You are now aware of your obligation to provide badly needed professional services to your clients. You now have the knowledge you need to market your services ethically and aggressively. My task is ended; yours begins.

A

Glossary

Accelerated Cost Recovery System. A method for depreciating property that permits a person to recover the cost of tangible property more quickly. The property must either be used in the person's trade or business or be held for the production of income. See also *depreciation* and *straight-line depreciation*.

Accrual method of accounting. An accounting method that determines income by events that establish right to the income. It is the right to income, and not the actual receipt of income, that determines the amount included in gross income. See also *cash receipts method of accounting*.

ACRS. See *accelerated cost recovery system*.

AcSEC. Accounting Standards Executive Committee

Adjustable rate mortgage. Loans that have interest rates (and some monthly payments) that change periodically; the rates may change every year, every three years, or every five years. Changes are based on a variety of financial indices. See also *fixed rate mortgage*.

Adjusted gross income. Gross income, reduced by allowable adjustments, before calculation of federal income tax. The deductions from gross income that determine adjusted gross income are called "above the line" deductions.

AFCPE. Association for Financial Counseling and Planning Education

AFS. Academy of Financial Services

AGI. See *adjusted gross income*.

AICPA. American Institute of Certified Public Accountants

Alternative minimum tax. A tax for taxpayers who have large write-offs from those investments that are deemed to be "preference items."

Amortization. The reduction of the principal of a loan by regular payments. In general, a method for reducing debt or for recovering the cost of intangible assets. This includes such practices as depreciation, depletion, prepaid expenses, and deferred charges. See also *depreciation*.

Annuitant. The person who is entitled to receive periodic payments of money, according to an annuity contract.

Annuity. A contract made between an insurance company and an individual. The insurance company agrees to provide an income (either fixed or variable in amount) for a specified period of time in exchange for a specified amount of money. Private annuities can also be arranged between two individuals.

ARM. See *adjustable rate mortgage*.

ARSC. Accounting and Review Services Committee

ASB. Accounting Standards Board

Asset. Any possession that has monetary value.

Back-end load. A sales charge due upon the sale, transfer, or disposition of an investment.

Balloon payment. The final payment due on a mortgage with monthly payments that are set up similar to a conventional fixed rate 30-year mortgage. The balloon payment comes due at the end of a much shorter period and represents the entire outstanding loan balance, an amount substantially larger than previous payments.

Bear market. A market that is sharply declining because investors believe that stock prices, or the market as a whole, will fall.

Beneficiary. The person designated to receive the death proceeds or death benefit of a life insurance policy or annuity. Also, the person designated to receive the benefits of a trust estate. A beneficiary can be an individual, a company, or an organization.

Bid and asked. A bid price is the highest price that someone is willing to pay for a stock. The asked price is the lowest price at which someone is willing to sell.

Blue chip stock. A common stock that is highly esteemed as an investment based on the following criteria: earnings in good or bad times, over a long period of time; 25 years or more of paying quarterly cash dividends; leadership in solid, established industries, coupled with solid expectations for continued success. See also *cyclical stock, defensive stock, growth stock, income stock,* and *speculative stock*.

Blue-sky laws. A popular name for laws enacted by various states to protect the public against securities fraud. The term originated during a case in which the Supreme Court upheld an early state securities act, which was passed to control schemes that had "no more substance than so many feet of blue sky."

Bond. A long-term debt instrument. A bond evidences the issuer's promise to pay interest at a stated rate and to repay the principal at a specified maturity date.

Bond fund. A mutual fund invested completely in bonds.

Bond rating. The investment quality of a bond as determined by independent rating services, such as Moody's Investors Service or Standard and Poor's Corporation.

Book value. An accounting term for the value assigned to an asset after all debts and liabilities have been subtracted.

Broker. An agent who buys and sells securities for others. A commission is charged for this service. See also *dealer*.

Broker-dealer. A person or firm that buys and sells securities for others and also for its own account. With some exceptions, broker-dealers must register with the Securities and Exchange Commission (SEC) and with the state securities commissioner in each state where they transact business.

Bull market. A market that is sharply advancing because investors believe that stock prices, or the market as a whole, will rise.

Buydown. A subsidy of the mortgage interest rate (usually by developers) to lower the mortgage rate.

Cafeteria plan. A written qualified plan under which all employee participants may choose among two or more benefits consisting of cash and statutory nontaxable benefits.

Callable bond. See *redeemable bond*.

Call option. An option to buy a specified number of shares at a definite price within a specified period of time. See also *put option*.

Capital gain or **Capital loss.** Profit or loss from the sale of exchange of capital assets, such as securities or real estate.

Capital growth. An increase in the value of a tangible investment.

Capital loss. See *capital gain*.

Capital stock. All shares that represent equity ownership of a business, including common and preferred stock.

Capitalization. The total book value of securities that are issued by a corporation. Capitalization may include bonds, preferred and common stock, and surplus.

Cash or deferred compensation plan. A retirement plan that allows employees to defer taxation on a portion of their compensation by permitting the employer to contribute that portion to a qualified retirement plan.

Cash receipts method of accounting. A method that taxes income as it is actually received by the taxpayer. See also *accrual method of accounting.*

Cash surrender value. The amount of money that is payable to an investor in exchange for a life insurance policy or annuity that has been canceled.

Casualty and theft loss. Personal losses of property that are deductible (within limits). These losses must not be connected with the person's trade or business, or any transaction entered into for profit; typical losses result from fire, storm, shipwreck or other casualty, or theft.

CD. See *Certificate of Deposit.*

CEBS. Certified Employee Benefits Specialist

Certificate. The piece of paper that evidences ownership of the stock or bond of a corporation.

Certificate of Deposit. A certificate for a Time Deposit in a commercial bank that earns a specified rate of interest over a given time. These certificates, also called CDs, are usually subject to penalties for early withdrawal.

CFA. Chartered Financial Analyst

CFP. Certified Financial Planner and College for Financial Planning

ChFC. Chartered Financial Consultant

Clifford Trust. A trust in which the beneficiary receives income for a term of at least ten years and one day. The principal is returned to the owner upon termination of the trust. See also *spousal remainder trust.*

Closed-end investment company. An investment company that issues a fixed number of shares and does not redeem them. See also *investment company* and *open-end investment company.*

CLU. Chartered Life Underwriter

CODA. See *cash or deferred compensation plan.*

Commercial paper. Short-term promissory notes that are generally issued by "well-known" corporate borrowers and have varying maturity periods.

Commission. A fee for providing services such as buying or selling securities or property.

Common stock. Securities that represent an ownership interest in a corporation. Stock ownership entitles an individual to share in the net assets, the net income, and some decision-making authority of the corporation.

Common stock fund. A mutual fund that invests its assets only in common stocks.

Community property. Property acquired during a marriage and held to be owned equally by husband and wife. This applies only in states that have laws providing for such ownership.

Compound interest. Payment of interest upon interest that may be determined daily, weekly, monthly, annually, or over any specified period of time.

Constructive receipt. A tax law doctrine that requires a person to report income (including capital gains) in the year that the person received the right to the income.

Convertible time insurance. An insurance policy that permits conversion to a permanent or endowment form. The conversion can be made without evidence of insurability.

Coordination benefit. An insurance provision that prevents duplicate payment for coverage when more than one policy is involved.

Corporate bond. Evidence of indebtedness of a corporation. The corporation promises to pay the principal amount at the end of a specified term, along with interest at a fixed rate. Bondholders have priority over both preferred and common stockholders.

Corporation. An organization chartered by a state government. This term generally refers to corporations engaged in business for profit although it includes some nonprofit corporations and municipalities that do not issue stock.

CPA. Certified Public Accountant

CPCU. Chartered Property and Casualty Underwriter

Credit life insurance. Term life insurance that pays off a loan if the borrower dies. This is sometimes required by lenders.

Cumulative preferred stock. A preferred stock with the provision that if one or more of its dividends are omitted, these arrears must be paid before dividends are paid on the common stock.

Current assets. Assets that can be converted easily to cash on short notice.

Current yield. The annual income of a security divided by its current price.

Cyclical Stock. Stock of a corporation that is dependent on the business cycle. See also *blue chip stock, defensive stock, growth stock, income stock,* and *speculative stock.*

Day order and **Open order.** Also known as GTC, or good-until-canceled, orders. An open order is an order to sell or buy a security that remains good until executed. A day order must be executed on the day that it is placed. See also *limit orders, odd-lot orders, stop-loss orders,* and *market orders.*

Dealer. An individual or firm in the securities business. A dealer acts as a principal, not an agent. Dealers generally buy for their own account and sell directly to customers from their inventory. The same individual or firm can function as either broker or dealer. See also *broker.*

Debenture. A promissory note that is not secured by a lien on any specific property. A debenture is backed by the general credit of the corporation. See also *bond.*

Defensive stock. Stock regarded as stable and comparatively safe, especially in periods of fluctuating business activity. See also *blue chip stock, cyclical stock, growth stock, income stock,* and *speculative stock.*

Deferred annuity. An annuity in which benefits begin at some future specified date. See also *variable annuity.*

Depletion allowance. Amounts allowed as a deduction for the recovery of capital invested in wasting assets, such as oil and gas. See also *depreciation.*

Depreciation. The write-off of the costs of an asset over a period of time to reflect its decrease in value. See also *Accelerated Cost Recovery System.*

Director. A person elected by the shareholders of a corporation to establish company policy. The directors elect the operating officers of the corporation.

Discount. The amount by which an investment sells below its par or face value.

Discount rate. The interest rate that is charged on loans from the Federal Reserve System to member banks.

Discretionary income. Income available for investment after essential living costs are paid.

Disposable income. The spending income of a wage earner after various withholding deductions.

Dividend. The pro rata proportion of net earnings paid to stockholders by a corporation. With preferred stock, dividends are usually fixed; with common shares, dividends vary with the profits of the company. See also *Ex-dividend*.

Dividend reinvestment plan. A device for automatically reinvesting dividends in additional shares. In the case of mutual funds, capital gains may also be reinvested.

Dollar cost averaging. The regular purchase of securities at a fixed dollar amount, not by number of shares.

Double taxation. The result of the taxation of corporate profits first as corporate income and then as taxable dividends to shareholders.

EA. Enrolled Agent

EE Bond. U.S. government savings bonds that sold at a 50 percent discount off face value. The denominations range between $50 and $10,000; they are redeemed at face value in 11 years. See also *HH Bond*.

Entitlement. The benefits payable under a program where an individual satisfies the eligibility requirements, such as Social Security.

Equity. The value of a person's ownership in real property or securities. For instance, the current market value of a home, less the principal remaining on its mortgage, is the equity of that property. Also, a person's total holdings, including real estate, stocks, vested interests in annuities or pensions, and so on.

Escrow. An account in which money or property is placed with an independent third party in order to assure that the terms of an agreement will be fulfilled.

Estate freeze. A technique for shifting the expected appreciation of an asset to the next generation before the appreciation has occurred.

Estate tax. Taxes imposed by the federal government (and by some state governments) on the taxable estate of a person who has died. See also *inheritance tax*.

Excess liability insurance. A policy that protects against loss in excess of coverage provided by another insurance contract.

Ex-dividend. A synonym for "without dividend."

Face amount. The amount, stated on the face of an insurance policy, that is paid at death or at contract maturity, less any policy loans or withdrawals made.

FAF. Financial Analysts Federation

Fair market value. The value of property established between a willing buyer and a willing seller in an arm's length transaction.

FASB. Financial Accounting Standards Board

Federal Reserve System. An independent U.S. government agency that controls the supply of money to the economy.

Fiduciary. One who acts for another in financial matters.

Finance charge. The cost for the use of borrowed money, usually expressed in terms of an annual percentage rate.

Financial plan. A forecast of income and expenditures over a specified period of time.

Financial planner. One who helps individuals in an ongoing process to arrange and coordinate their personal and financial affairs in order to achieve their objectives.

Financial professional. A broker, CPA, insurance agent, lawyer, trust officer, real estate agent, or other professional operating in the financial industry.

Fixed rate mortgage. A loan made on real property that has a constant interest rate over the life of the loan. See also *adjustable rate mortgage.*

Floating interest rate. An interest rate which fluctuates with changes in an established index, such as the prime rate.

FMV. See *fair market value.*

GASB. Governmental Accounting Standards Board

General Obligation Bond. Bonds issued by state and local governments and supported by their power to tax. See also *municipal bonds.*

General partner. A person who is usually actively engaged in the trade or business of a partnership. A general partner has unlimited personal liability in the partnership. See also *limited partner.*

General partnership. A form of business that has only general partners. Profits, losses, and deductions are passed through to the individual partners involved in the business. See also *limited partnership.*

Gift tax. Taxes imposed by the federal government on lifetime transfers of money or property as gifts.

Gift tax exclusion. The first $10,000 transferred to a person as a gift that may be excluded from gift taxes during each calendar year.

Government obligation. Instruments of the U.S. government public debt. Examples are Treasury bills, notes, bonds, savings bonds, and retirement plan bonds. These are fully backed by the U.S. government, as opposed to U.S. government agency securities.

Graduated payment mortgage. A loan that carries a fixed interest rate, but has variable monthly payments at first. Generally, the payments begin low and increase gradually.

Gross income. The total income that a person receives. This includes salary, interest, dividends, rent, royalties, and other readily recognized items of income. It also includes windfalls, discharge of indebtedness, compensation-in-kind, and promissory notes received as payment.

Group life insurance. Insurance offered to employees or group members on a group basis that often results in lower cost premiums and no medical examination.

Growing equity mortgage. Also known as a rapid payoff mortgage, it combines a fixed interest rate with changing monthly payments.

Growth stock. The stock of a company with a record of relatively rapid growth earnings. The price/earnings ratio may be smaller than speculative stocks but greater than blue chip stocks. See also *blue chip stock, cyclical stock, defensive stock, income stock,* and *speculative stock.*

GTC order. See *day order.*

HH Bonds. U.S. government savings bonds which pay 7.5 percent per year, semiannually. These are exchangeable for series EE Bonds.

IAFP. International Association for Financial Planning

IBCFP. International Board of Standards and Practices for Certified Financial Planners

ICFA. Institute of Chartered Financial Analysts

ICFP. Institute of Certified Financial Planners

Incentive stock option. A type of qualified option that usually enables an employee to purchase stock at a bargain price.

Income stock. Stock purchased for its current income. See also *blue chip stock, cyclical stock, defensive stock, growth stock,* and *speculative stock.*

Indexing of taxes. A provision that allows adjustment for inflation in certain provisions of the tax code. Examples include personal exemptions, the zero-bracket amount, and the tax rate schedules.

Individual Retirement Account. A tax-favored retirement plan that can be established by any individual who has earned income, as well as a spouse not working outside the home (spousal IRA). Contributions to an IRA can establish significant income tax deductions, as they are tax deductible. Earnings are not taxed until the funds are withdrawn, usually during retirement.

Inflation. A sustained rise in the price level of goods and services. Inflation is generally caused by demand pull and cost shove on prices.

Inheritance tax. Taxes imposed by some states on the passing of a deceased person's estate property to the heirs. It is a tax upon the heir's right to receive his share of the estate. See also *estate tax.*

Interest. Payments made to a lender by a borrower for the use of the money.

Inter vivos trust. Also known as a living trust. Established during the lifetime of the grantor, it may be revocable or irrevocable.

Investment. The use of money to make money.

Investment adviser. A person who provides advice to the public concerning the purchase or sale of securities. Investment advisers are generally required to register with the SEC.

Investment Advisers Act of 1940. An act passed by Congress that empowers the Securities and Exchange Commission to register and regulate investment advisers.

Investment banker. Also known as an underwriter. The person or firm that acts as the intermediary between the corporation issuing new securities and the public.

Investment company. A regulated company that owns a portfolio of securities in other companies. The investment company sells shares in this portfolio to investors. See also *closed-end investment company* and *open-end investment company.*

Investment yield. The annual rate of return on an investment. See also *yield.*

IRA. See *individual retirement account.*

Irrevocable trust. A trust that may not be revoked by the grantor at any time. See also *revocable trust.*

ISO. See *incentive stock option.*

ITC. Investment Tax Credit

JD. Juris Doctorate

Joint and survivor annuity. An arrangement whereby the owner of the annuity elects to have payments continue to another person after his death.

Joint tenancy. A form of co-ownership whereby each joint tenant has an undivided interest in the whole property. When one joint tenant dies, his interest passes to the surviving joint tenant or tenants. The last surviving joint tenant obtains title to the entire property.

Keogh retirement plan. A form of qualified pension or profit sharing for an individual who has earned income from self-employment.

Level premium insurance. Insurance in which the yearly premium is the same over the life of the policy.

Leverage. The use of borrowed funds to increase the return on an investment.

Liability. A claim against a business or an individual.

Like kind exchange. The tax law provision that lets a taxpayer avoid taxes on the associated gain or loss when he exchanges property solely for property of "like kind." See also Rollover.

Limit order. An order to buy or sell stock that specifies the maximum price the buyer is willing to pay or the minimum price a seller is willing to accept. See also *day order and open order, stop-loss order,* and *market order.*

Limited partner. An investor who has limited personal liability in a partnership. See also *general partner.*

Limited partnership. A form of business whose partners include one or more general partners and one or more limited partners. Profits, losses, and deductions are passed through to the individuals involved in the business. See also *general partnership.*

Liquidity. The ability to readily convert an asset into cash.

Living trust. See *inter vivos trust.*

LLM. Master of Laws

Long-term capital gain or **Long-term capital loss.** See *capital gain or capital loss.*

Lump-sum distribution. The complete distribution of benefits from a pension or profit-sharing plan in a single year.

MAI. Member Appraisal Institute

Margin. The amount paid by customers when a broker's credit is used to buy securities; the remainder is loaned by the trader. When an investor buys on margin, he hopes the price will go up fast enough to cover his loan and thereby increase his buying power. If prices drop, however, he will also increase his losses.

Margin account. A securities account that a buyer opens with a broker. The buyer deposits the margin amount, and the broker advances the balance.

Margin call. A demand upon customers to put up money or securities with a broker. The call is made when the equity in a margin account declines below a minimum standard set by the Securities and Exchange Commission, or by the stock exchange, or by the brokerage firm.

Market order. An order to buy or sell stock at the best price obtainable in the market, with no price limit. See also *day order and open order, limit order, stop-loss order,* and *odd-lot order.*

Maturity. The date that a loan or bond comes due and is paid off.

Money market. Markets in which short-term low risk securities are traded.

Money market fund. A mutual fund that specializes in investing in short-term securities with low risk.

Mortgage. A lien on property that is created by pledging the property as security for repayment of a loan. The property is transferred to the lender if the borrower defaults.

Municipal bond. The debt obligations of states, cities, towns, school districts, and public authorities. There are two principal types of municipal bonds: general obligation bonds and revenue bonds. In general, interest paid on municipal bonds is exempt from federal taxes.

Municipal bond fund. A mutual fund that specializes in investing in municipal bonds. Investors enjoy federal income tax exemptions on dividends.

Mutual fund. A fund that pools the dollars of many people and that undertakes to invest those dollars more productively than the individuals could for themselves.

NAPFA. National Association of Personal Financial Advisors

NASD. National Association of Securities Dealers. The NASD is a self-regulatory organization empowered by the Securities and Exchange Commission to regulate the activities of brokers and dealers in the over-the-counter market.

NASDAQ. National Association of Securities Dealers Automated Quotations. An automated information network that provides brokers and dealers with price quotations on securities listed with the over-the-counter market.

Net asset value. The value of an investor's portion of the actual portfolio securities held by an investment company.

No-load mutual fund. A fund that charges no sales commissions to the purchaser.

Nominal yield. The interest rate stated on the face of a bond. This does not include any paid discount or premium.

Nonrefundable tax credit. A tax credit that reduces a taxpayer's income tax liability. There is no refund if the credit is larger than the tax owed. See also *refundable tax credit*.

Nonrecourse loan. A secured liability for which the borrower is not personally liable. See *recourse loan*.

Odd-lot order. An order of less than one hundred shares. See also *day order and open order, limit order*, and *market order*.

Open-end investment company. An investment company that has outstanding redeemable shares. Generally, it continuously offers new shares to the public and redeems its outstanding shares upon demand.

Open order. See *day order and open order*.

Option. A contract that involves the right to buy or sell securities at specified prices within a specified time.

Ordinary income. Income that is taxed at ordinary rates instead of preferential rates.

Permanent insurance or **Whole life insurance.** Any type of life insurance, other than term, with the following characteristics: a cash value that can be borrowed, used as collateral, or withdrawn by surrendering the policy; a lump-sum benefit payable at death.

Personal financial planning. The process of coordinating a broad range of financial services, products, and strategies that are consistent with the client's goals and values. The process must develop and maintain a plan of action to reach the client's personal objectives. The plan must respond to changes in goals and environment, reflect the client's stage of life, and include transfer of wealth at death.

Personal property. Generally, any property other than real estate.

PFP. See *personal financial planning*.

Portfolio. All assets held by a mutual fund at any specific time. Also, the total investments held by an individual.

Portfolio mix. A combination or selection of investments, including stocks, bonds, real estate, and selected limited partnership interests.

Preferred stock. The equity capital stock of a corporation. This has priority over common stock for the payment of dividends, or the distribution of corporate assets if the company liquidates.

Price/earnings ratio. The price of a share of common stock divided by the earnings per share for a one-year period.

Prime rate. The interest rate that major banks charge their best customers.

Principal. The amount of money that is financed, borrowed, or invested.

Probate. A court-supervised transfer of a deceased person's assets. Literally, the process of proving that the written will of the deceased is valid.

Proceeds. The amount payable under a life insurance policy upon the death of the insured. The proceeds consist of the face amount of the contract, plus accumulated dividends (if any), plus whatever amounts may be payable on riders, less any money owed to the life insurance company on the policy in the form of loans and interest on those loans.

Profit sharing. A defined contribution plan established by an employer to provide benefits to employees; the benefits vary according to profits of the corporation.

Put option. An option to sell a specified number of shares at a definite price within a specified period of time. See also *call option.*

Rapid payoff mortgage. See *growing equity mortgage.*

Real estate investment trust. Also known as an REIT. An organization that concentrates investments in real estate.

Record date. The date that a shareholder must be registered on a company's books in order to receive a declared dividend or to vote on company matters.

Recourse loan. A secured liability for which the borrower is personally liable. See *nonrecourse loan.*

Redeemable bond. Also known as callable bonds. These may be paid at the option of the issuer during a specified period prior to maturity.

Refundable tax credit. A tax credit that provides a taxpayer with a refund if the credit is greater than the tax owed. See also *nonrefundable tax credit.*

REIT. See *real estate investment trust.*

Repurchase agreement. Money market agreements in which the seller agrees to repurchase the securities at a fixed date at a higher price.

Retirement plan. A tax-favored employer benefit plan that defers taxation of contributions until retirement. This can be established by any business, whether incorporated or not. Employees as well as business owners participate on a nondiscriminatory basis. Contributions are deductible as a business expense; contribution and benefit limits may fluctuate from year to year.

Revenue bond. Bonds payable out of revenue from the operation of public facilities or from a special source of revenue; they are not payable out of general tax collections. See also *municipal bond, special assessment bond,* and *tax-exempt security.*

Revocable trust. A trust that may be terminated by the grantor at any time. See also *irrevocable trust.*

RHU. Registered Health Underwriter.

RIA. Registered Investment Adviser

RM. Residential Manager

Rollover. The nonrecognition of gain or loss when amounts realized are transferred into similar types of property, such as from one qualified plan to another, or from the sale of a principal residence into a new residence. See also *like kind exchange.*

RR. Registered Representative

Savings bond. See *EE Bond* and *HH Bond.*

S Corporation. A corporation that has elected to be treated similarly to a partnership for tax purposes. A method of incorporating a business to allow profits and losses and tax considerations to pass through to the individual shareholders.

SEC. Securities and Exchange Commission

Security. An investment of money in a common enterprise with the expectation of profit from the effort of others.

Selling short. The sale of stock that an investor either does not own and, therefore, must borrow to settle an account; or does own but does not wish to deliver.

Short-term capital gain or **Short-term capital loss.** See *capital gain or capital loss.*

Special assessment bond. Bonds that cover the cost of improving facilities. Property owners who are directly benefited by the improvements are assessed for the improvement with the assessment spread over a series of years. See also *municipal bond, revenue bond,* and *tax-exempt security.*

Speculative stock. Unproven stocks or new stock issues of corporations, with high price/earnings ratios. See also *blue chip stock, cyclical stock, defensive stock, growth stock,* and *income stock.*

Spousal remainder trust. A trust that shifts income to a beneficiary in a lower tax bracket during the period of the trust. The principal is paid to the grantor's spouse when the trust terminates. See also *Clifford Trust.*

SRO. Self-regulatory organization

Stock option. The opportunity for employees or underwriters to buy stock in a company at favorable prices and terms. The prices and terms are defined in a stock option.

Stop-loss order. An order to buy at a price above or to sell at a price below the current market price. See also *day order and open order, limit order,* and *market order.*

Straight-line depreciation. A method for depreciating tangible property in equal amounts each year. See also *ACRS* and *depreciation.*

Street name. Securities that are held in the name of the broker rather than the customer.

Tax avoidance. Legal methods of reducing income tax liabilities. See also *tax evasion.*

Tax credit. Expenditures that can be used to offset tax liabilities. Tax credits are subtracted directly from tax liability. See also *refundable tax credit* and *nonrefundable tax credit.*

Tax evasion. Illegal methods of reducing income tax liabilities. See also *tax avoidance.*

Tax-exempt bond. The interest income on some bonds that is exempt from federal income taxation. Generally, the securities of states, cities, and other public authorities are exempt. Municipal bonds are often called "tax-exempts."

Tax-exempt income. Certain kinds of income not subject to income tax. Included for U.S. taxpayers are income from most state and municipal bonds, social security payments, dividends up to specified sums, and veterans' pensions.

Tax-exempt interest. Interest earned on tax-exempt securities that is not included in gross income for federal income tax purposes. In most states, the income from municipal bonds is tax-exempt to state residents.

Tax exempt security. Certain obligations issued by state and local governments, the interest of which is exempt from federal income tax. See also *municipal bonds, revenue bond,* and *special assessment bond.*

Tax shelter. A device whereby a taxpayer may shelter income from tax. An investment that provides tax savings by creating losses to offset taxable income. Examples include investments in oil drilling or certain real estate activities.

Tenancy in common. A form of co-ownership whereby, upon the death of a co-owner, his interest passes to his estate and not the surviving owner or owners.

Term life insurance. Insurance that covers a limited specific period of time. One type of term insurance (convertible term) can be exchanged for other types of insurance, even if the policy holder would not otherwise qualify. See also *whole life insurance* and *universal life insurance.*

Testamentary trust. A trust created by the deceased's will; this is an irrevocable trust. See also *inter vivos trust.*

Treasury bill. Short-term U.S. government paper sold at auction through Federal Reserve Banks. These are sold at a discount with maturities of 13, 26, and 52 weeks. The minimum denominations are $10,000, with multiples of $5000 above this.

Treasury bond. A U.S. government long-term security, sold to the public and having a maturity greater than ten years. These are offered in denominations ranging from $1000 to $1,000,000, with various maturities.

Treasury note. U.S. government paper that has a fixed maturity of not less than one year and not more than ten years. Treasury notes are issued in denominations of $1000 and $5000. Notes maturing in four years or longer are available in minimum denominations of $1000; notes maturing in less than four years are available in minimum denominations of $5000.

Treasury stock. A stock issued by a company but later reacquired. It can be held in the company's treasury indefinitely, reissued to the public, or retired. Treasury stock receives no dividends and has no vote while held by the company.

Trust. A legal arrangement by which title to property is given to one party to manage for the benefit of a beneficiary or beneficiaries.

Trustee. An individual or corporation appointed, or required by law, to administer or execute the trust for the beneficiaries of the trust.

Underwriter. See *investment banker.*

Unified credit. A credit that can be used to reduce a federal estate tax liability. See also *estate tax.*

Unit investment trust. A limited portfolio of bonds or other securities in which investors may purchase shares. It differs from a mutual fund in that no new securities are added to the portfolio.

Universal life insurance. Life insurance consisting of a term portion and a cash accumulation portion. This type of policy provides for current market rates of interest, and flexible premium payments that are not fixed in timing or amount. See also *term life insurance* and *whole life insurance.*

Variable annuity. A form of annuity whereby the benefit varies with the performance of an investment. See also *deferred annuity.*

Vesting. The minimum period required for a participant in a qualified plan to receive benefits from the plan.

Whole life insurance. Life insurance providing for regular premiums, regular death benefits, and cash values that can be borrowed against, or withdrawn upon surrender of the policy. See also *permanent insurance, term life insurance,* and *universal life insurance.*

Will. A declaration of a person's wishes concerning the disposition of his property after death, the guardianship of his children, and the administration of his estate. A will is executed in accordance with certain legal requirements.

Yield. Also known as investment return. The dividends or interest paid that are expressed as a percentage of the original price. The return on a stock is calculated by dividing the total of dividends paid in the preceding 12 months by the original price.

Zero-bracket amount. The amount of personal deductions permitted in lieu of itemized deductions.

B

List of Software

Abacus Data Systems, Inc.
2775 Via DeLa Valle
Suite 201
Del Mar, CA 92014
    FASTPLAN

Advanced Micro Applications Corporation
Utah State University
Post Office Box 1228
Logan, UT 84322
    PFP—Microcomputer Program for Personal Financial Planning

Barnes, Stork & Mitchell
932 Santa Cruz Avenue
Menlo Park, CA 94025
    Prophet System

Financial Planning Consultants, Inc.
Financial Planning Building
Post Office Box 429
Middletown, OH 45042
    Comprehensive Personal Financial Plan

Financial Planning Systems
537 East 300 South
Salt Lake City, UT 84102
    Client Financial and Estate Planning System

Kinnard Softplans
2953 Brogden Street, NE
Hillsboro, OR 97123
    L.I.F.E. Goals

Leonard Financial Planning
4513 Creedmoor Road
Raleigh, NC 27622
  Leonard Financial Planning

Life-Work Planning Corporation
1267 Cook Avenue
Lakewood, OH 44107
  FINPLAN—Financial Planner's Diagnostic Tool

Lumen Systems, Inc.
Post Office Box 9893
Englewood, NJ 07631
  The Personal Financial Planner

Micro Planning Systems
1499 Bayshore Highway
Suite 214
Burlingame, CA 94040
  The Professional Financial Planning System

Money Tree Software
760 Madison, SW
Corvallis, OR 97333
  Money Plan

Sawhney Software
888 Seventh Avenue
New York, NY 10106
  FUND-IT

Softbridge Microsystems Corporation
186 Alewife Brook Parkway
Cambridge, MA 02138
  The Softbridge Financial Planner

Sterling Wentworth Corporation
2744 Aspen Circle
Salt Lake City, UT 84109
  Planner

Sumit Financial Systems, Inc.
12620 120th Avenue, NE
Suite 201
Kirkland, WA 98034
  Plan Master

The American College
270 Bryn Mawr Avenue
Bryn Mawr, PA 19010
  Money Manager

Unified Management Corporation
20 N. Meridian Street
Indianapolis, IN 46204
  COM-PLAN

Bibliography

American Institute of Certified Public Accountants. *Issues Involving Registration Under the Investment Advisers Act of 1940*. New York: AICPA, 1986.

Amling, Frederick. *Investments: An Introduction to Analysis and Management*. 5th ed. Englewood Cliffs: Prentice-Hall, 1984.

Amling, Frederick and Droms, William. *The Dow Jones-Irwin Guide to Personal Financial Planning*. Homewood: Dow Jones-Irwin, 1982.

Apilado, Vincent P. and Morehart, Thomas B. *Personal Financial Management*. St. Paul: West, 1980.

Ball, Dianne, ed. *CPA Marketing Report*. Atlanta: Professional Publications Inc., May, 1984.

Band, Richard. "A Billionaire's Simple Secret of Successful Investing." *Personal Finance* (Reprint Series No. M1026). Ed. Richard Band. Arlington: KCI Communications Inc., 1986.

Bandler, Richard and Grinder, John. *Frogs Into Princes*. Moab: Real People Press, 1979.

Beasley, Bruce. "All of the Above." *Financial Planning*. Atlanta: International Association for Financial Planning, Inc., March, 1986, pp.111–117.

Bissett, Lesley D., ed. *Client Finder II*. Reston: Reston Publishing Company, Inc., 1984.

Bohn, Robert F. "Financial Planning and Services: A Historical Update." *Proceedings of the IAFP Academic Symposium*. New York: International Association for Financial Planning, 1985.

Bonoma, Thomas V. *The Marketing Edge*. New York: Free Press, 1985.

Bovee, Tim. "K Mart to Test-Market Financial Services in 31 Stores." *The Daily Breeze*, 22 January 1985.

Calero, Henry and Nierenberg, Gerald I. *How to Read a Person like a Book*. New York: Hawthorn Books, 1971.

California Certified Public Accountants Foundation. "Adding Personal Financial Planning to Your Practice." *Advanced Personal Financial Planning Certificate Program* (Course Prospectus Flyer), July 1986.

College for Financial Planning. *1984 Bulletin*. Denver: College for Financial Planning, 1984.

Creviston, Carlene. *Personal Finance Today.* St. Paul: West Publishing Co., 1979.

Droms, William G. "Educational and Certification Opportunities for Personal Financial Planning Practitioners." *AICPA Conference Manual,* American Institute of Certified Public Accountants, 1985.

Elam, Houston G. *Marketing for the Non-Marketing Executive.* New York: American Management Association, 1978.

Fabozzi, Frank J., ed. *Readings in Investment Management.* Homewood: Richard D. Irwin, 1983.

Fast, Julius. *Body Language.* New York: Evans, 1970.

Fresques, Linda, ed. *Outlook.* Palo Alto: California Society of Certified Public Accountants, Spring, 1986.

Friedman, Paul G., ed. *The Pryor Report* (Vol. I, No. 5), Shawnee Mission: Fred Pryor Seminars, Inc., January, 1985.

Goldsmith, Charles. *Selling Skills for CPAs: How to Bring In New Business.* New York: McGraw-Hill Book Company, 1985.

Groves, Ray S. *Family Financial Planning, 1979.* Ernest and Whinney, 1979.

Hallman, G. Victor and Rosenbloom, Jerry S. *Personal Financial Planning.* 2nd ed. New York: McGraw Hill, 1981.

————. *Personal Financial Planning.* 3rd ed. New York: McGraw-Hill Book Company, 1983.

Haller, Ellis. "How to Pick a Financial Adviser." *U.S. News and World Report,* 30 June, 1980.

Huebner, S. and Black, K. *Life Insurance.* 10th ed. Englewood Cliffs: Prentice-Hall, 1983.

IDS. *Financial Planning—How It Works for You.* Minneapolis: IDS Brochure, 1987.

International Association for Financial Planning. *Building a Capital Base,* Atlanta: IAFP, 1984.

Johnson, Kerry L. "How to Win a Client's Trust Quickly." *California Planner,* May, 1986, p.11.

Jones, H. Stanley. *Personal Financial Planning: New Opportunities for the Professional Accountant.* Fairfield: Professional Focus, 1984.

Jones, Landon Y., ed. *Americans and Their Money/4.* New York: Time, 1986.

Kess, Sidney and Westlin, Bertil. *Estate Planning Guide.* Chicago: Commerce Clearing House, 1982.

Lauterbach, Jeffrey R. "Survey of the Competition." *AICPA Conference Manual,* American Institute of Certified Public Accountants, 1985.

Ledgerwood, Ian, ed. *Modern Maturity.* Long Beach: American Association of Retired Persons, June–July, 1985.

MacKenzie, Dennis J. *The Calculating Financial Planner.* Ventura: Portfolio's Inc., 1985.

Management Analysis Center, Inc. *Opportunities for Certified Public Accountants to Provide Financial and Business Advisory Services.* Cambridge: Management Analysis Center, Inc., 1984.

Mandino, Og. *The Greatest Salesman in the World.* New York: Frederick Fell, Inc., 1968.

Mattauch, Gene, ed. "Personal Financial Planning: An Increasingly Popular Perk." *Small Business Report,* Monterey: Business Research and Communications, March, 1985, pp.67–72.

Martin, Timothy L., ed. *Accountants IBMicro Report* (Vol. I, No. 3), Atlanta: Professional Publications Inc., October, 1984.

————. *CPA Computer Report* (Vol. III, No. 3), Atlanta: Professional Publications Inc., September, 1984.

McCaffrey, Mike. *Personal Marketing Strategies.* New York: Prentice-Hall, 1983.

McGill, Dan M. *Fundamentals of Private Pensions.* 5th ed. Homewood: Richard D. Irwin, 1984.

Mehr, Robert. *Fundamentals of Insurance.* Homewood: Richard D. Irwin, 1983.

Meier, Ronald P., ed. *The CPA Financial Planner* (Vol. I, No. 2), Kingwood: Professional Investment Planning, Inc., August, 1984.

Molloy, John T. *Dress for Success.* New York: Peter H. Wyden, 1975.

Nuccio, Sal. *Guide to Personal Finance.* New York: Harper and Row, 1967.

Owens, William, E., ed. *Public Accounting Report* (Vol. VII, No. 12), Atlanta: Professional Publications Inc., December, 1984.

Richards, Robert, et al. *The Financial Planner's Tax Almanac, 1984.* Homewood: Dow Jones-Irwin, 1984.

Roberts, J. Michael, ed. *California Planner* (Vol. III, No. 2), Sacramento: December, 1985.

———. *California Planner* (Vol. III, No. 2), Sacramento: February, 1986.

Roehm, Harper A., et al. *A Survey of Consumer Attitude Toward Financial Planning, Financial Services, and Financial Planners.* New York: Roehm, Castellano, Karns, 1986.

Rostvold, Gerhard N. *Economic and Financial Survival in the 1980'$.* Corona del Mar: Urbanomics Publications, 1979.

Shildneck, Barbara J., ed. *Journal of Accountancy.* New York: American Institute of Certified Public Accountants, July 1985.

———. *Journal of Accountancy.* New York: American Institute of Certified Public Accountants, December, 1985.

———. "Boosting the Profession with Effective PR." *Journal of Accountancy,* New York: American Institute of Certified Public Accountants, February, 1986, p.76.

Sigerson, Bartlett J.D., ed. *Tax Management Financial Planning Journal* (Vol. I, No. 11), Washington, DC: Tax Management, Inc., October, 1985.

———. *Tax Management Financial Planning Journal* (Vol. I, No. 15), Washington, DC: Tax Management, Inc., December 1985.

Silverburg, Michael. *Introduction to Financial Planning.* Ventura: Portfolio's Inc., Financial Training Center, 1983.

Slapak, Gregg, et al. *1985 Marketing CPA Firm Services Conference.* Palo Alto: California Certified Public Accountants Foundation for Education and Research, 1985.

Sommerfield, Ray M. *Federal Taxes and Management Decisions.* Homewood: Richard D. Irwin, 1984.

Tax Management Inc. *Financial Planning: Process and Practice.* Washington, DC: Tax Management Inc., 1985.

Thompson, Gordon and Tuchman, Gary. *Financial Planning in the 1980s: Opportunities and Strategies for Success.* Menlo Park: SRI International, 1979.

U.S. Department of Commerce. *Current Business Reports 1985 Service Annual Survey.* U.S. Department of Commerce, Bureau of Census, 1985.

Veres, Robert N., ed. *Financial Planning.* Atlanta: International Association for Financial Planning, Inc., January, 1986.

———. *Financial Planning.* Atlanta: International Association for Financial Planning, Inc., February, 1986.

Walters, Ralph. "Advertising and Solicitation—A Matter of Judgement." *Monthly Statement,* Palo Alto: California Society of Certified Public Accountants, June 1986, p.2.

———. "The Making of a Professional." *Monthly Statement,* Palo Alto: California Society of Certified Public Accountants, June 1986, p.10.

Weiner, Steve. "Banks Hire Retailing Consultants for Help In Becoming Financial-Products 'Stores'." *Wall Street Journal,* 20 May 1986.

Weiss, Stuart and Phillips, Peter. "Putting a Tighter Leash on Financial Planners." *Business Week,* July, 1985, pp.113–114.

Whalen, John, ed. "AICPA Proposes Ethics Changes." *Monthly Statement,* Palo Alto: California Society of Certified Public Accountants, June 1986, p.1.

———. "Vincent Discusses Ethics of Contingent Fees at Conference." *Monthly Statement,* Palo Alto: California Society of Certified Public Accountants, June 1986, p.1.

Wilson, James H. "The CPA's Role in Personal Financial Planning." *AICPA Conference Manual,* American Institute of Certified Public Accountants, 1985.

Yearly, Midge, ed. *CPA Personnel Report* (Vol. III, No. 3), Atlanta: Professional Publications Inc., October, 1984.

Index